THE PLAYHOUSES OF OUR GRANDPARENTS

ENGLISH TRANSLATION: JONATHAN SLY, JANE PECK AND THEDA BRADDOCK-GOUTARD
WITH THE COLLABORATION OF HÉLÈNE GAUDY IN WRITING THE TEXTS.
GRAPHIC CREATION: NOÉMIE LEVAIN

WWW.ACTES-SUD.FR

NICOLAS HENRY

THE PLAYHOUSES OF OUR GRANDPARENTS

ACTES SUD

THE PLAYHOUSE SETS THE STAGE, ALL AROUND THE WORLD

Growing up, our "playhouses" were our imaginary hideaways, sanctuaries where we felt protected, surrounded by our favorite things. Our own little theater set where sheets metamorphosed into oceans, and piles of books became islands inhabited by Indians, Pygmies or Robinson Crusoe. Whether created in the backyard or under the covers in our bedroom, when we designed and built a children's fort, den, or playhouse, we invented a whole new world in which to play, dream and let our imaginations run free. When I was little my Grandfather taught me the art of woodworking and my grandmother that of sewing. Later as an adult, quite naturally I turned back to my grandparents when I wished to relive some of those magical moments we had shared, when gestures spoke louder than words; and it was there and then that I took my very first photographs of my own grandparents. From these first images, the project « The Playhouses of Our Grandparents » was born: my personal quest to seek out and meet our elders and give them a voice. I wanted to explore with grandparents all over the world this intriguing form of child's play, what seemed to be an excellent medium for passing on memories, philosophy and wisdom. So I set out to discover the world, with nothing more than my camera, a bag of rope, clothespins and some studio spotlights. ¶ With every new encounter I would show people those first photographs of my grandparents' playhouses – photographs I had glued in a sketchbook, or other shots taken in towns, villages or countries where I'd just been. This photo-journal explained my ideas better than any verbal description ever could have. Along the way, I realized how the Playhouse is a universal concept. Inside every one of us, lies the youthful spirit of a child who revels in creating, with everyday items around him, a world invented entirely by his imagination. ¶ When arriving in a village, I would search out my "accomplice." Often this was someone around my age who was inspired to convince his own grandparents to join in the adventure of

"I am the bonds I weave."
Théodore Monod

making a playhouse. Explaining the concept of building a children's fort was always a good way to get creative juices flowing. Based on the concept that, for me, any grandparent was perfect for the part, my accomplice would often start by presenting me a member of his own family, a neighbor or key community figure. Given the magic of word-of-mouth and human curiosity, the invitation to participate in playhouse-building spread like wildfire and gradually more and more people came forth to participate. This enthusiastic support meant we could build and photograph a new playhouse every day. ¶ Over time, my installations became bigger and more elaborate, built primarily outdoors, often on symbolic sites, so that what might start as a simple photo-shoot would often turn into a full-fledged theater set. Playhouses were built from the stuff of elders' lives, objects from their past and present, the very foundations of their existence. Utensils, knick-knacks and all kinds of tools were then arranged and staged, juxtaposed according to individual ideas and the tales the grandparents would tell during the course of installation. The Playhouse gradually became a vehicle for freedom of speech, a setting where memories, revelations and the joy of sharing reigned. ¶ Sometimes, up to forty people would collaborate, with more than a hundred spectators gathering around to watch the work in progress. This theatrical setting and captive audience often set the stage for spontaneous oratory outbursts from members of the community. From a single playhouse, countless words sprung forth. ¶ ¶ Three key elements are essential in contributing to the success of this kind of spontaneous show. ¶ First, we must have a story to tell, as, when we do, the world welcomes us with open arms. While sharing the pages of my photo-journal, sometimes I'd end up telling the story of my grandparents a good dozen times a day. I'd willingly turn over my book to curious villagers, accepting that it would undoubtedly suffer in the hands of children's unbridled enthusiasm. As the journal was passed around, steadily would grow the gossip, rumors and "buzz" about the mysterious makeshift theater taking shape in the village. As time passed, I became

Stars are pretty white things that live far away and no one really hates. Nobody ever says, "I don't like stars", because they outlive everyone. ¶ Sometimes, stars explode into a million tiny fragments, but not one falls to Earth for they bounce off the air that protects us, high above the clouds. People say that when they see a shooting star, all their troubles disappear. When you see a shooting star, what you wish for will come true. But if you make a wish, don't tell anyone. When a shooting star flashes across the sky, your wish stays in its trail and thus gives birth to a new star. Not only does your wish come true but also, that's how stars are born.

JOSÉPHINE NYOUNAI IN HER GARDEN WITH THE LEAVES OF HER TREE FROM AFRICA, LES MESNULS, FRANCE.

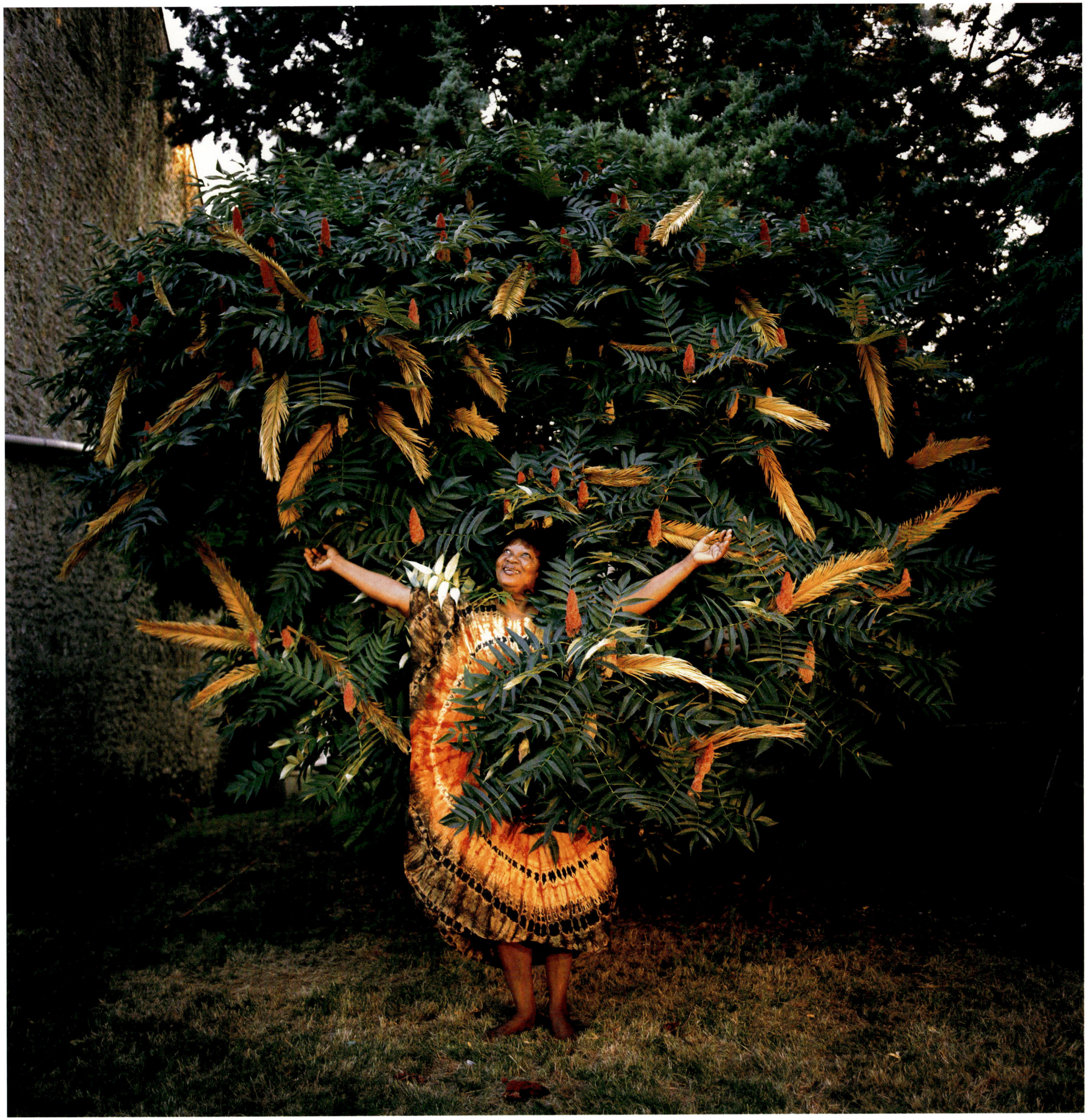

more comfortable with my role as traveling show master and as the doors of imagination opened wider, so did those of the villagers - offering food and shelter, but also, at the same time, a certain sense of responsibility to guarantee the success of the show. ¶ Secondly, imagination is needed in order to compensate for the modesty of the tools at one's disposition during the building process. In more urban settings, playhouse building often resembled that kind of "living out of a box" atmosphere that one encounters when moving, inspiration fueled by digging through cartons and pouring over old family photo albums. While in the countryside, a pair of scissors could be transformed into a machete, gaskets linked together to resemble creeping vines and tangled bark made to look like the rope of a swing. To create solid arbors and arches, I'd split bamboo in quarters and once we had a solid frame we were able to pin large leaves in place using thorns. In the glare of the sunlight or that of my spotlights, these large vegetal screens would produce a greenish stained-glass-window effect. ¶ I'd dig with my bare hands to unearth stones to use as wedges to hold stakes in place. When the ground was too hard, heavy counterweights were attached to the feet of structures, while stays were attached at the pinnacle. When there were no tree trunks around to use for support, I'd bind up clumps of grass and affix the ropes to them. There is always strength in solidarity and when it came to draping things, often the lightest member of the tribe or community was sent scurrying up a tree with safety ropes around his waist in order to attach sheets or other elements. ¶ During the building process, each of these movements evokes a spirit of authenticity, that of simple and honest individuals, like the sailor hoisting his sails or practicing the art of knot-tying, the farmer devising cunning ploys to keep his beasts in check, and even kids building a tree-house. In the end, we're imitating the movements of billions of skilled anonymous laborers who make up half of the population today, those men who naively and majestically live in harmony with Nature and build impressive architectural structures with only their bare hands. ¶ The third element is that of spoken word. As the result of long hours of respectful listening, my playhouse journal is full of hundreds of pages of strange and mysterious anecdotes. As my subjects recount their stories, in the process of taking copious notes, I too become a storyteller. Interviews with grandparents took place in the context of each playhouse; their messages are hidden in the foundation of the designs, and are the wind behind my creative direction. When the rhythm of construction and telling of stories were in sync, and providing that the installation didn't collapse for any unforeseen reason, the recounting of the grandparent's stories could become colorful speeches addressed to a sometimes rather large and rowdy audience. The support of an attentive crowd helped nourish the exuberance of oration. My Playhouse photographs are not classic studio shots featuring rigid figures staring vaguely out to sea, nor stances of unaffected poseurs wearing artificial attitudes. The joy expressed on my subject's faces is that of a loving gaze one bestows on someone they care about. ¶ Often at the end of a shoot, after we'd managed to clean everything up and put away all our "toys", we'd gather together for an end of evening chat, a lively debriefing where everyone dug deep into their memories and reflections, contributing eagerly in the hopes of adding their own words to that of the elders and thus their own personal touch to the pages of my journal. ¶ ¶ The Playhouse project took me to forty countries where I produced over four hundred portraits. The innate map-reading skills of my friend Thomas often set my morning compass straight on those days when I was unable to recall which part of the world we had landed in. His sense of direction and ability to tame the most uncooperative vehicles saved us from many scrapes, like guiding us through masses of thick fog and navigating a sea of Tata trucks hurtling down Nepalese or Andes mountain slopes, so close you could feel their door handles brushing against yours. The further you go from big cities, the smaller airplanes become and you have to run to be the first to fill the hold. We spent long evenings working out the best strategies to ensure how our three hundred and thirty pounds of lighting equipment would travel on with us to new destinations. We'd strap our spotlights and batteries to beasts of burden, on the narrow bridges of riverboats or onto rooftops of buses. ¶ For long months I paid constant attention to the moods of the sky: from the way the wind influences the movement of the clouds to the process of how formations take shape and dissolve as influenced by altitude and reflections from the sea, acting as a giant mirror. The position of the sun provided an essential indicator for arranging the playhouse set and adjusting the orientation of the camera. Through Thomas's diligence and expertise in lighting we managed to make the most of both artificial and natural lights. We were able to capture moments of grace, ephemeral and symbolic. Like that moment at day's end, when color is majestically splashed across the sky somehow mirroring the joyous contentment felt by these grandparents in the twilight of their lives. ¶ The world into which our grandparents were born was one where people often lived and died all together under the same roof or canvas tent. Today the transmission of language, history and traditions, as well as our knowledge of nature and biodiversity, is highly influenced by media and education systems. The verbiage of the television holds more value than the wise words coming from our grandmothers. The disillusionment felt by many urban dwellers comes from the fact that they are daily spectators of a success they will never share. They feed off nostalgic memories of a time when man did not live alone in the middle of the crowd. Today, global models have replaced passed-down family traditions. In rural settings, we are now producing generations unsuitable for a community way of life, incapable of deriving survival solutions from nature. The figure of an elder no longer commands the respect it once did. Once upon a time, grandparents were synonymous with authority and wisdom; today they are often seen as weak and lonely. ¶ During the Playhouse adventures we laughed and cried every day and I realized over time, that joy and creation are the best weapons we have to fight the tragedy of the human condition. Transformed into kings and queens for a day, the grandparents I met around the world taught me to have faith in the extraordinary ability of human beings to open up to one another. Living with a genuine willingness and brave heart to welcome the unknown can help us transform our perspective about the world and our fellow human beings. To do this, just build a playhouse with a few yards of rope and some pieces of wood, and then declare it your palace. From beneath this taffeta, raffia and batik, the words of our elders ring out, and thus the story begins... NICOLAS HENRY

One day my great grand-daughter Victoria called me and said "Great-Grandma, Great-Grandma, you know what? It's a boy!" She was 3 years old and her baby brother had just been born. Together with your grandfather, we turned towards the window looking out on the forest; we wrapped our arms around each other and hugged for a long time. ¶ The passing of time does not erase our emotions, but has further intensified our love. We have survived starvation, bombings, and exodus, so we decided to grow a large garden for our children. All that you see here, I've made myself. I sew, I embroider, I knit. ¶ What I have a hard time understanding today is that we can buy a gift in a store. The time and thought someone consecrates to another when making something, that is a true gift.

GENEVIÈVE GIRAUX, GRANDMOTHER OF NICOLAS HENRY, IN HER SITTING ROOM LOOKING OUT OVER RAMBOUILLET FOREST, FRANCE.

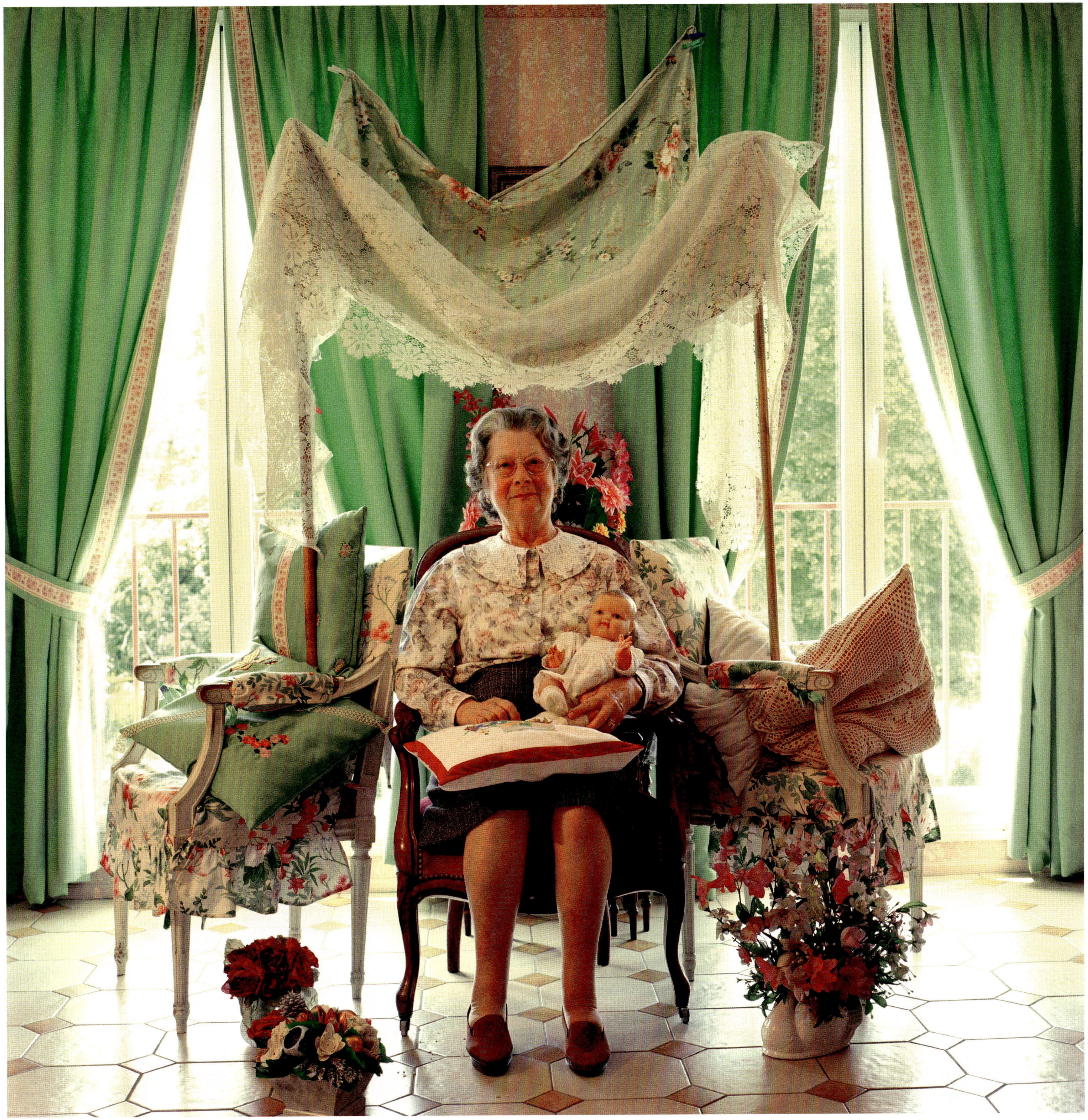

MARIA CELIA GREFA AGUINDA ¶ AIAIR RANDES
FAILLE BHATTA ¶ BERYL JOHNSON ¶ ESPIRITA
NUMAZAWA ¶ KO NAKAJIMA ¶ THOMAS CH
AGUINDA ¶ AIAIR RANDES ¶ MALEY KUNNAPH
BERYL JOHNSON ¶ ESPIRITA LOPEZ MAMAN
KO NAKAJIMA ¶ THOMAS CHARLEY ¶ WOO K
RANDES ¶ MALEY KUNNAPHAN ¶ YENI TEMPA
ESPIRITA LOPEZ MAMANI ¶ ROLYN THOMP
THOMAS CHARLEY ¶ WOO KWONG ¶ MARIA C
KUNNAPHAN ¶ YENI TEMPA ¶ SOTIMA ¶ FAILL
MAMANI ¶ ROLYN THOMPSON ¶ YOSUÉ NUM
WOO KWONG ¶ MARIA CELIA GREFA AGUIND
TEMPA ¶ SOTIMA ¶ FAILLE BHATTA ¶ BERYL
THOMPSON ¶ YOSUÉ NUMAZAWA ¶ KO NAKAJ
CELIA GREFA AGUINDA ¶ AIAIR RANDES ¶ MALE
SOTIMA ¶ FAILLE BHATTA ¶ BERYL JOHNSO
MAMANI ¶ ROLYN THOMPSON ¶ YOSUÉ NUMAZ
KWONG ¶ MARIA CELIA GREFA AGUINDA ¶ AIAI
SOTIMA ¶ FAILLE BHATTA ¶ BERYL JOHNSON ¶

THE PLAYHOUSE
WHERE MYSTERY LIVES

In the great stones, where beastly spirits dwell, so live our stories. Here on the surface, we see traces of ghostly silhouettes. We, the Quichuas, live with spirits in the forest. The plants enable us to communicate with nature. When you drink the Ayahuasca, a dream leads you through time, to your past, your present and your future. This is what ties the bonds between man, water, animals and plants. The enlightenment it brings, this is the sense of responsibility that makes you a human being. ¶ Since the time our river was bridged our children have set out in every direction. To be a mother is the the greatest of joys but now our children have wings like a bird and one day, we shall find ourselves alone. There are hardly any great trees left today. Our forest is, itself, an orphan. I believe that we start to lose our roots when future generations no longer spend their lives together. One day, it will be too late and our land will no longer bear future generations.

MARIA CELIA GREFA AGUINDA AT THE FOOT OF ONE OF THE LAST GREAT TREES, AMAZONIAN FOREST, ECUADOR.

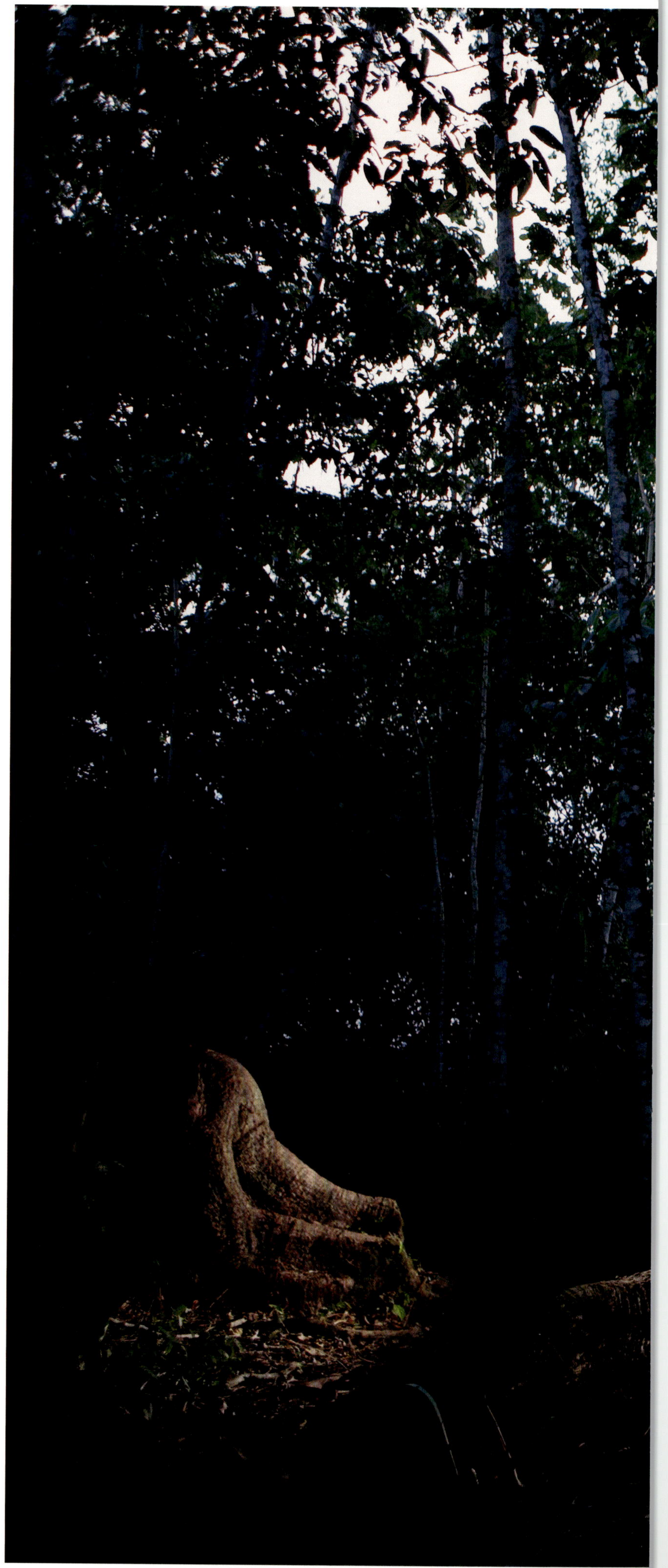

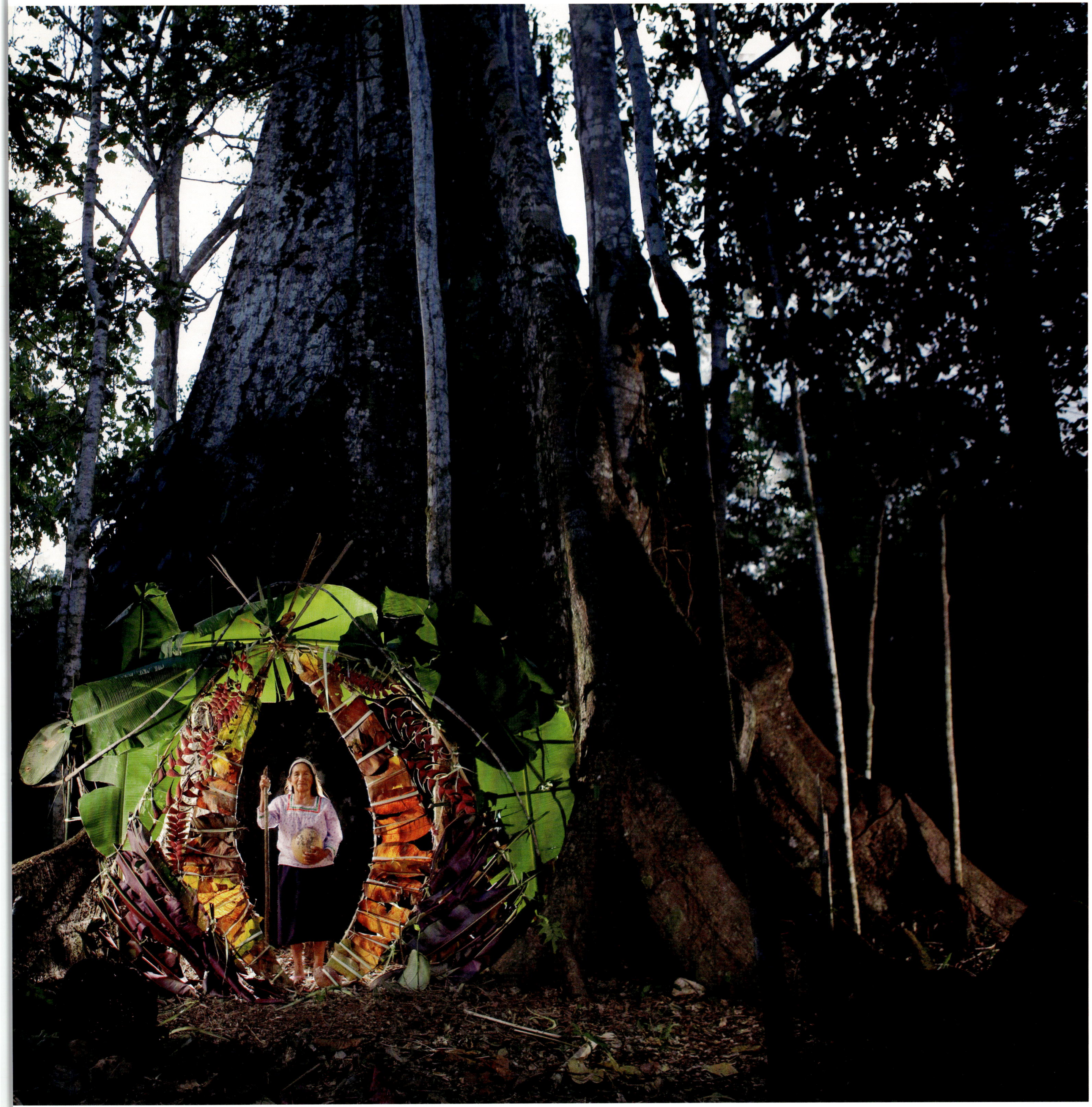

The spirit of nature

took possession of my body to teach me about the masks. Yesterday, it spoke of your arrival. The laughter of the children in our village gathered us together as we set off deep into the jungle to rebuild the House of Secrets. ¶ Women never turn their gaze to the stone and the drum. The pig's tooth that I wear represents my grade, my value according to tradition. Once you bring together the taro, the rice and the yam, you may kill a pig. The dances performed by the society of men are witnesses to this new grade. When you move up a rank, the ceremonies are rich with the colors in nature that surround us. ¶ Today we have forgotten our traditions because, for a long time, the religion that was brought to us by boats forbade our practices. Our ancestors did not believe that there was a God yet that God took care of us. He respected mankind while never ceasing to laugh.

AIAIR RANDES AT THE SITE OF THE MYSTERY HOUSE, LORBAAP, VANUATU.

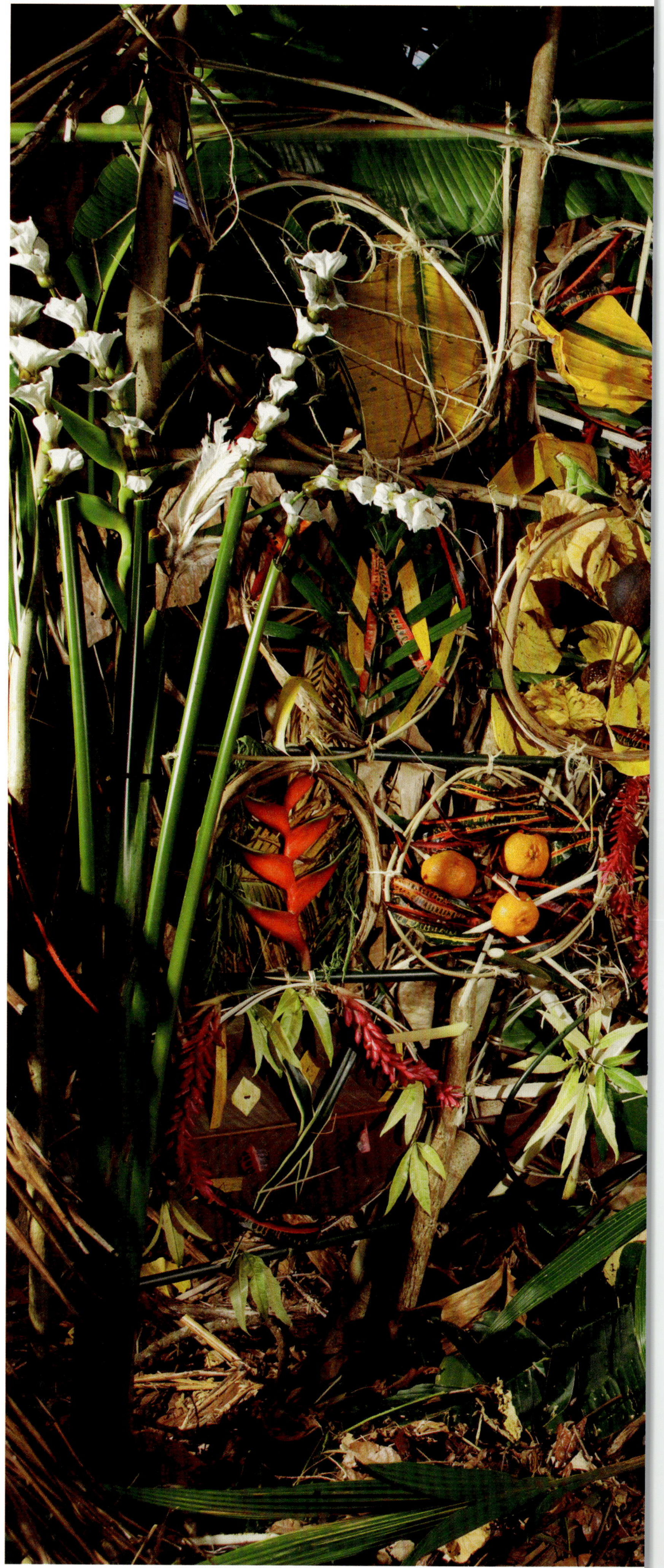

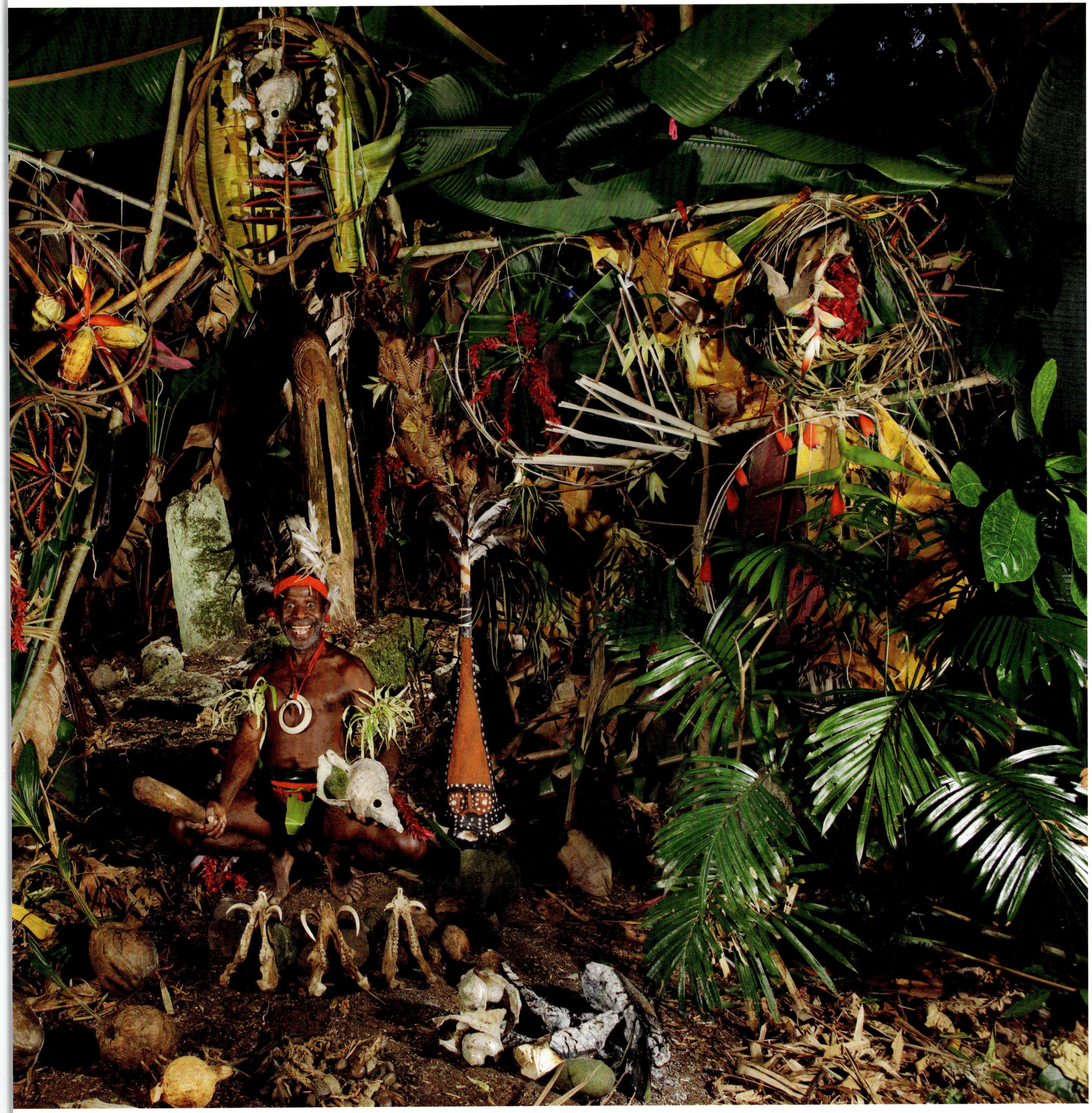

Buddha is at the summit of the hierarchy. When you are good, it is he who leads you along the path to paradise. He shines over all the spirits to whom our temple pays hommage. The care I give them is an expression of my respect. I know how to please them and make sure they are comfortable. I would love to live even longer so as to continue going to the temple. And according to the teachings of Buddha, I would attain peace by letting go of my desires. ¶ My husband and I are shamans. When we enter a state of trance, the spirits voice themselves through our mouths. In the beginning, they spoke an odd language that no one understood but before long they began to speak Thai. Now, people come from afar to speak with them and we offer answers to their questions. ¶ Spirits are like children: one must give them food, tenderness and, at times, even money. In order to thank them I make garlands from cloth, I burn candles and incense and I give them offerings of fruit.

MALEY KUNNAPHAN IN THE TEMPLE OF THE FAMILY HOME, RIVER KWAI BRIDGE, THAILAND.

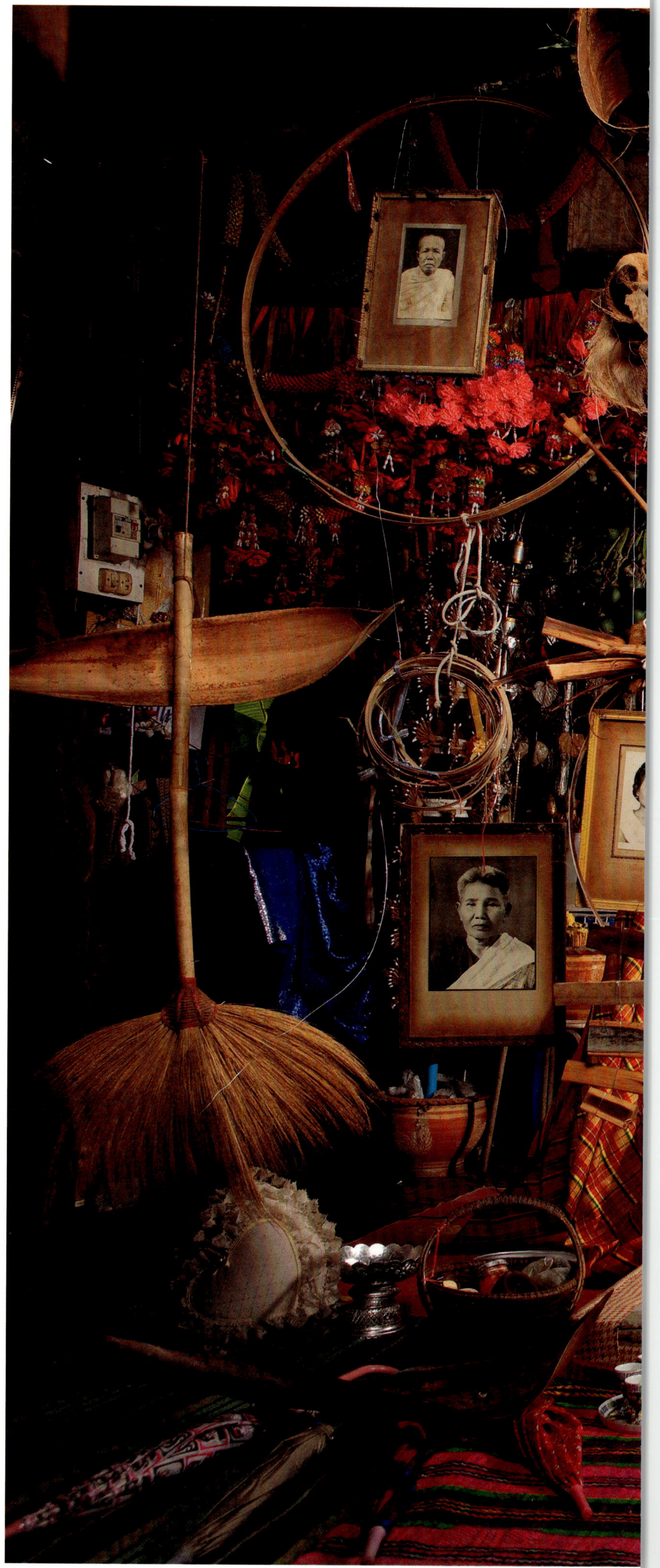

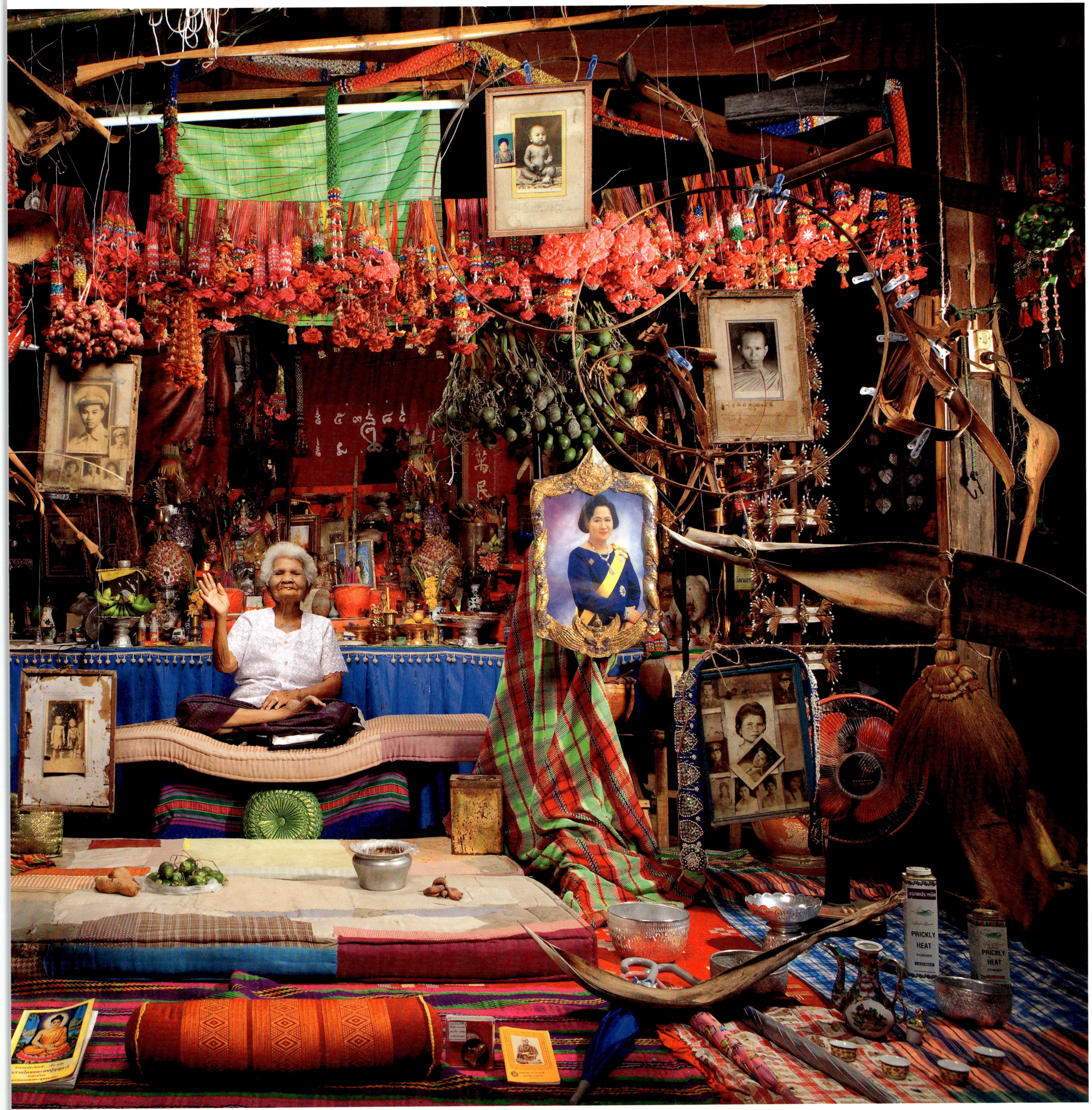
PRICKLY HEAT POWDER
PRICKLY HEAT POWDER

My dreams tell me that the dead are not dead. When I watch human beings I tell myself that there is something in all of us that can never end, something that is infinite. Death cannot be the last act. I believe our presence lives on forever among men. We are born amongst the stars, already bearing our futures. We must know from where we have come in order to know where we will go. Every day, I ask my ancestors to help my children achieve what I could not. ¶ When my wife joined me here, the Earth began to nurture us. Here in the tata, our earthen house, when I hunt an animal, I sacrifice it on the mound of soil that represents my father. His spirit walks ahead followed by that of the animal. Together, they bring me happiness to grow our family, the opportunity, for us, to be more human with humans and more natural with nature.

YENI TEMPA, SOTIMA AND THE ANCESTORS, BEFORE THEIR *TATA*, SOMBA COUNTRY, BENIN.

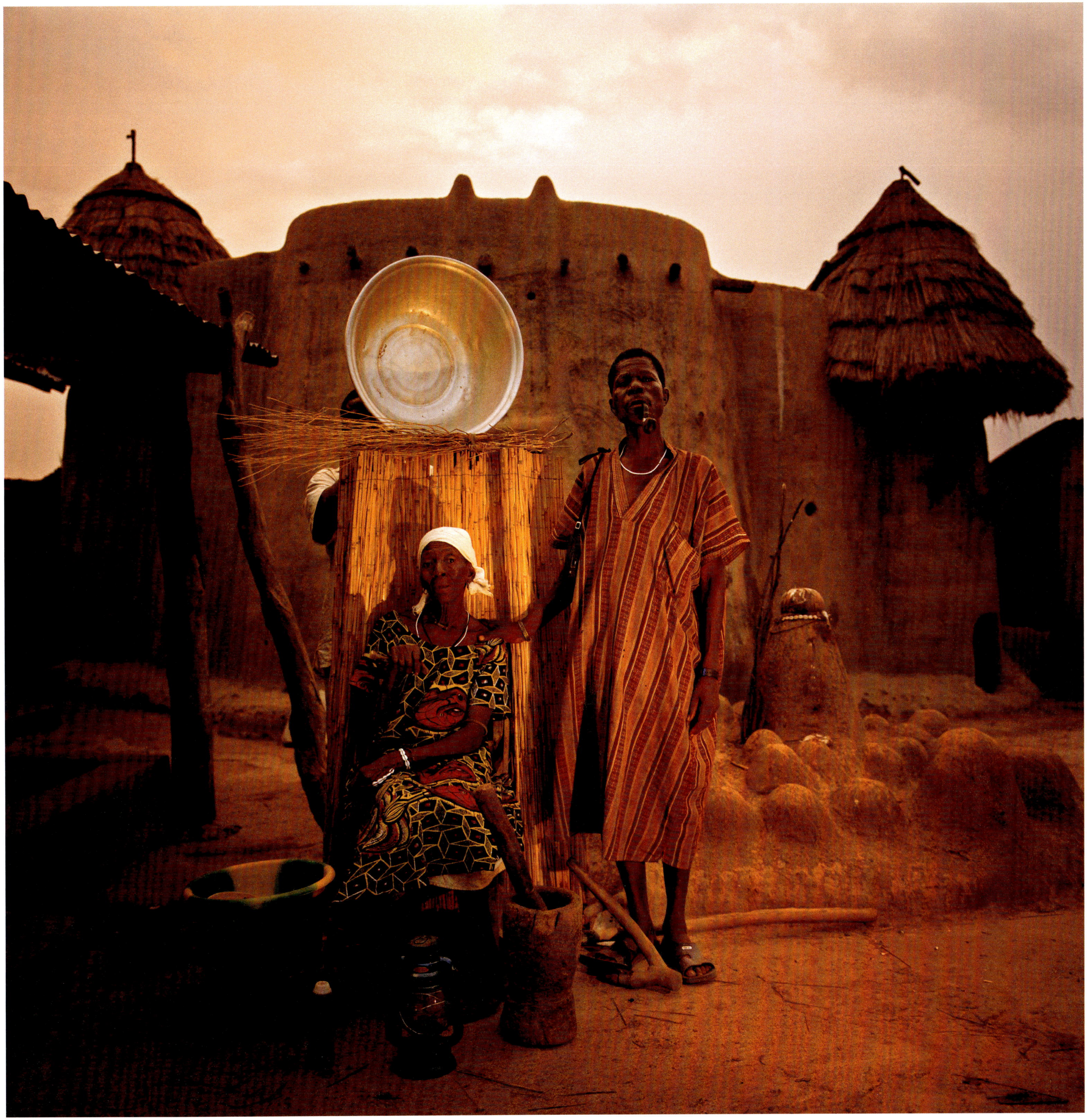

All of our gods have their own distinct character and they accompany us through each moment of our lives. When you are sick you ask Shiva for help. He has the force of the elephant. He is the god of the mountain, who lives above us, smoking grass, with a cobra draped over his shoulders to keep him warm. His son, Ganesh, who has the head of an elephant, helps you get through the obstacles life puts before you. Kali is the anger that sets itself against your enemies and sucks their blood. Lakshmi, depicted as a cow, will give you money if you pray to her. As for Saroti, she can bring you knowledge. ¶ We each have a favorite god and our parents teach us their background. If we take the paths that climb up into the mountains, it is Buddha's presence that accompanies us through life. When our sons come of age, they cut off the head of a goat to alleviate Kali's anger. Then they mount the peaks to seek advice from the lamas who make the rain fall with their drums. ¶ Tika Day is a very important day for us. The young help the elders by sharing what they own, and in each house, the elders bless them in return. They apply pigment and rice to their foreheads so that their wishes may come true.

FAILLE BHATTA, GANESH, SHIVA, KALI, LAKSHMI AND OTHER GODS, DURALI, NEPAL.

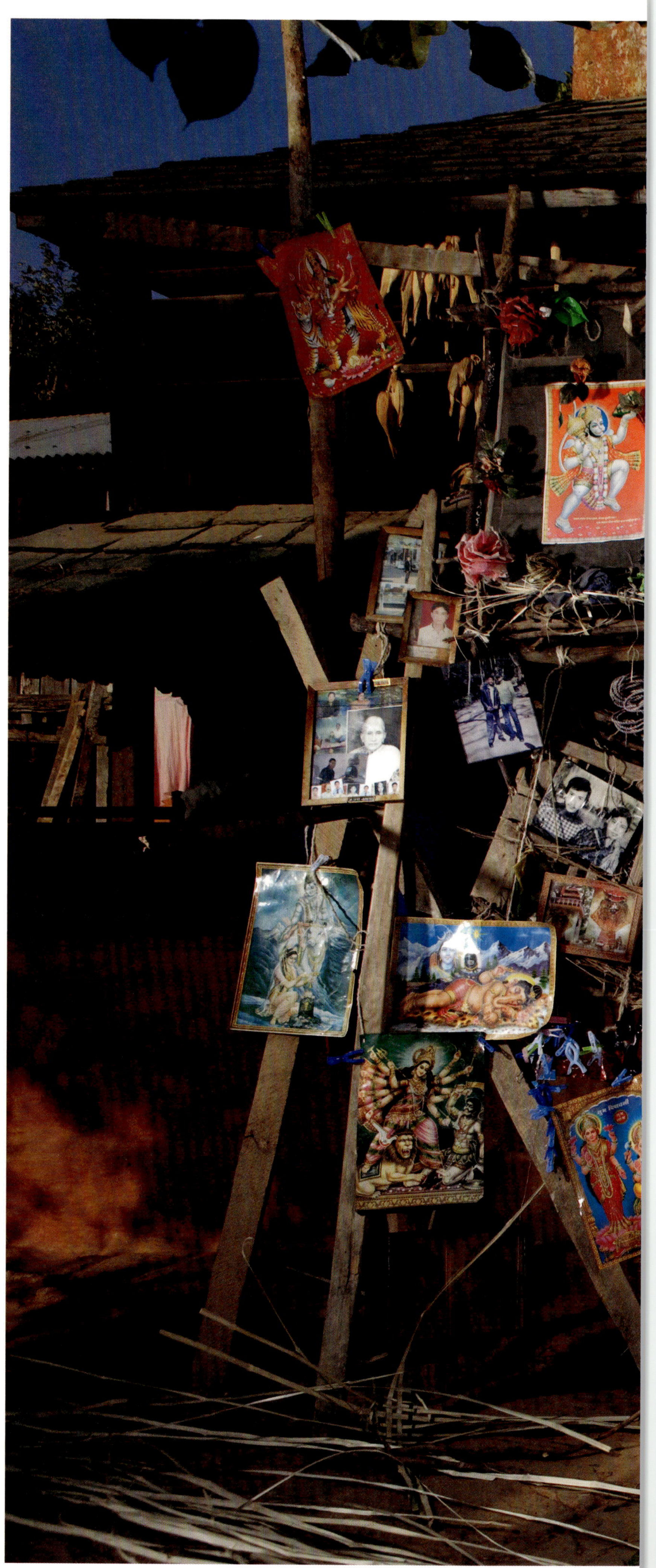

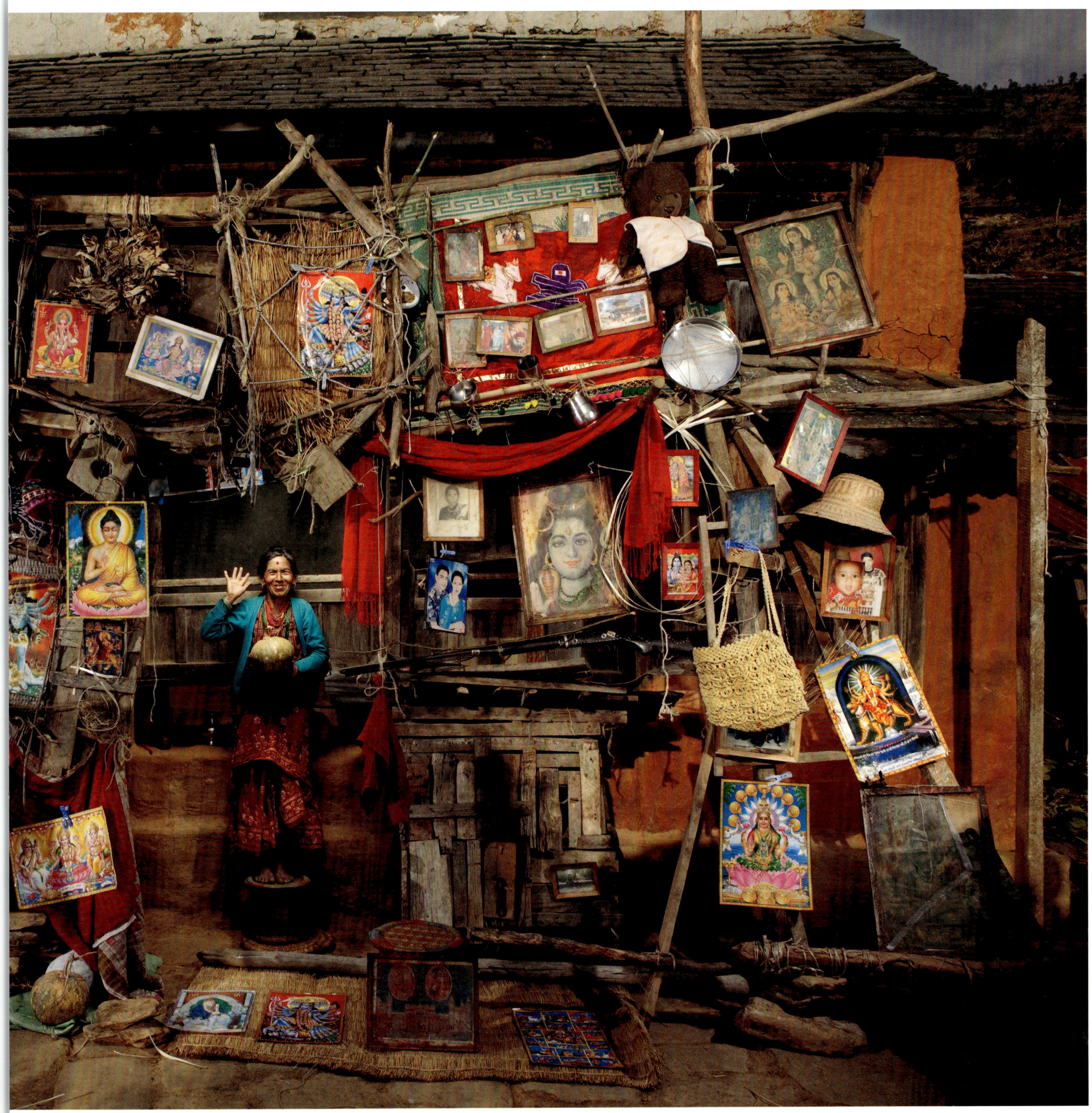

Since the dawn of time we have used the ochre of chalk cliffs to paint our bodies. During traditional ceremonies, the drawings on our skin reflect our family ties. The dots symbolize the desert, and the lines, our region of four rivers. My husband comes from these dots and I from these lines. He comes from the desert and I from the rivers. I come from water. People here are known as Adnyamathanha, people of the rocks. We are on the land of black kangaroos and emus. We are on the land of snakes. But they have become aggressive, as nature has changed, transformed by man. Maybe there are too many vehicles that disturb them. So, I put on my "Lady Bird" dress, the color of a ladybug, which is known to bring good luck, and I take the didgeridoo my son made me with his father's family in the north, and tranquillity and harmony surround me. ¶ I was born with good fortune. I am one of the only women in our village to have been able to leave for studies in Adelaide. I know how to read and I can swim, which is very rare here. Drought is getting worse and worse. Rivers are slowly and surely losing water. From time to time I let the children swim in my water reserve, just so they can feel the pleasure of bathing. My husband comes from the desert and I from the rivers. I come from the lines, I come from water. This is the land that runs through me.

BERYL JOHNSON, SPOTS AND LINES, VADHALEENA, AUSTRALIA.

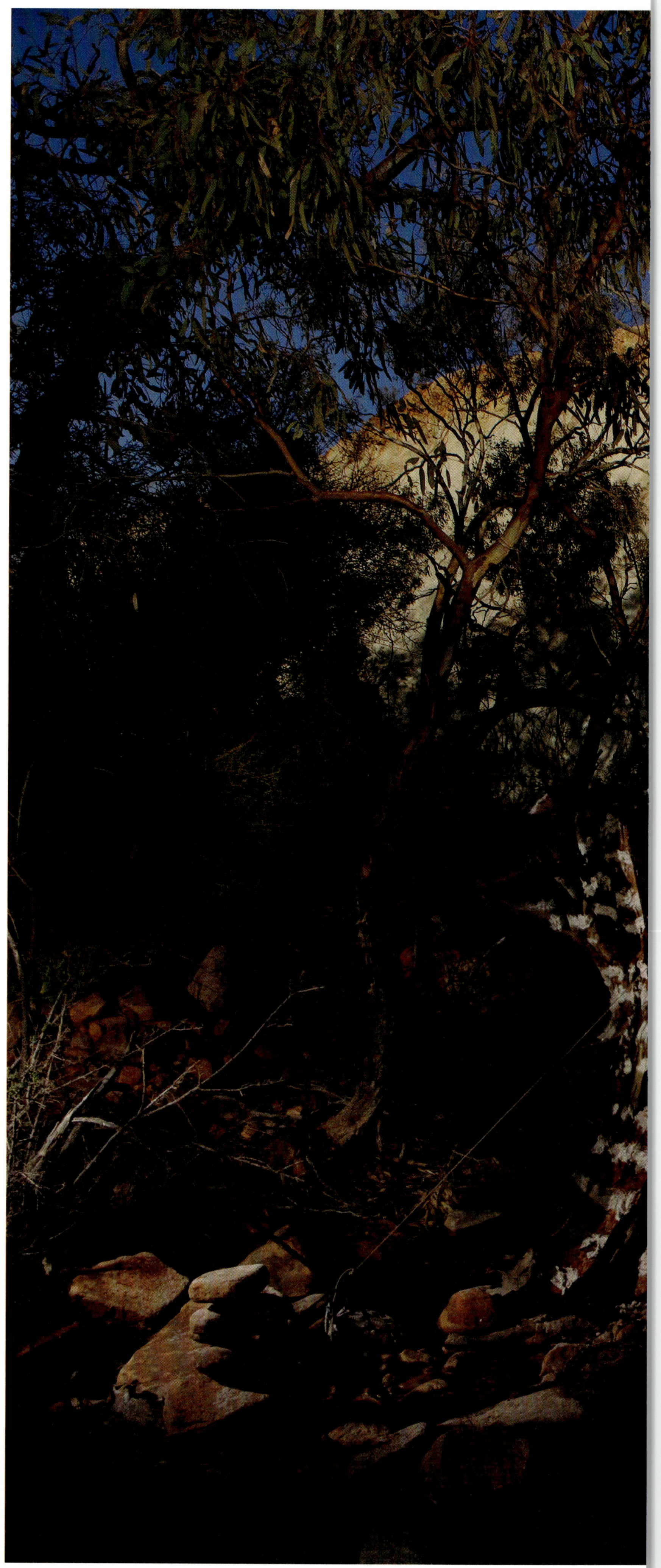

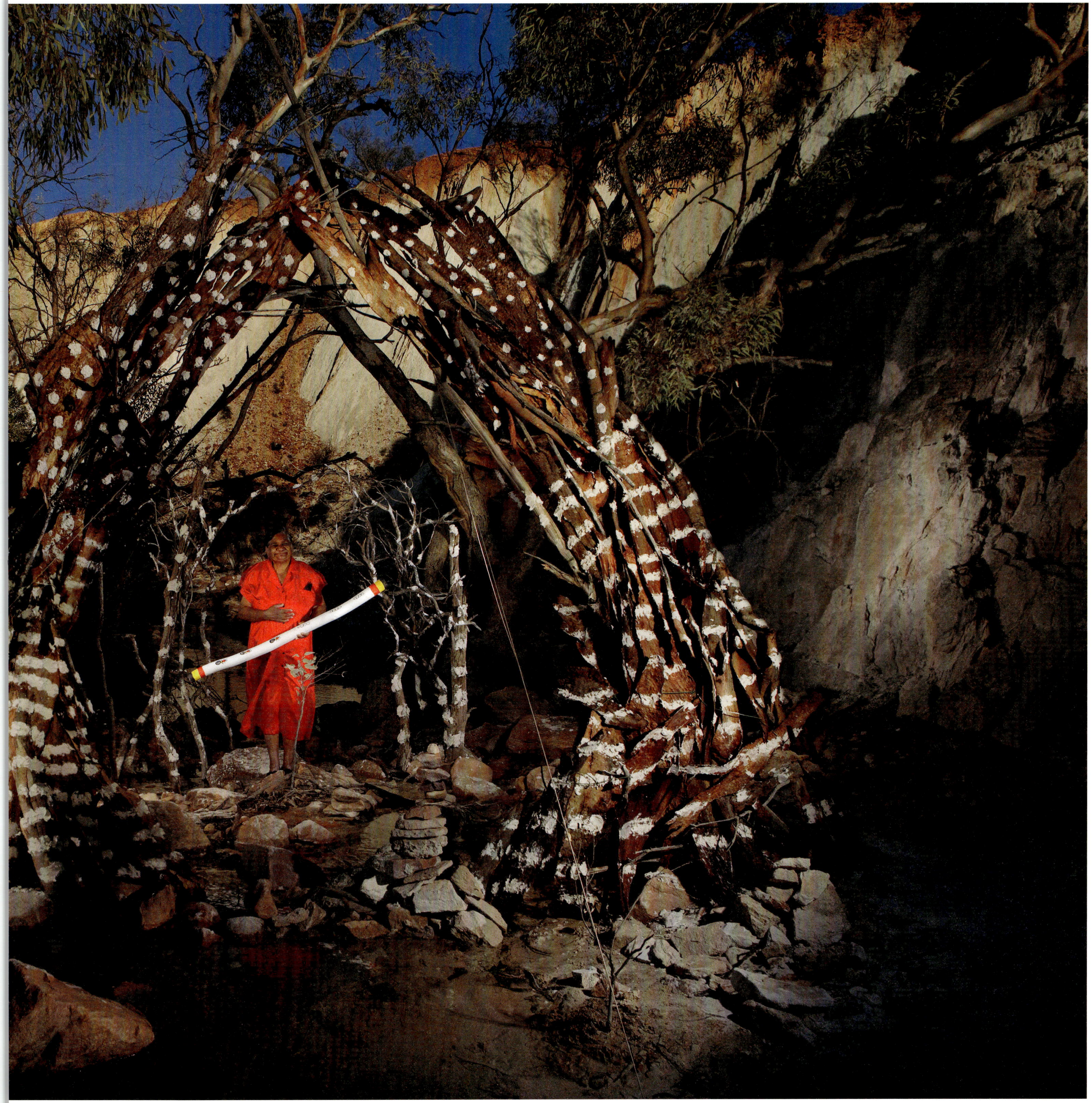

In the desert, days are scorching hot and nights bitterly cold. We have always used the tall grasses that grow in the oasis near the giant cacti to make hats. When I was a child we would also use them to make socks and gloves. ¶ Our shaman is the one who has a relationship with the forces of nature and that of the mountain. He is the one to set the dates of the harvest and for planting. He cares for us with plants and peyotl, the cactus that generates visions that enable us to communicate with the gods. ¶ The water of the Cordillera is a vital element in our lives. Today, man only believes in himself. The gringos of Santiago marry our daughters and bring tourists who take baths in our deserts. I wash my clothes myself in order to save water. Before, everything was much greener. This was back when there was no country. If I have one dream it is to be able to cross over all of these invisible borders to go see the eternal snow on the peaks of the volcanoes.

ESPIRITA LOPEZ MAMANI IN THE OASIS IN THE MIDDLE OF THE DESERT, SAN PEDRO, ATACAMA, CHILE.

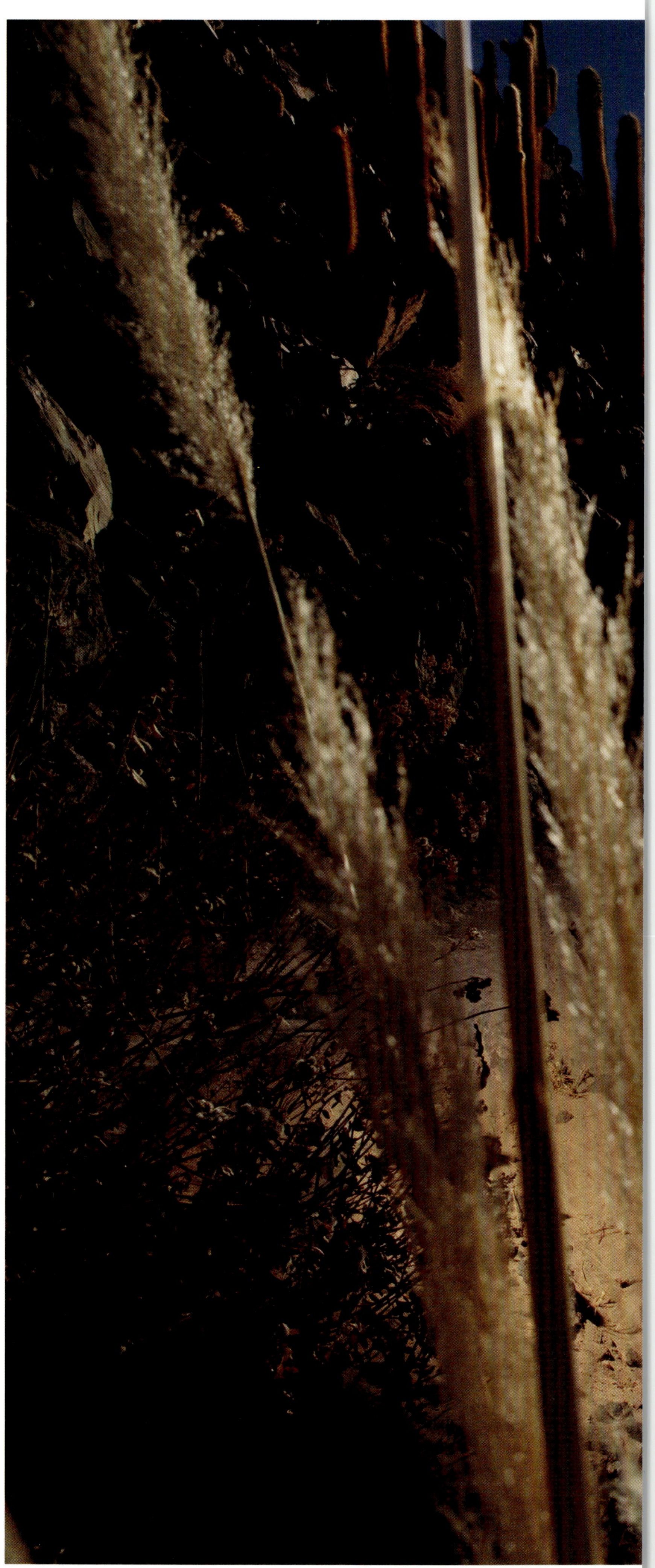

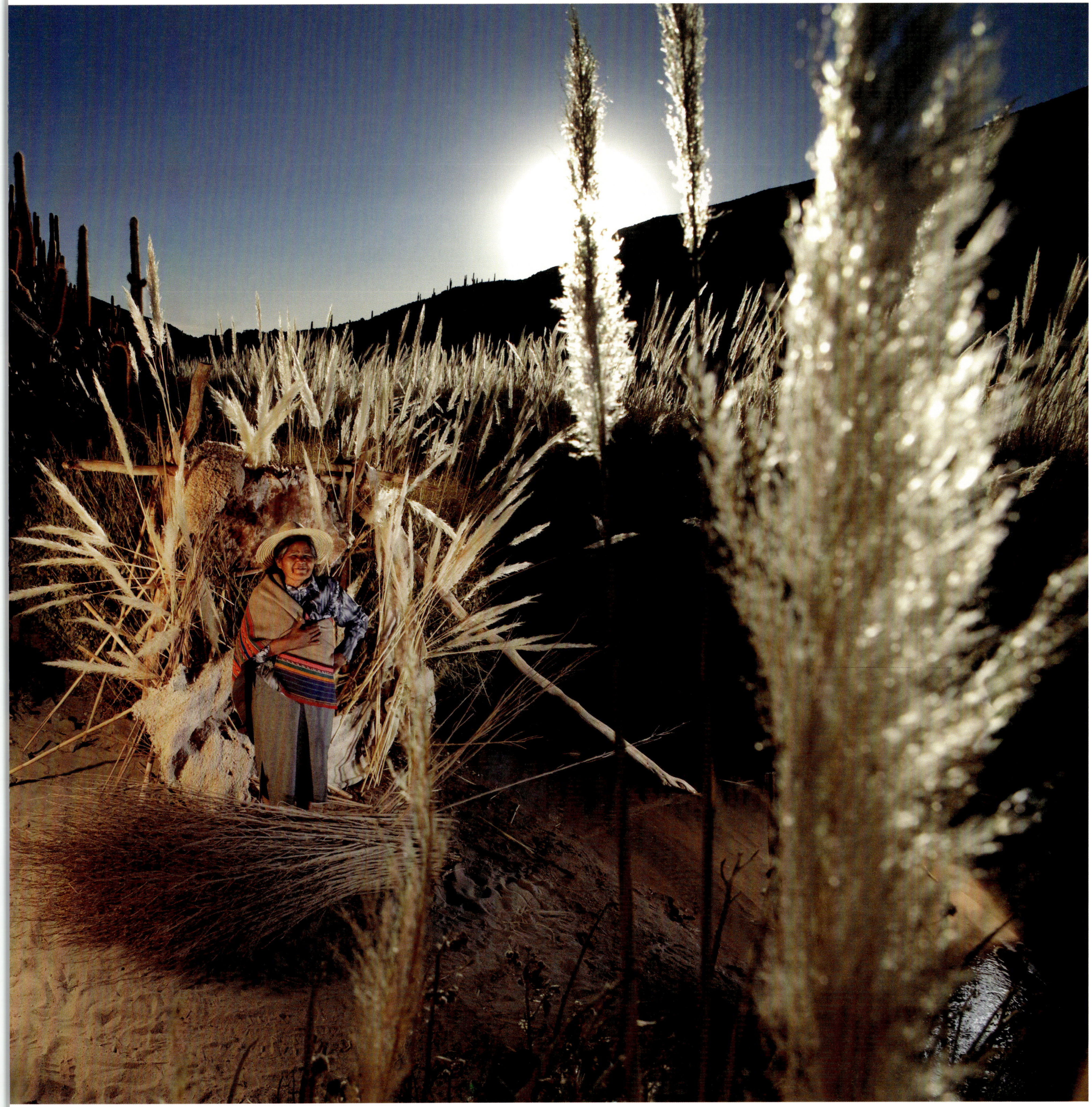

Inside the forest lives our memories, watching us. Our plants and their colors nurture our bodies and our mind. As time goes by, we end up looking like the world in which we live. ¶ In paradise and in our garden lives the spirit of nature's creator who gives us everything. Europeans believe that things don't have souls, but sometimes when you walk beneath the leaves, you hear voices speaking to you. When the new moon comes, everything is dark and rain seems imminent. This isn't a good day to set out into the forest. The tall trees here are sacred, as spirits inhabit them. If you want to cut them down or to burn them, you must do the "Tamafa", the ceremony with a chicken and Kava root. ¶ When the season comes where mangoes are plentiful, we get drunk off their sugar and dance through the villages. The river is the path that leads us to the gardens. This is where I bathe. It is the source of life and the only path that connects the sea to the mountains.

ROLYN THOMPSON AND THE EYE OF THE FOREST, ON THE GARDEN PATH, VINTUA, VANUATU.

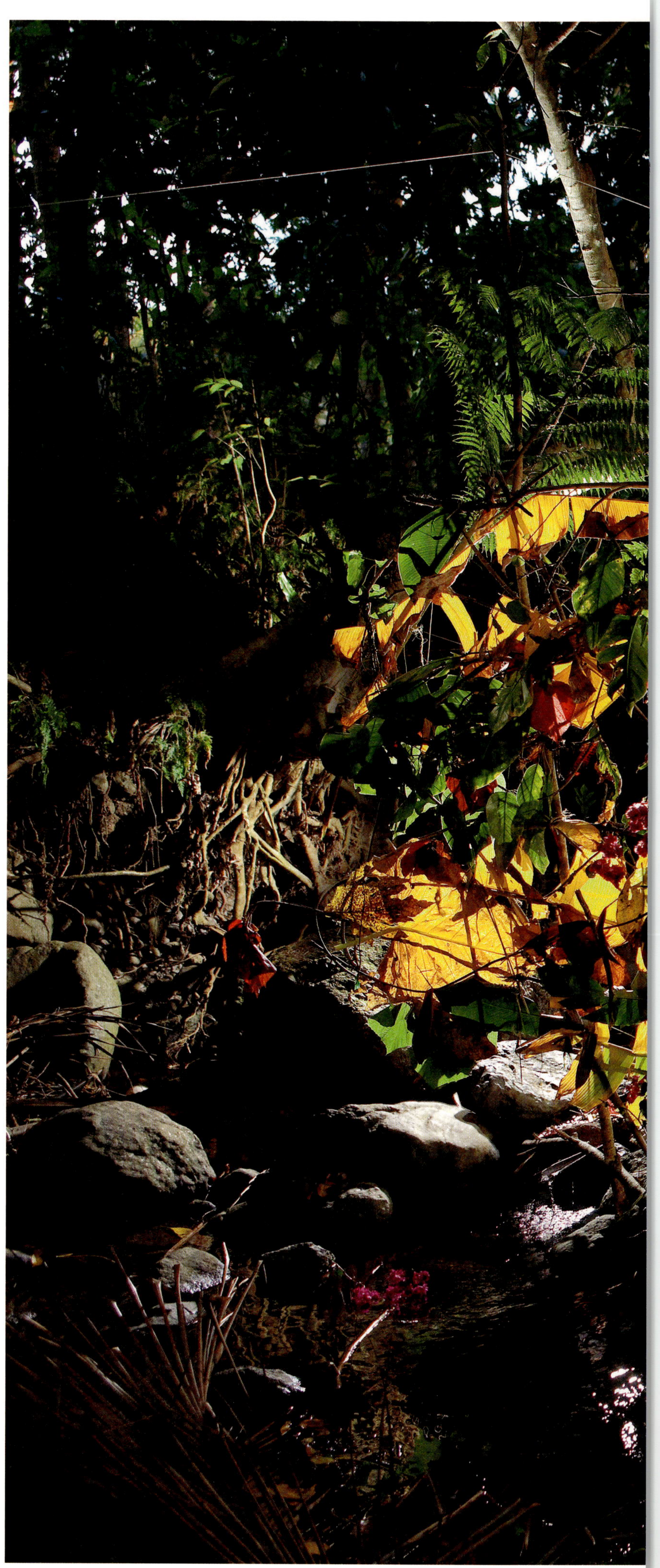

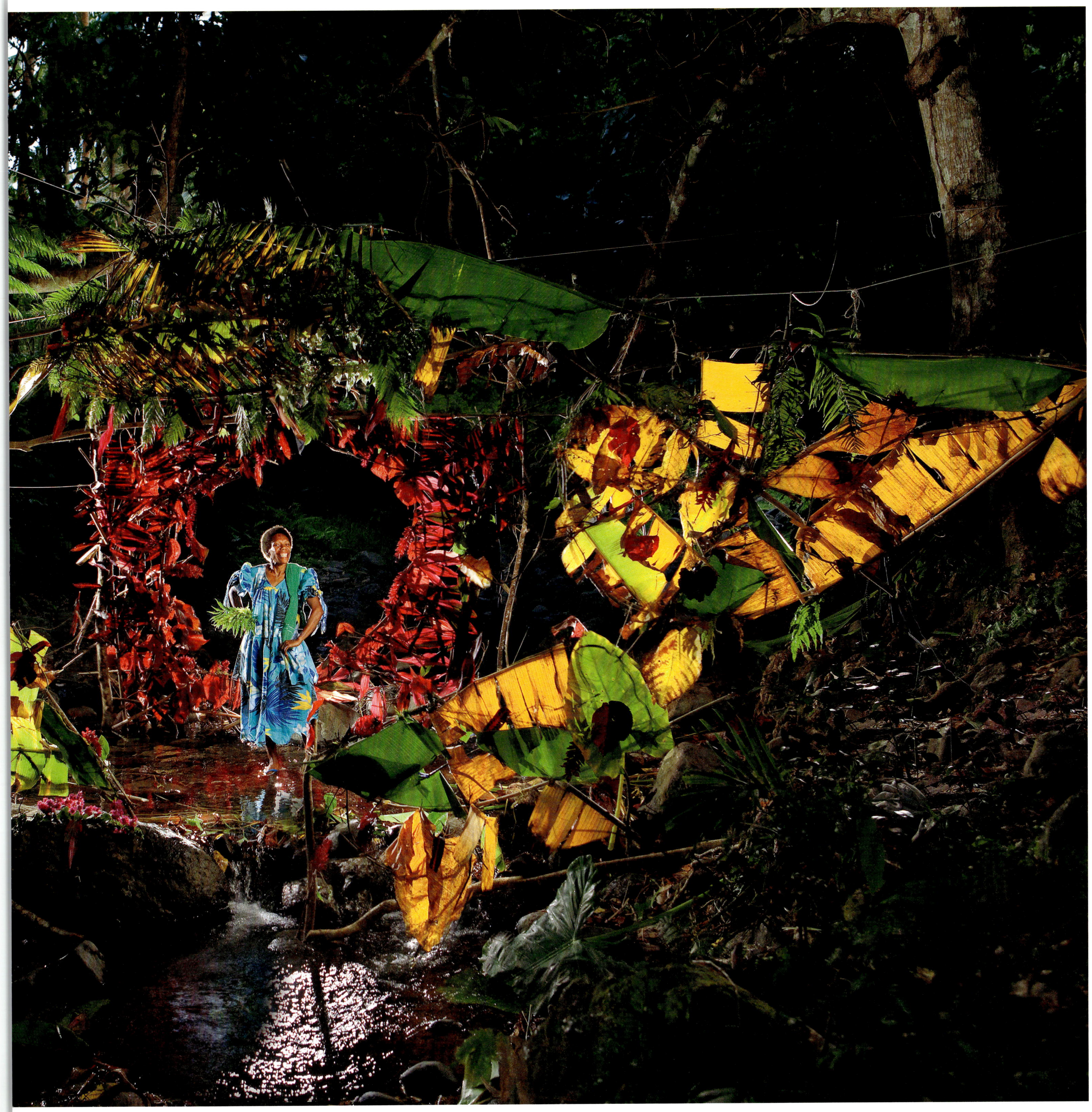

When man landed on the moon I was in front of my television, very surprised that anyone was so eager to go there. There are no plants, nor water, nor oxygen. Nothing but rocks, dust and cold. I wonder sometimes what goes through these men's minds that make them want to go so far. Maybe we need to teach them to look around themselves for something new. ¶ Our children go to Tokyo to study and when they come back, they can't find work. So generations no longer live together. Me, I took care of my parents and those of my husband's. My children should do the same, give and receive, if they want to understand the meaning of our lives. The retirement homes and the aged who die alone, that is sad. For me, we must lead life in a natural way; live and die with our family. ¶ The winter here is long and hard. We impatiently await spring and the bloom of the flowers. Then comes the time of festivities. Each year, it's a rebirth. This miracle, I don't wish to understand as, in the mystery, lives joy.

YOSUE NUMAZAWA AND THE SCARECROWS OF THE SEASONS, YAMAGATA, JAPAN.

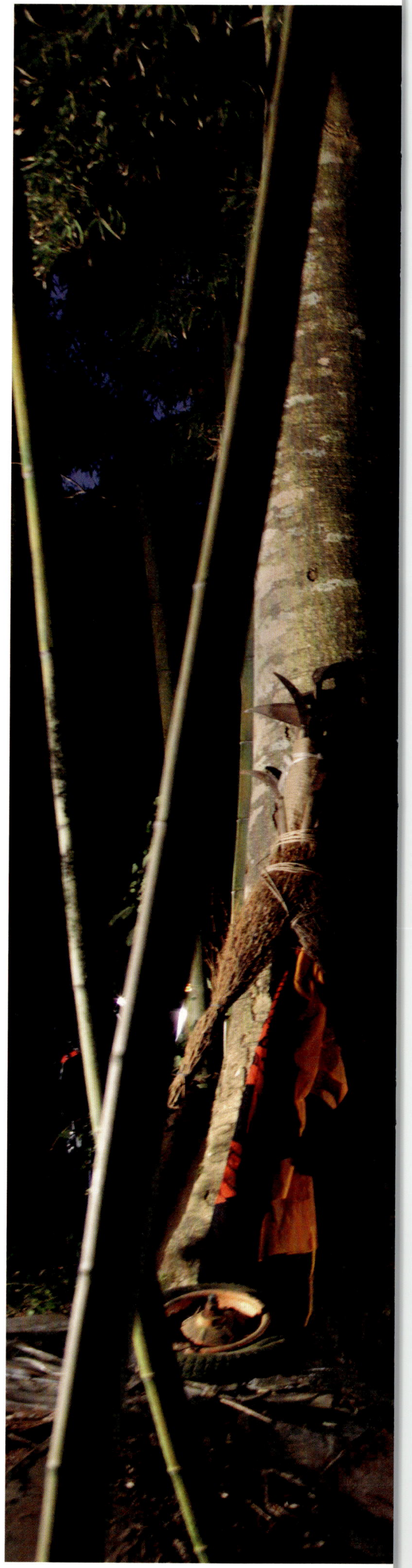

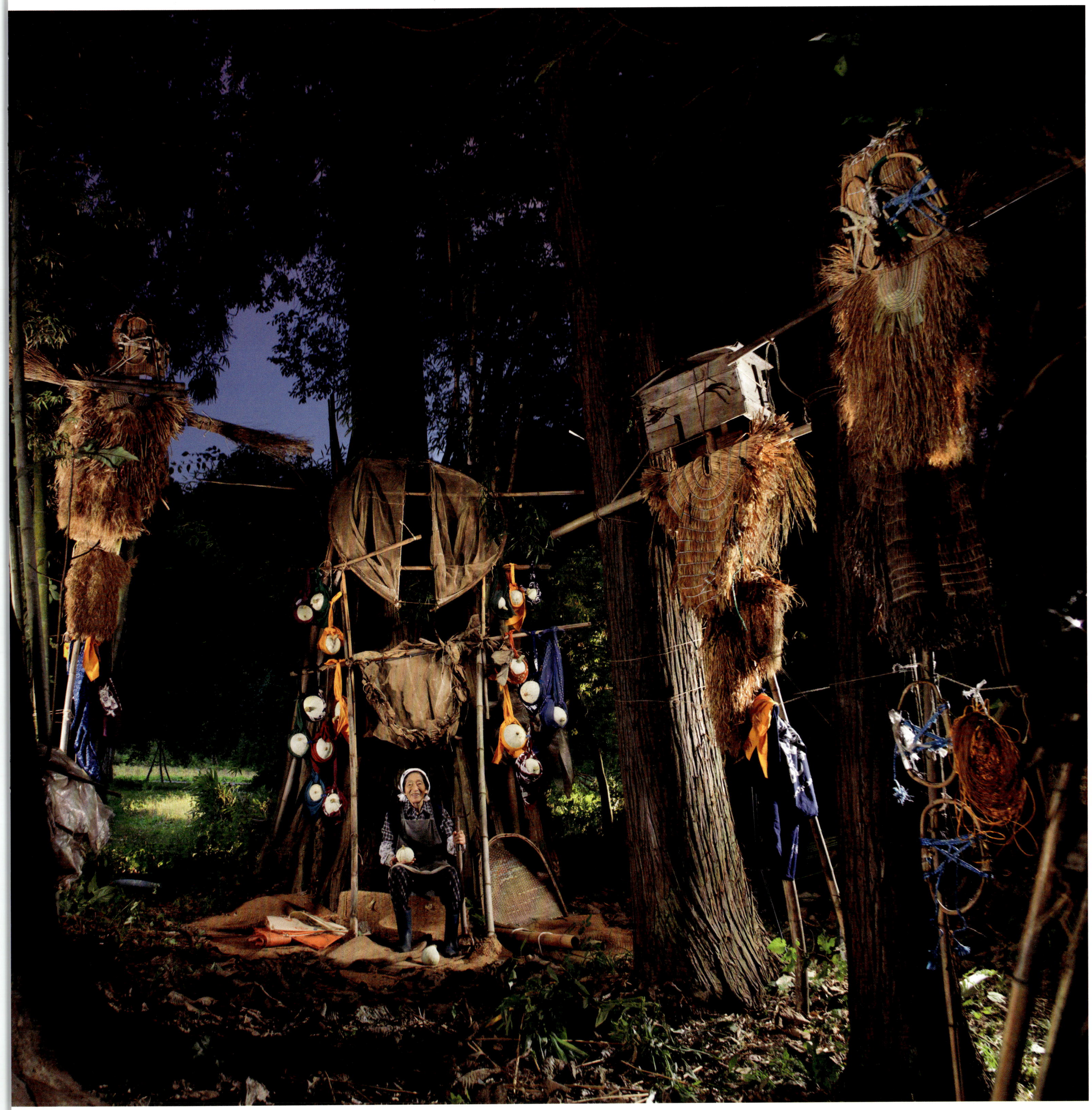

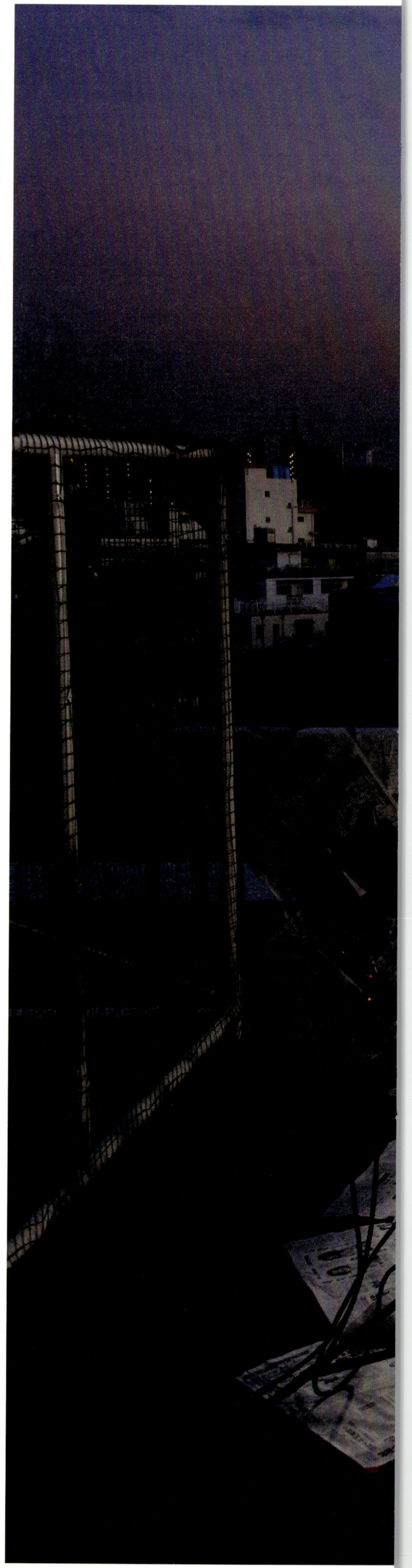

Robots, androids, and artificial intelligence are like new consciences. They have immense potential, and are the instruments of my creation. Technology and biology will one day merge. We will create hybrids of half-humans and half-machines. Personally, I already feel as though I am a product of this transformation. I am half-man, half-machine, and that means the beginning of chaos! ¶ The first major events of chaotic science were biotechnology and cloning. But that was only the beginning: after Newton and Einstein, chaos science will be the third revolution. The first two have made the Earth sick. The third shall determine our destiny. ¶ Japan is already full of robots. They're everywhere. Robotic legs that allow the handicapped to walk, robotic fish that cause farmed fish to move, drones that wage war, as in Afghanistan… ¶ What worries me is that man will one day create a superhuman. Artificial intelligence would control humanity and take over. Everybody lined up in rows, devoid of consciousness, dominated by machines. Nothing but wires in the brain and Big Brother watching over us. We would succumb to absolute fascism. Will it ever be possible to turn back the clock? Maybe, one day, we'll simply want to become human again.

KO NAKAJIMA, CONNECTED TO THE MACHINES OF HIS OWN CREATION, ROOFTOPS OF TOKYO, JAPAN.

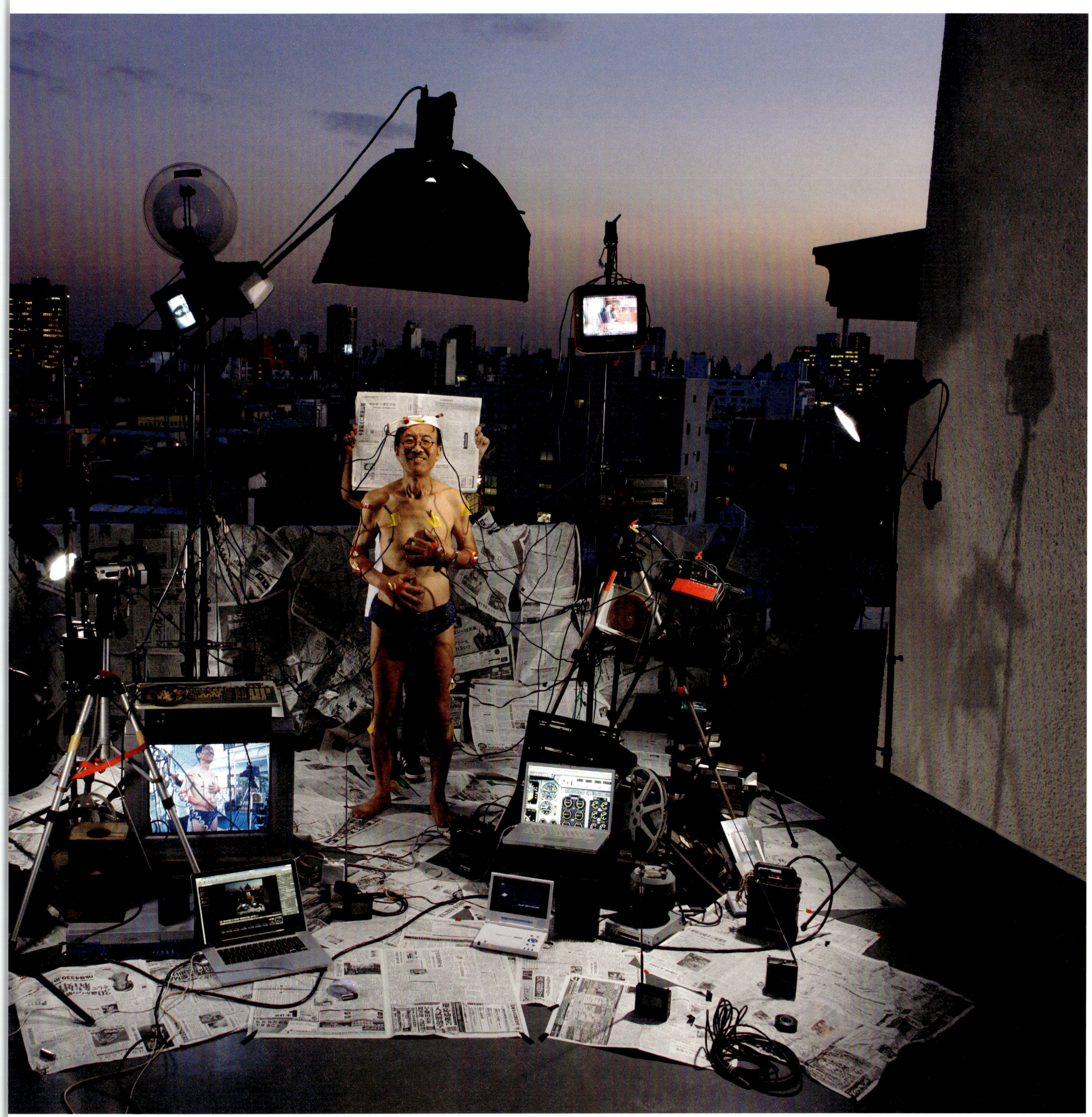

Every night I go out to sea with my nightlight, and my bow and arrows. I put out my lines when the fish come out to eat the crabs. I dive down to take in my arms the turtles that sleep around these reefs. I will go great distances to search out the kind of giant conque that can feed an entire family. We live at the base of a volcano that sometimes takes on the color of the setting sun. When it bursts out in anger, huge black stones go flying across the sky. ¶ One day, someone used the magic of our custom to make the rain come. On the waves of the sea, he abandoned leaves that transformed the weather and by his fault a cyclone came. Trees were destroyed; houses of wood and coconuts were carried away. We had nothing left. Then, a helicopter appeared. It left us tents and food to survive. If I could have flown with him, I would have brought back an enormous fish to feed the entire village.

THOMAS CHARLEY AND HIS HELICOPTER FISH, TANA, VANUATU.

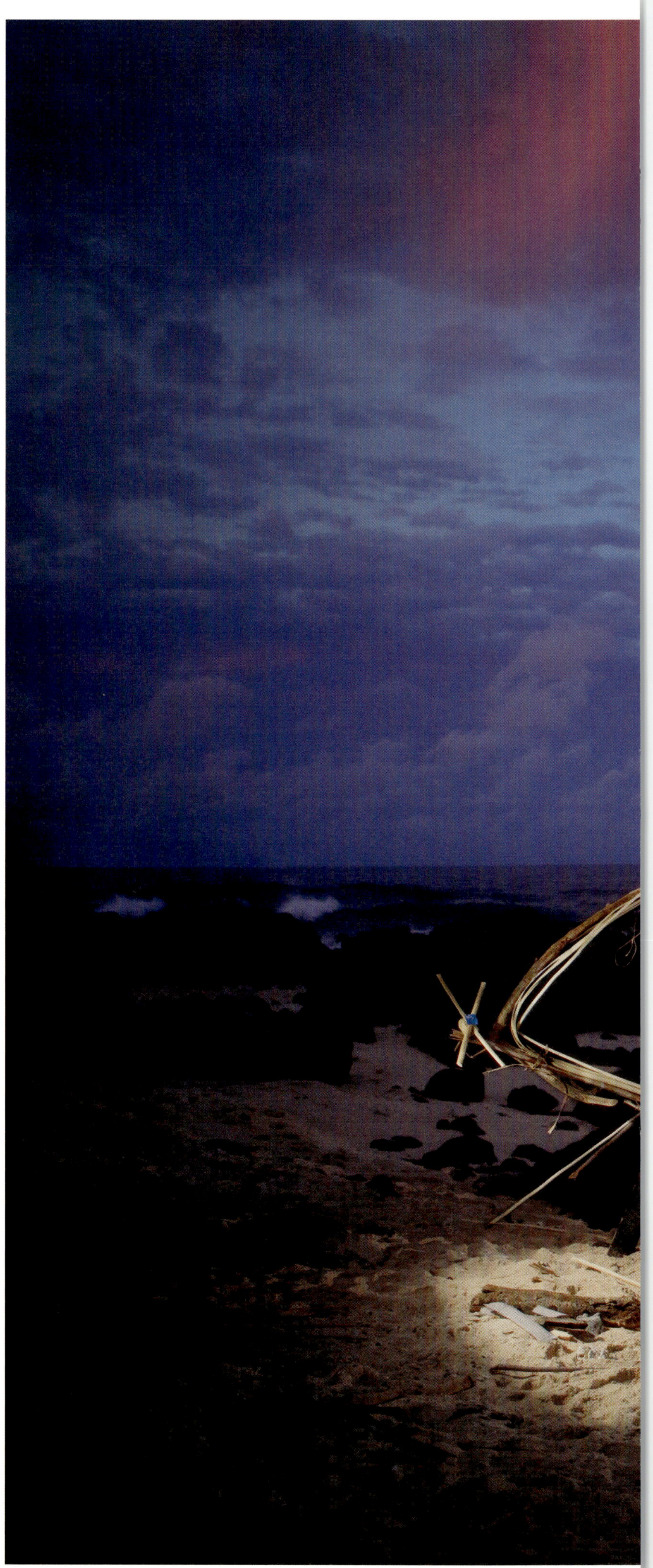

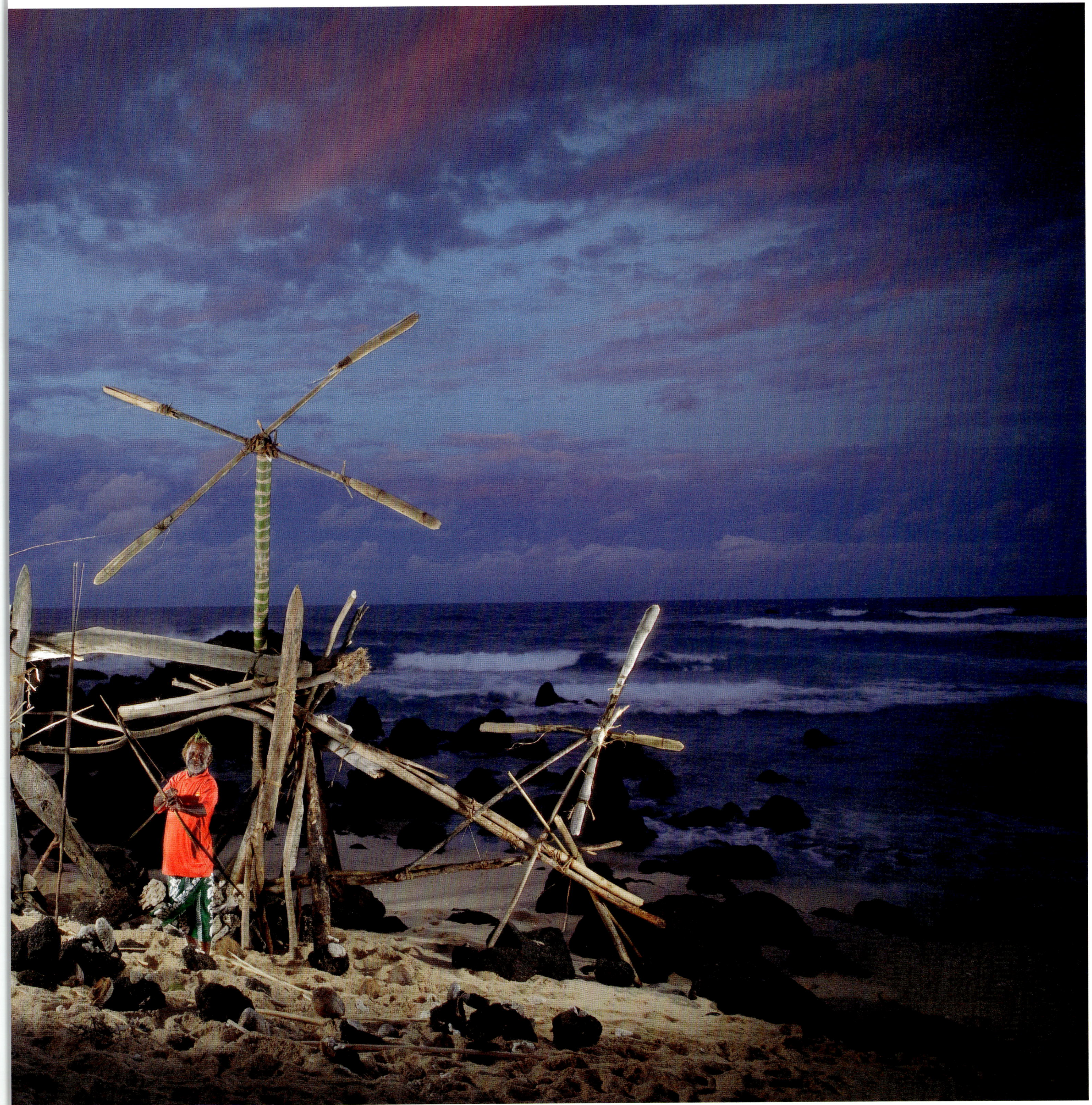

I was 8 years old when I came to China. That was the age I started to work. For years I lived in the noise and chaos of constructions sites, building house on top of house. We built a world amongst clouds of dust that I can still feel in my lungs. Today, our towers are so high that soon they will block out all daylight. ¶ I was very ill when I met my master. He asked me to sit in an invisible chair. Each day, I came back to see him. Each day, for an entire year, I was immobile. ¶ These days, at dawn, in the depths of the garden, the elders join me to practice tai chi. Our search for harmony and equilibrium draws our attention to the tree. Its roots will accompany us in our destiny, even if man no longer knows how to live with the seeds that give fruit.

WOO KWONG HOU DOING TAI-CHI ON A ROOFTOP IN HONG KONG.

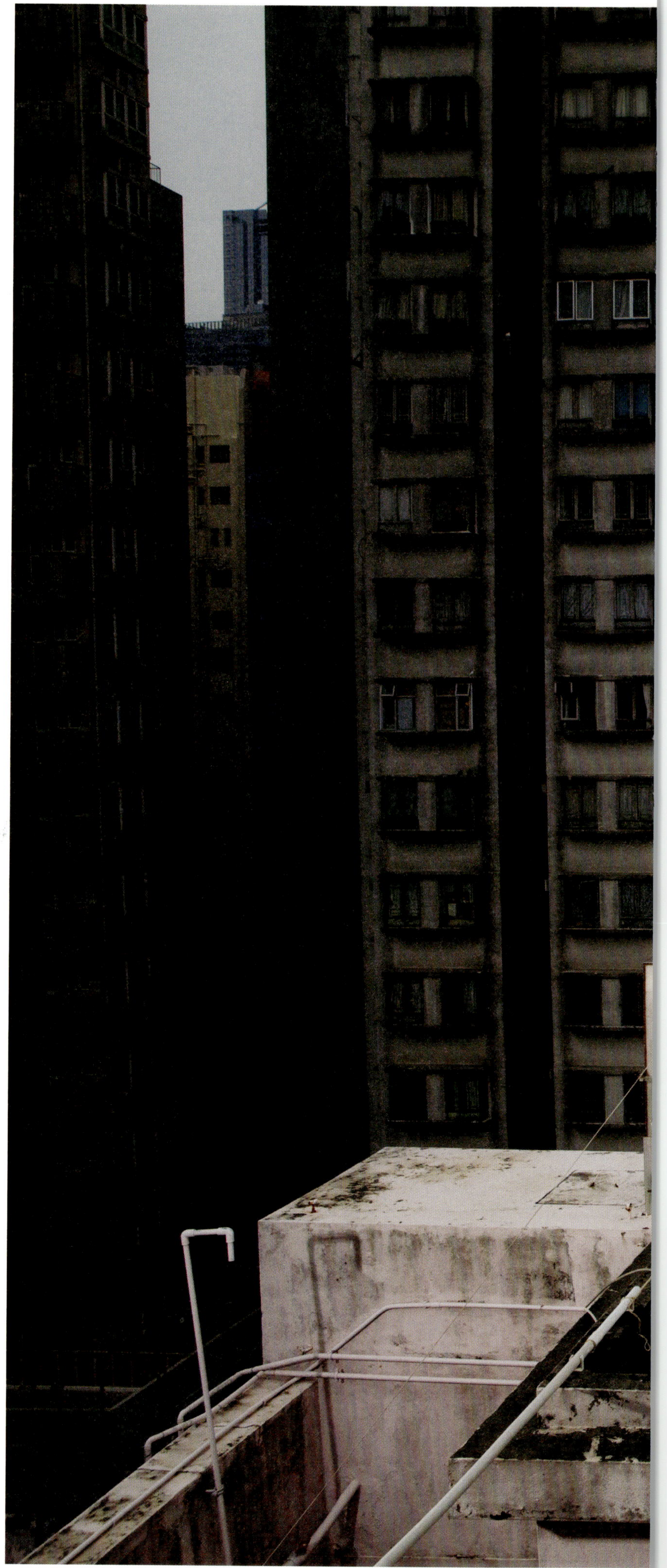

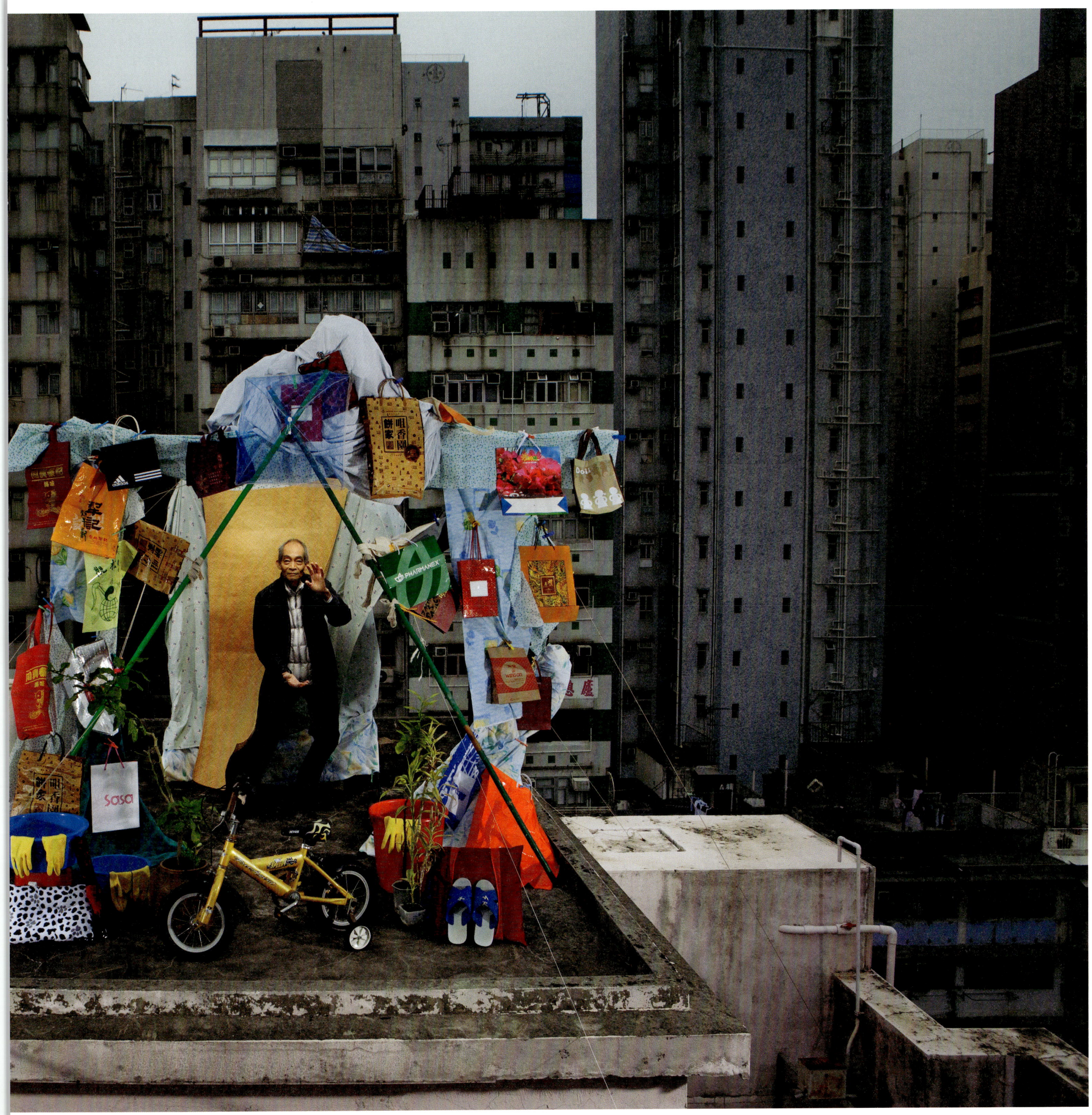
adidas
PHARMANEX
sasa

AMÉRICA GERMINA NARVAEZ ¶ PENG VARIKUL
NICOLAS JACKY ¶ JAMIL SALAMI KAWALDEH
RAYMUNDO GERMANO DA CRUZ ¶ TAE LEA
VARIKUL ¶ SEGUNDO MANUEL COUCHA ¶ HE
KAWALDEH ¶ WAYAN RETU ¶ MADE RENI ¶ LE
TAE LEAMAN ¶ AMÉRICA GERMINA NARVAEZ ¶
HENRI SUQUET ¶ NICOLAS JACKY ¶ JAMIL SAL
CAPITAINE RAYMUNDO GERMANO DA CRUZ ¶
PENG VARIKUL ¶ SEGUNDO MANUEL COUCHA ¶
KAWALDEH ¶ WAYAN RETU ¶ MADE RENI ¶ LE
TAE LEAMAN ¶ AMÉRICA GERMINA NARVAEZ ¶
HENRI SUQUET ¶ NICOLAS JACKY ¶ JAMIL SAL
CAPITAINE RAYMUNDO GERMANO DA CRUZ ¶
PENG VARIKUL ¶ SEGUNDO MANUEL COUCH
SALAMI KAWALDEH ¶ WAYAN RETU ¶ MADE RE
GERMANO DA CRUZ ¶ TAE LEAMAN ¶ AMÉRICA
PENG VARIKUL ¶ SEGUNDO MANUEL COUCH
SALAMI KAWALDEH ¶ WAYAN RETU ¶ MADE R
CRUZ ¶ TAE LEAMAN ¶ AMÉRICA GERMINA N

THE PLAYHOUSE
BUILT IN THE DEAD TREE

In my grandmothers' time, we used to say that the old trees should not be cut down for they are the monuments from our past. They have been a part of history, that of the Quecha, the Mapuche and Aymara people; then, along came the Spanish and the creation of borders. The old trees are relics of ancient times. ¶ The white flag that my children carry waves above the roofs in our village. It whispers our growing anger to the breeze: a factory will be built on the geysers, on the territory of our ancestors. These geysers are the life, the force of the land, and its breath. They give us water to cultivate our land, which little by little, is turning into a desert. ¶ Perhaps one day, our children who have left to study will come back to teach us how to build a different world. But school doesn't teach them the consciousness of a living earth, the essence of nature. They don't learn how to make fire, read the sky, understand the meaning of different lights, all that which we learned from our parents. Tomorrow, if we don't pass along our wisdom, the drum will cease to beat and the homes will be built in dead trees.

AMERICA GERMINA NARVAEZ AND HER GRANDCHILDREN, ATACAMA, CHILE.

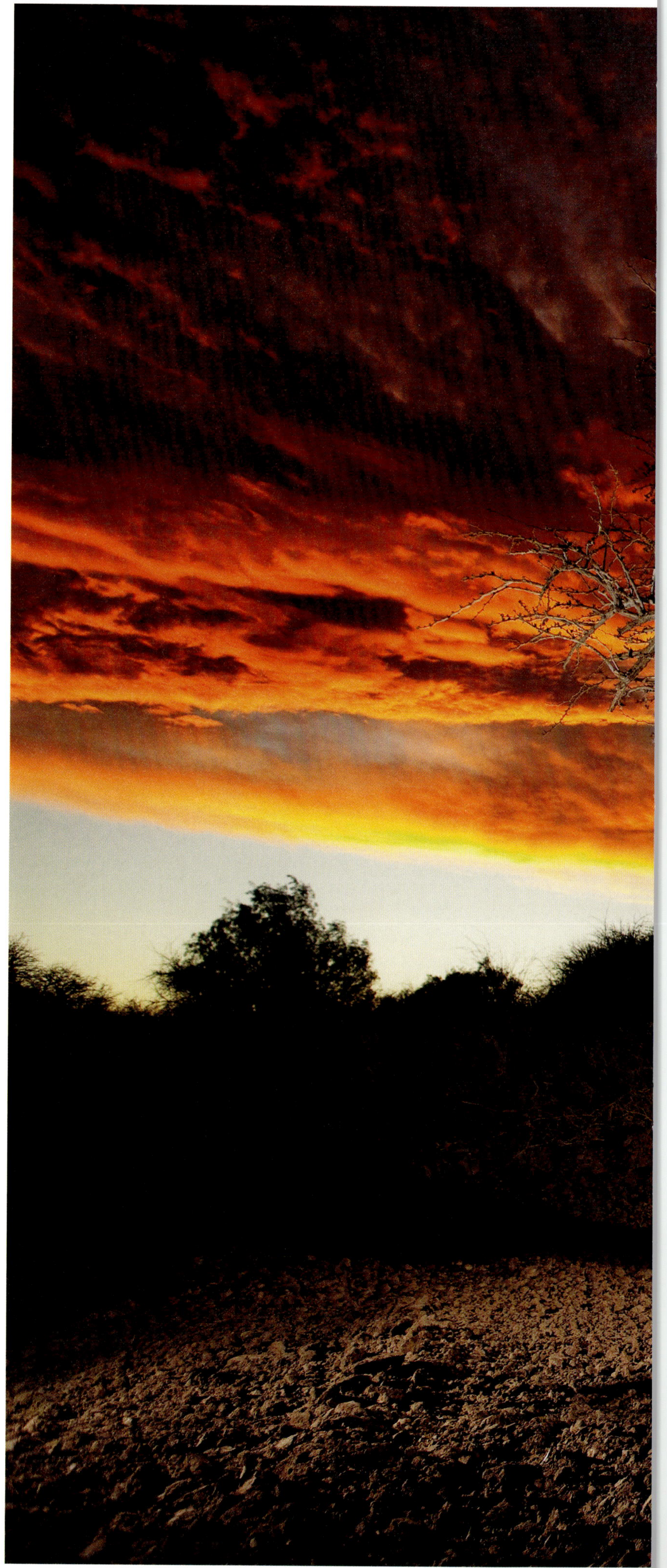

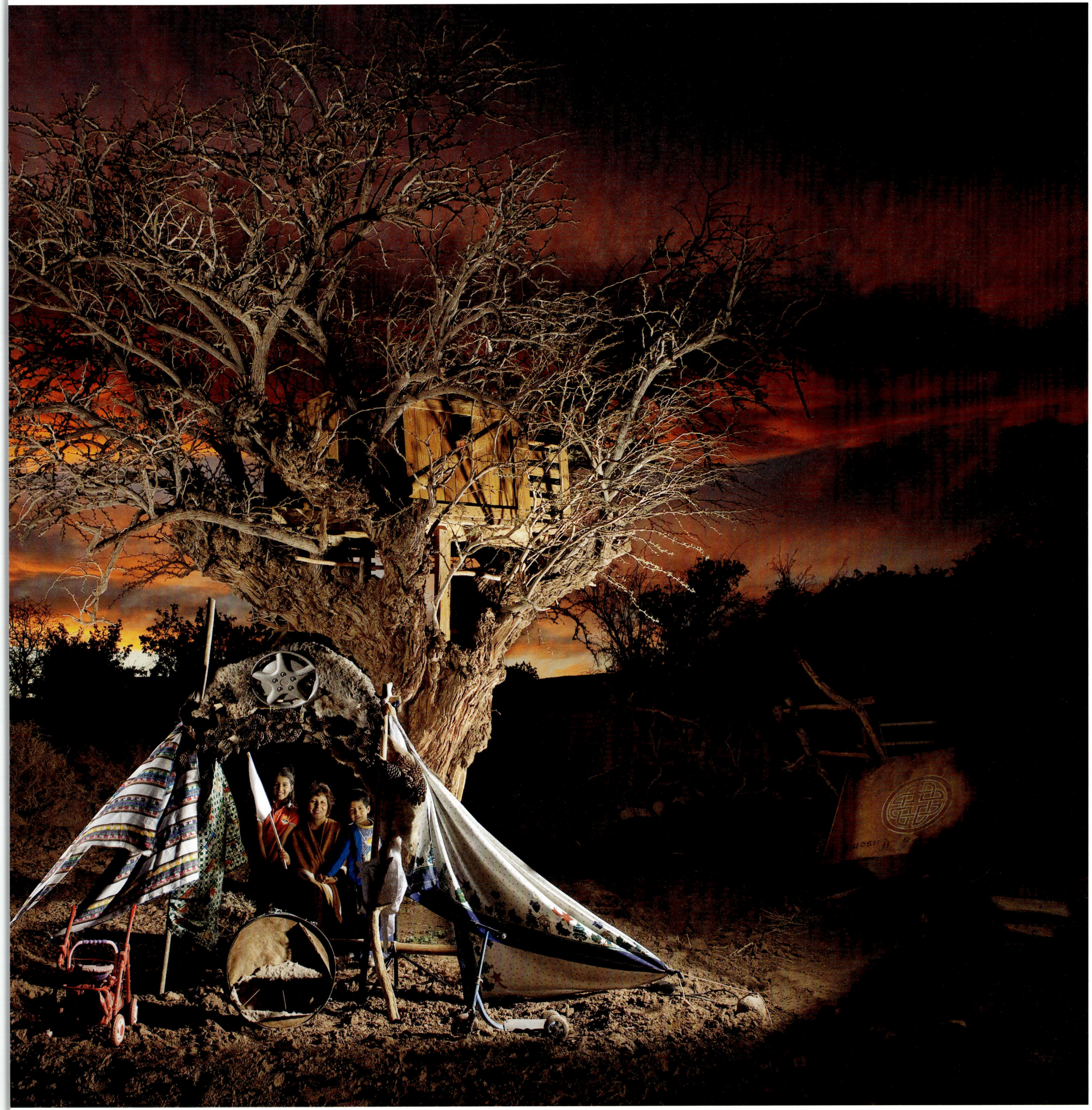

It was 9 o'clock that morning when the sea rolled in, like the great tides. The wave was enormous, as high as a mountain. Families ran inland with their children. I saw my house on the edge of the water collapse under the strain of the tsunami. We spent several nights in the forest, not knowing what new phenomenons to expect. Now, when I go afar to fight big fish, I am scared of the big waves and the wind. I am constantly studying the lights and the movement of the ocean. ¶ When I was younger, my wife drowned while we were fishing. It is difficult to raise our children alone, even more so as the sea has changed. Since motorboats arrived there are fewer and fewer fish. And fifty years ago, the beach was much larger. I think one day we shall have to leave, as our islands will have been swallowed up by the sea. ¶ These hardships give us the experience we need to overcome new difficulties and my love for my children will always allow me to start anew.

PENG VARIKUL, CAMPING IN HIS TREE ABOVE THE SEA, KOH MUK ISLAND, THAILAND.

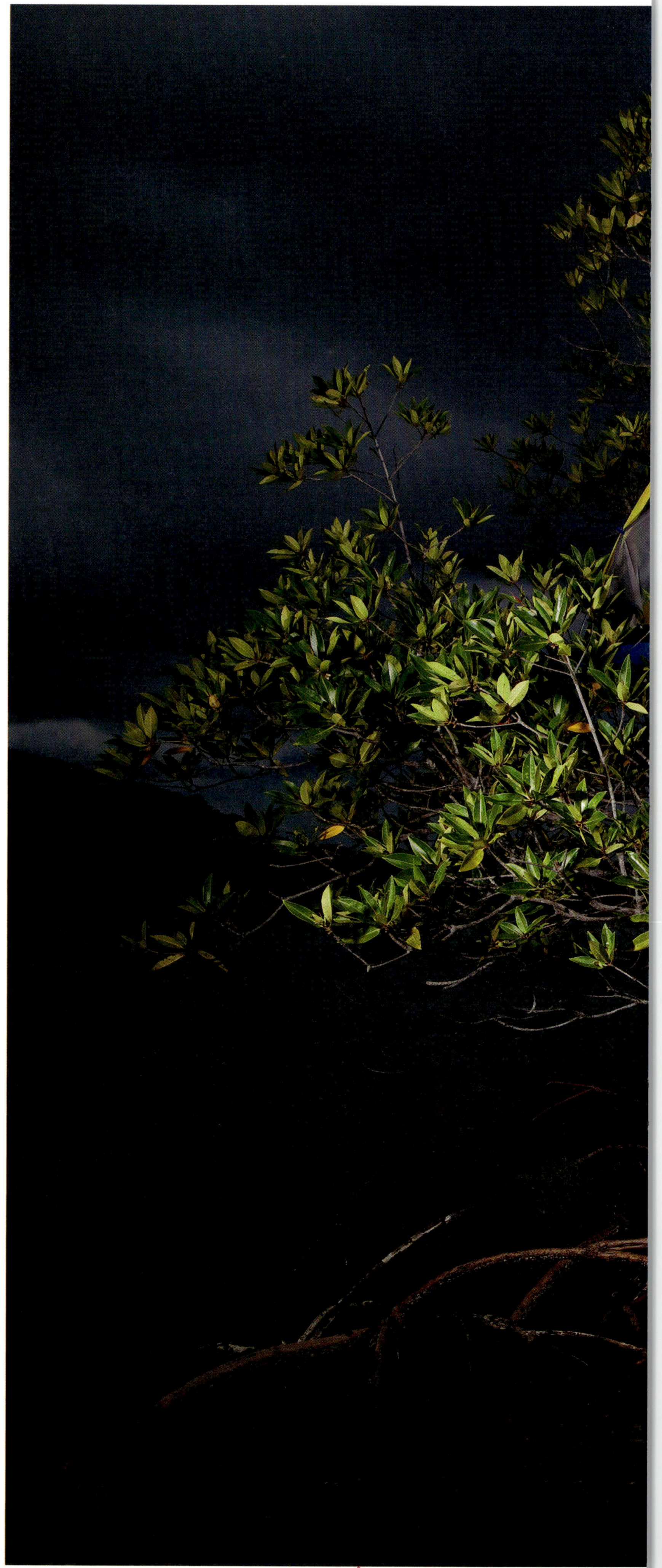

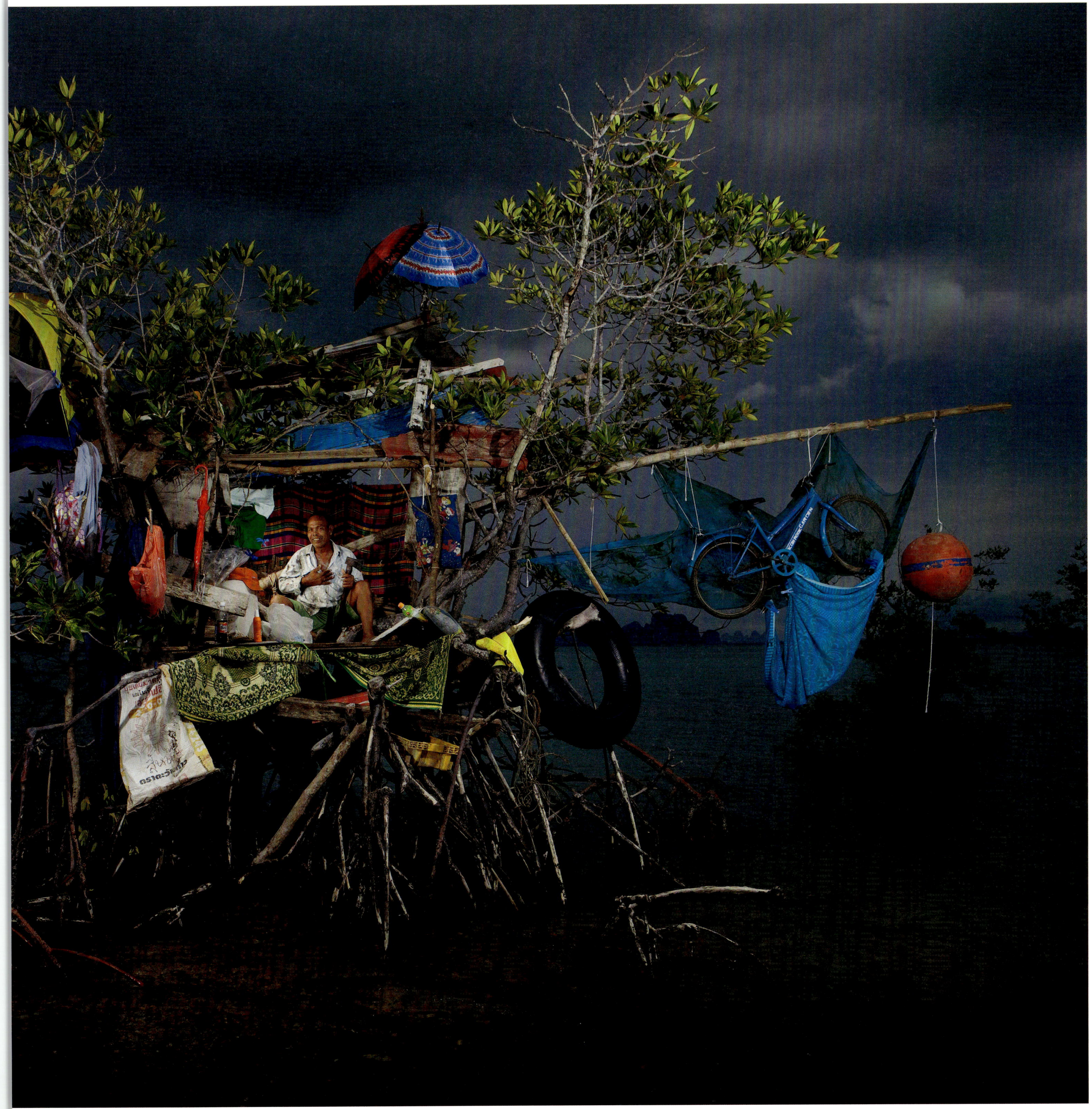

Our village is in the shape of a condor, the spirit of our mountains. We are like the immense shadow of its wings spread through the sky. Several years ago, the army came to train in our region. There were explosions near the volcano and the condors disappeared. Today, we are like a shadow of a bygone age. ¶ Pachamama, our mother earth, has fallen ill. The snow and ice are disappearing. The climate has changed and the desert gains ground with each day that passes. In our community, we are so poor that we must help each other out. In order for the village to survive, we welcome strangers. Their money allows us to keep our children at our sides instead of sending them to the slums. Thus our families are able to stay together. We can continue to cultivate our native plants and raise our animals. We can continue to lead the cows out to the pasture on the big mountain, higher and higher until one day, one of us sees a new condor whose spirit will return to live amongst us.

SEGUNDO MANUEL COUCHA IN THE VILLAGE OF CASA CONDOR, AT THE FOOT OF THE CHIMBORAZO VOLCANO, ECUADOR.

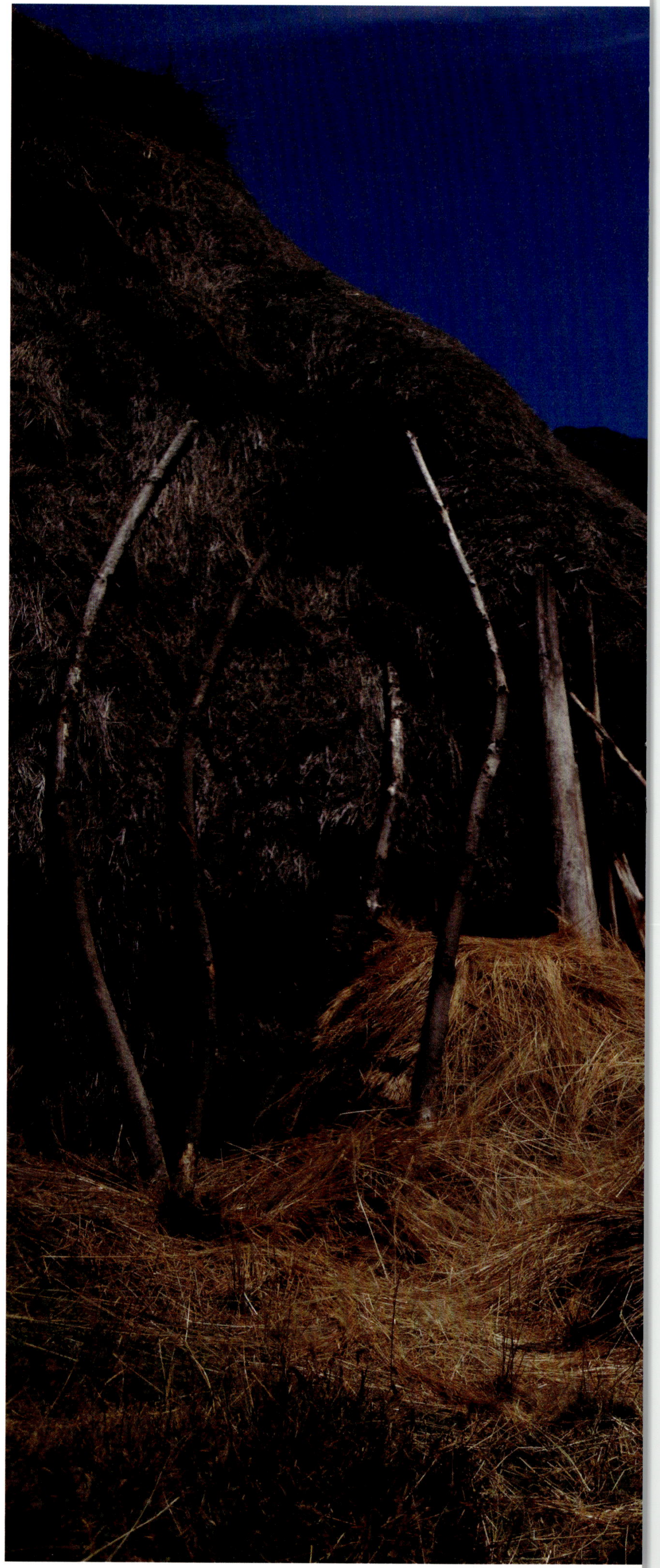

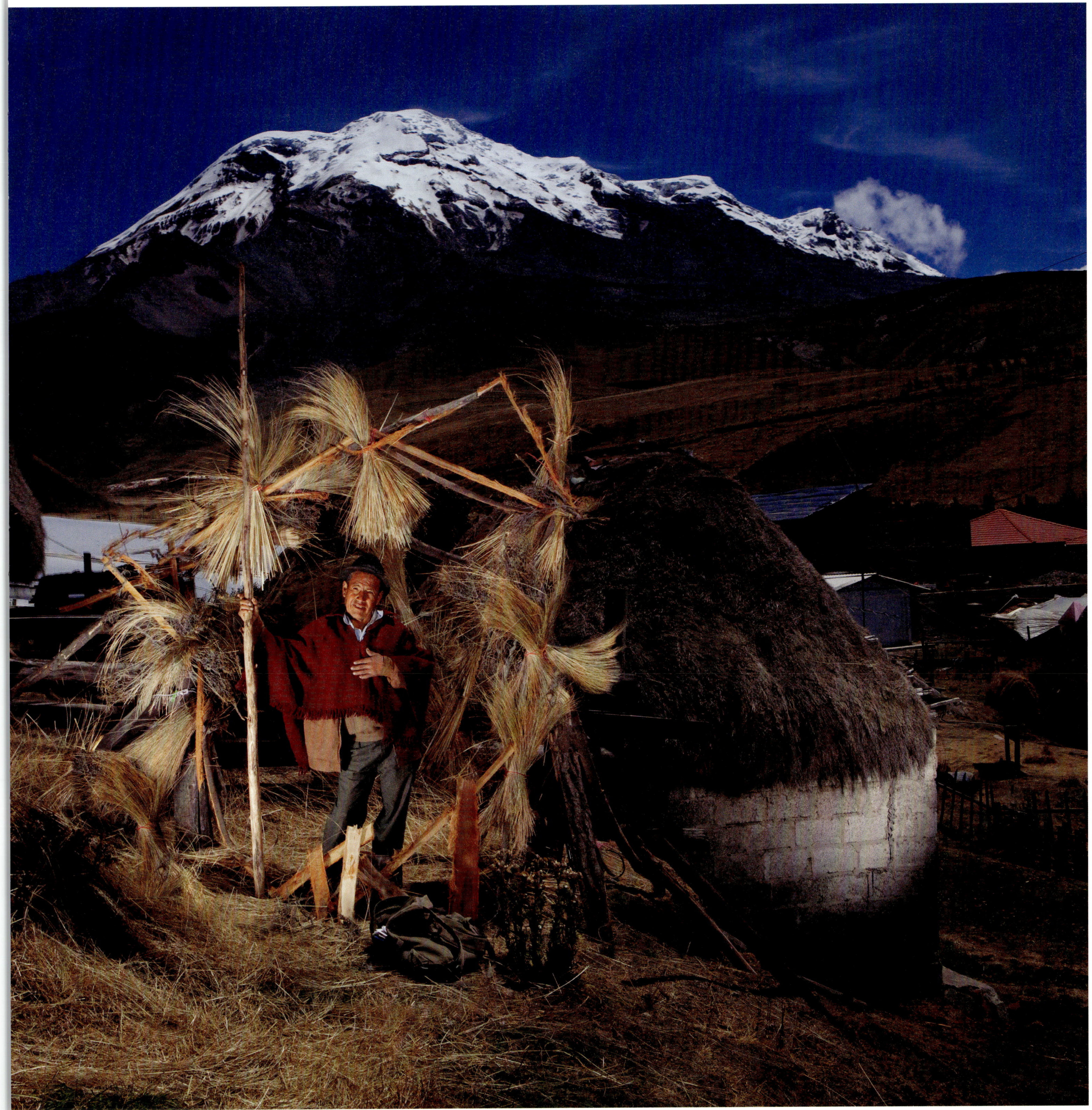

These days, the people we meet at sea no longer know the bow from the stern on their boats. When I was 13, I dropped out of school and set out on Le Cambodge, a 175-meter long ship. I had a good quartermaster who trained you by yelling. One spilled drop of paint and he would yell "I'm going to make you eat that, you idiot!" Sometimes, in the middle of the night, my shipmate would put me in the harness and pull me up the mast with the winch, more than 50 meters above the water. Life was rough but we'd make our own pastis in the hold and with a bit of trading, we were able to make a decent living. ¶ Pollution has made the fish disappear, like an insecticide killing flies. It's been a long time since we've seen the blackbirds and robins! We have thrown soil and concrete onto the seabeds where the fish and sea urchins reproduce. And the fewer fish there are, the more subsidies we give to the huge boats with their enormous nets that trawl several hundred meters deep. At the same time, we've started to take in so many fish that we have to throw heaps of dead surplus back into the sea. That's why they've all disappeared. ¶ Since I retired 20 years ago, I've been skippering the coast guard boat. It's hard to count how many landlubbers we've saved. It's all volunteer action, costing nothing to save a life! Personally, I think it's better to die at night. That way we've lived one last day.

HENRI SUQUET, FISHERMAN AND RESCUER AT SEA, ON THE BOAT SNSM, BANDOL, FRANCE.

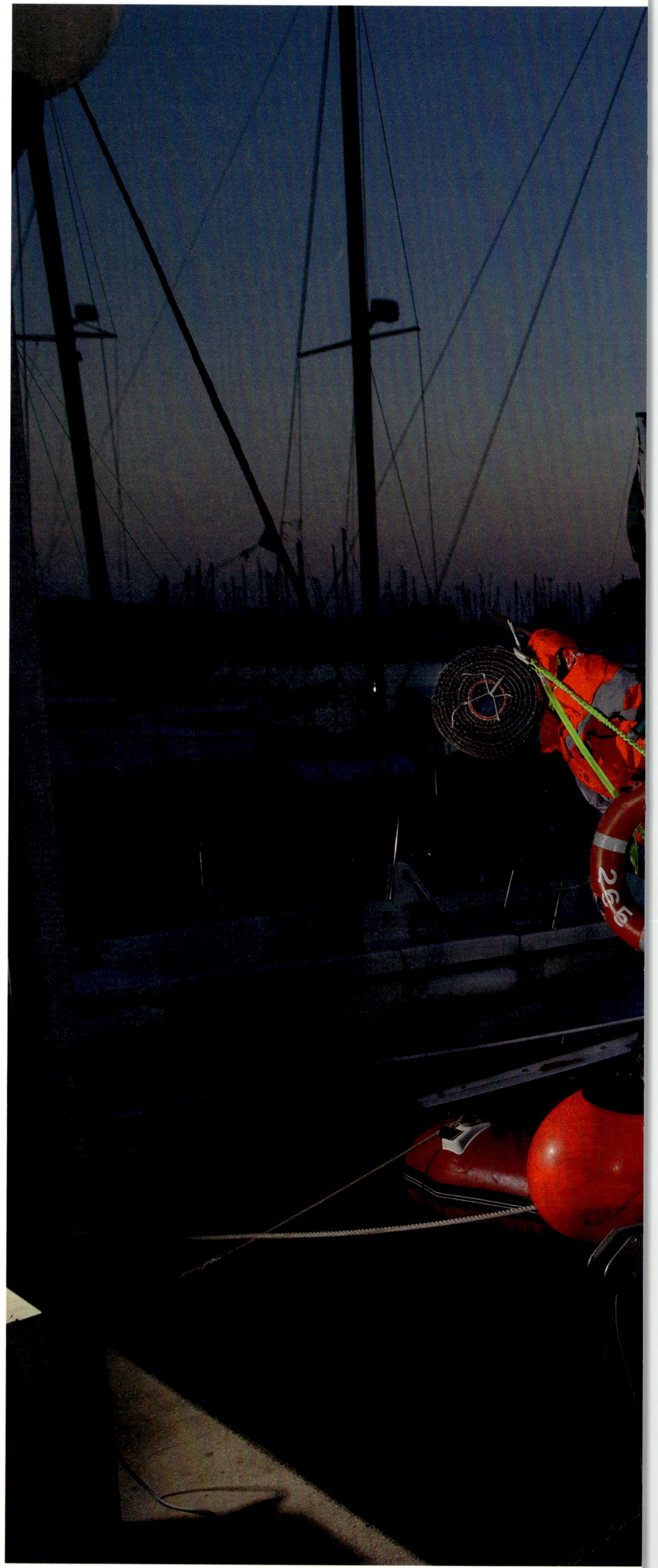

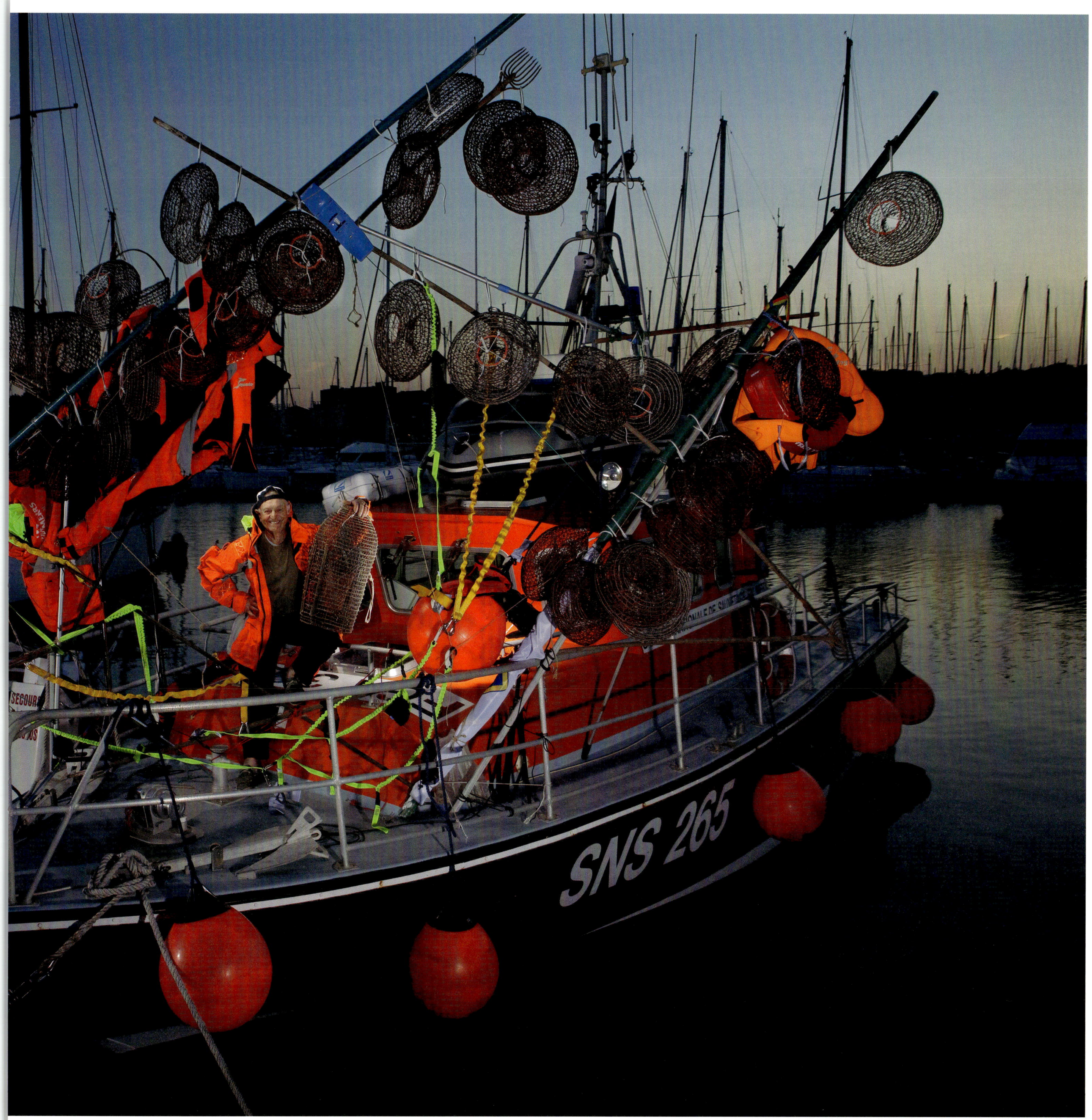
SNS 265

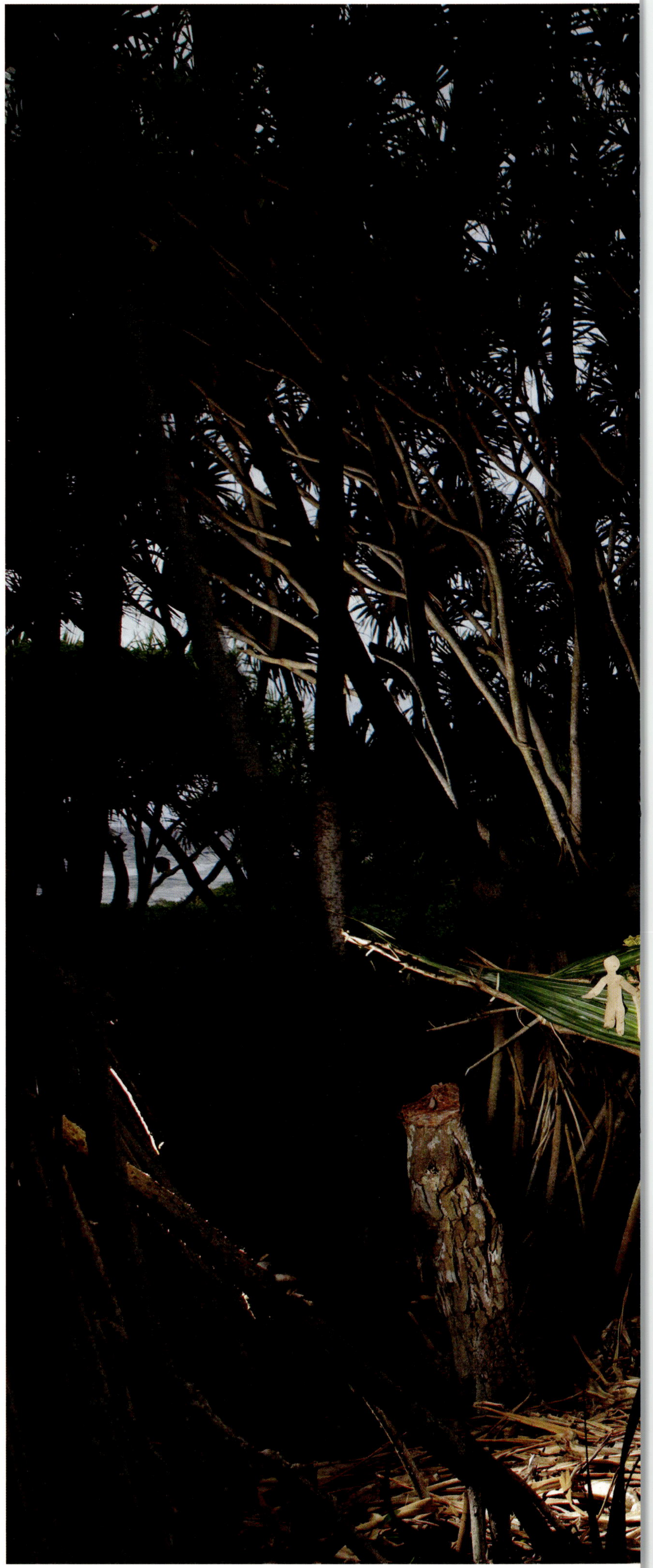

I am a traditional doctor. I seek out plants that grow near the volcano. According to our beliefs, it is the volcano that nurtures our land. At the edge of the ocean and in the gardens of the mountain, nature is, for me, an immense pharmacy. I heal with local plants that exist only on Tanna Island. Our medicine complements that of the white man, who knows about the diseases that came by boats. ¶ It was my father who taught me everything I know and I try to share this knowlege with my own son. It's becoming harder and harder to find certain plants that have been gradually disappearing. The population has risen and there are fewer unspoiled plots of land. Some say it's the pollution that has changed our climate. What is certain is that the sea level has risen and that droughts and cyclones have become more frequent. ¶ In our grandfathers' time there were huge yams. Corn, bananas and fruit were never so beautiful. To keep healthy, it is food that counts the most. Many doctors dream of curing all the new diseases. As for me, I hope only that nature continues to thrive. In this way there will be fewer diseases and more plants to cure them.

NICOLAS JACKY IN THE PANDANUS FOREST OF PORT RESOLUTION, TANNA, VANUATU.

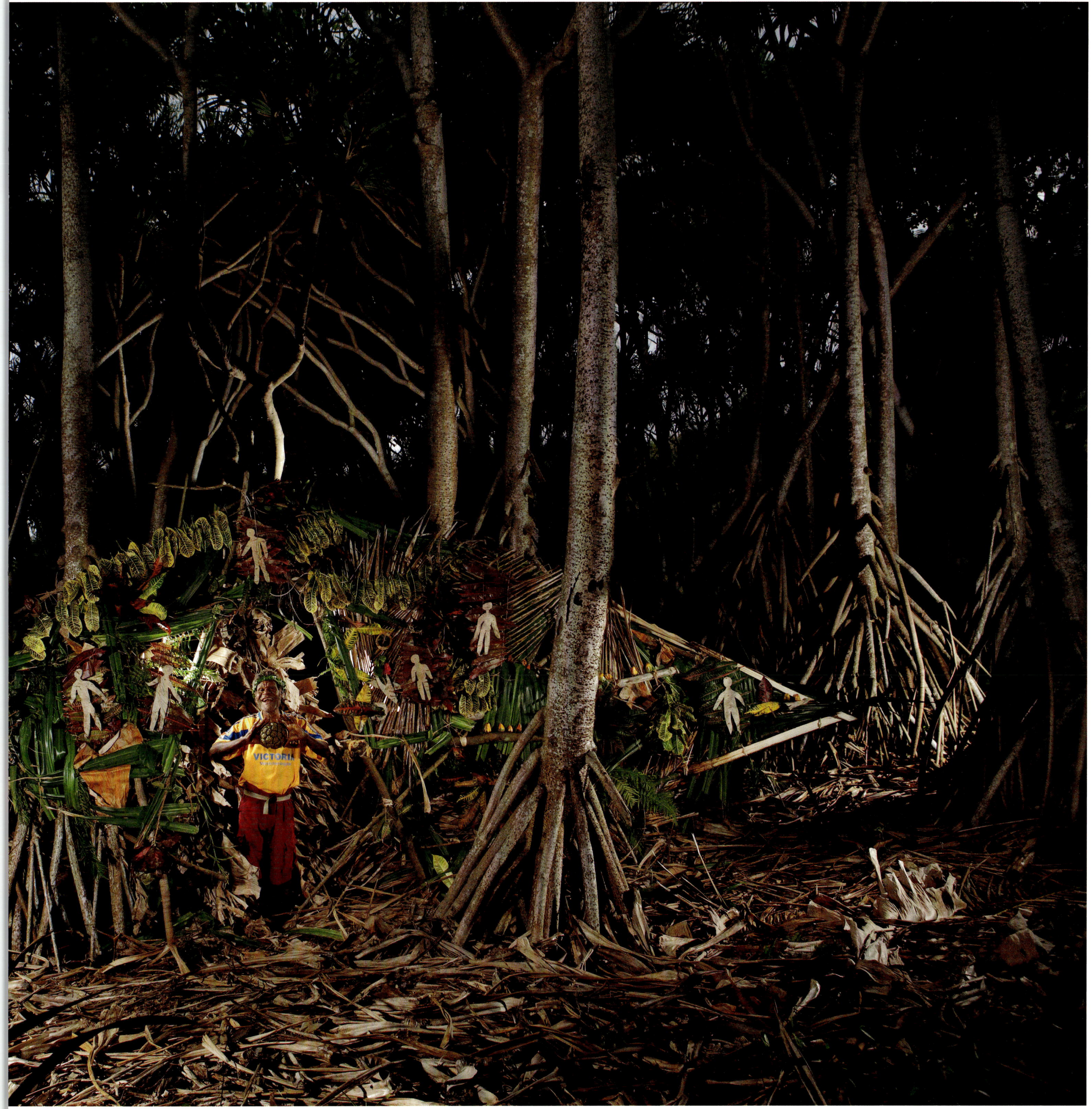

I have 12 children. In one year, I had two sons: the first in the beginning and the second at the end! I'm 50 now, my hair is white and I have no more teeth because I am so poor. When my son separated with the mother of his children, I sold everything to give him a new wife. ¶ I kiss my oil lamp because it protects me. Even after a month spent in the wild with my goats, I have a strong heart and am never afraid. Here, only the song of the muezzin, rising from afar, mingles with the sigh of the desert. One of my boys is always with me, walking alongside me. This is how the young discover a relationship with harmony. Each day, we walk and we eat only what nature gives us. We nourish ourselves with milk and cheese from our goats, flour, and birds and rabbits which we hunt. We sleep in grottoes and, sometimes, we hear the djinns talking. ¶ Nowadays, people don't get enough exercise. It's like they are nothing but fat stomachs on feet, like our camels who fall ill as they constantly eat the plastic that lies around. Sometimes we gather up pieces of plastic and we burn them in a huge bonfire to try to get rid of them. I would love for the glimmer of these flames to encourage us to once again live together, to be loyal brothers and friends.

JAMIL SALAMI KAWALDEH AND HIS GRANDSON, RAKAN AIMAN AND THE SCRIPTURES OF WOOD AND STONE, DANA, JORDAN.

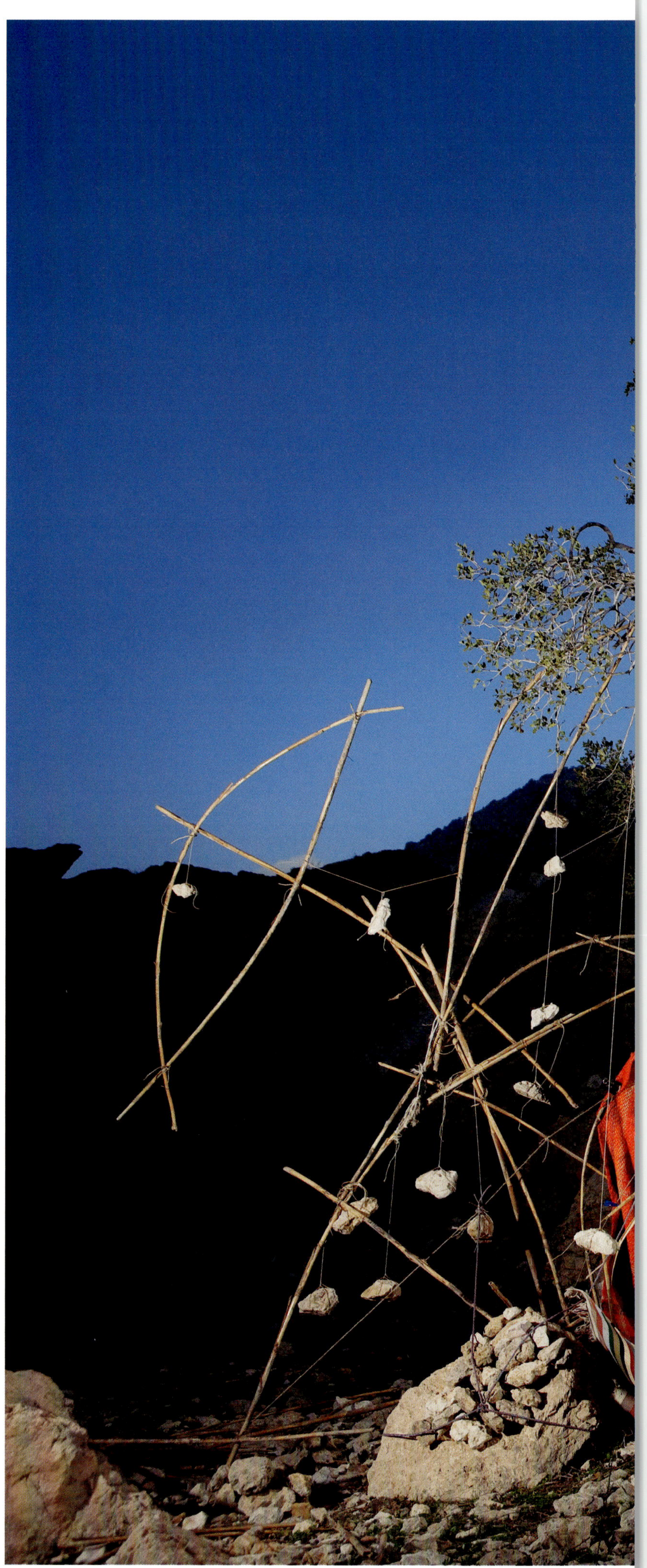

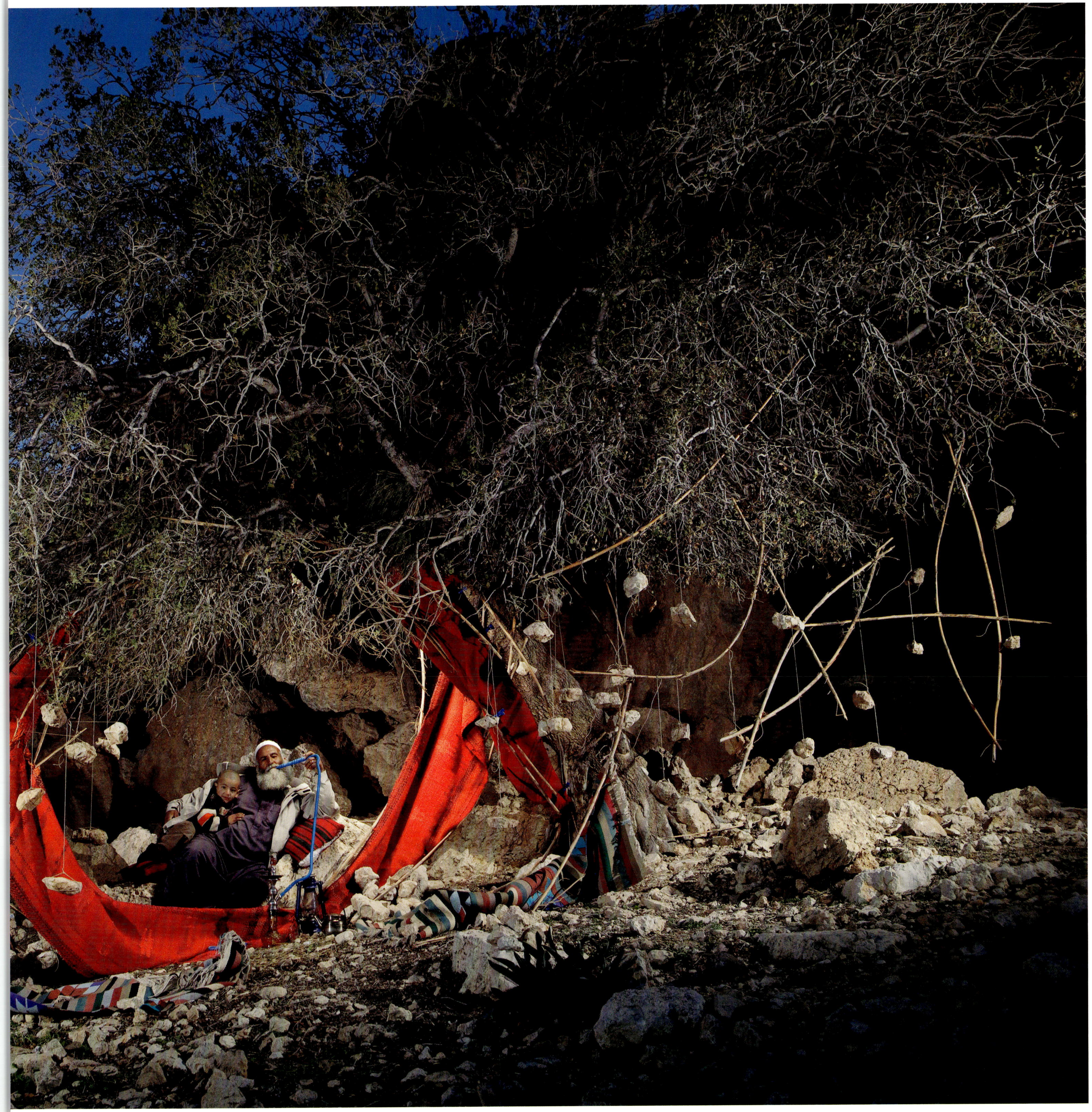

Our grandparents used to live to be at least 100. Death now comes calling at sixty. We exercise less and we consume far too many chemicals. They're everywhere, even in the fruits of our garden. Life is shorter but has become easier. Thanks to electricity we no longer have to search far and wide for wood and water to cook. We don't have to walk for an entire day to get to Denpasar. ¶ The modern world brings us diversity, but also competition as people show off what they have to everyone. Our children's education requires lots of money. Some are forced to sell their land just so their children can go to school, without knowing what tomorrow will bring. If the path of education does not allow the young to forge a life of their own their families will have absolutely nothing. ¶ Despite all of this, I still hold on to my ceremonial platter to honor Tuhan, our God. I pray that we shall never run short of clean water and that nature will one day make us healthy again.

WAYAN RETU, MADE RENI AND THE FACE CREATED WITH CATAMARAN FLOATS AND SAILS, AMED, BALI.

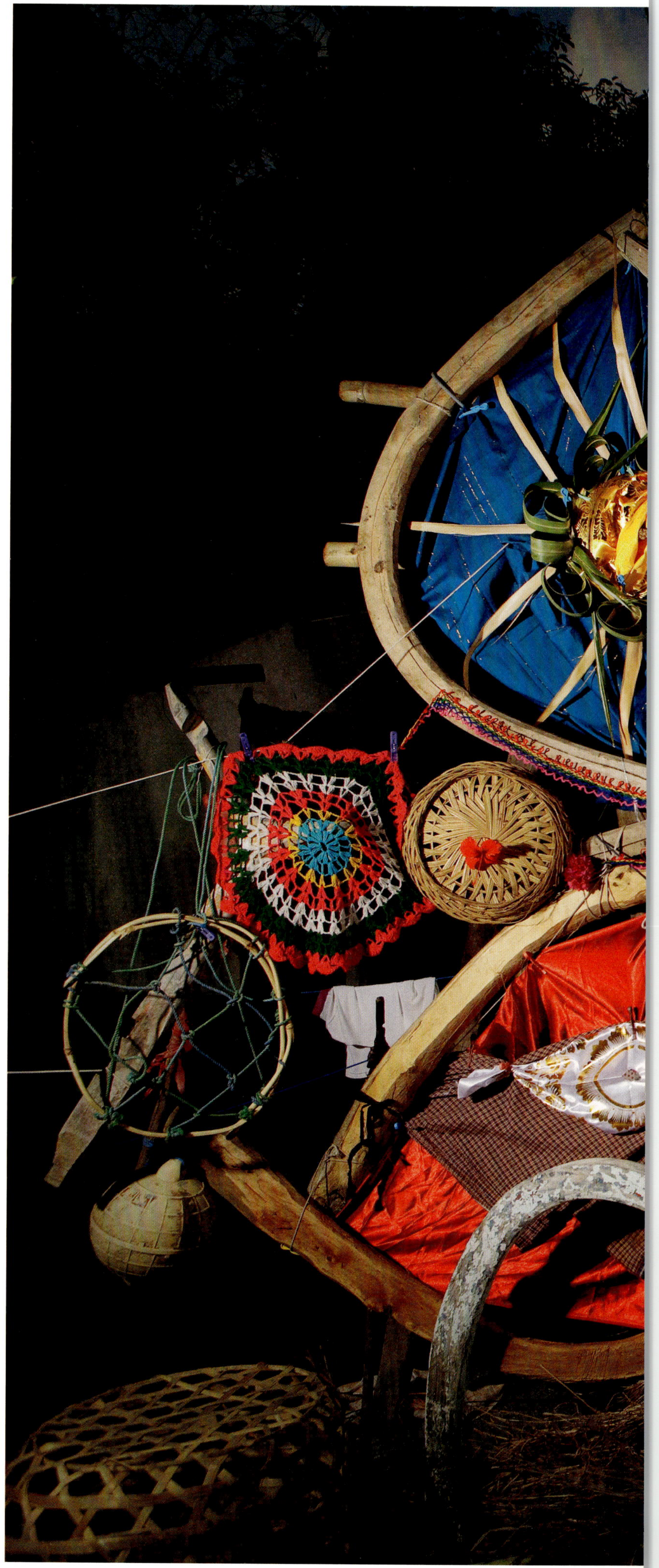

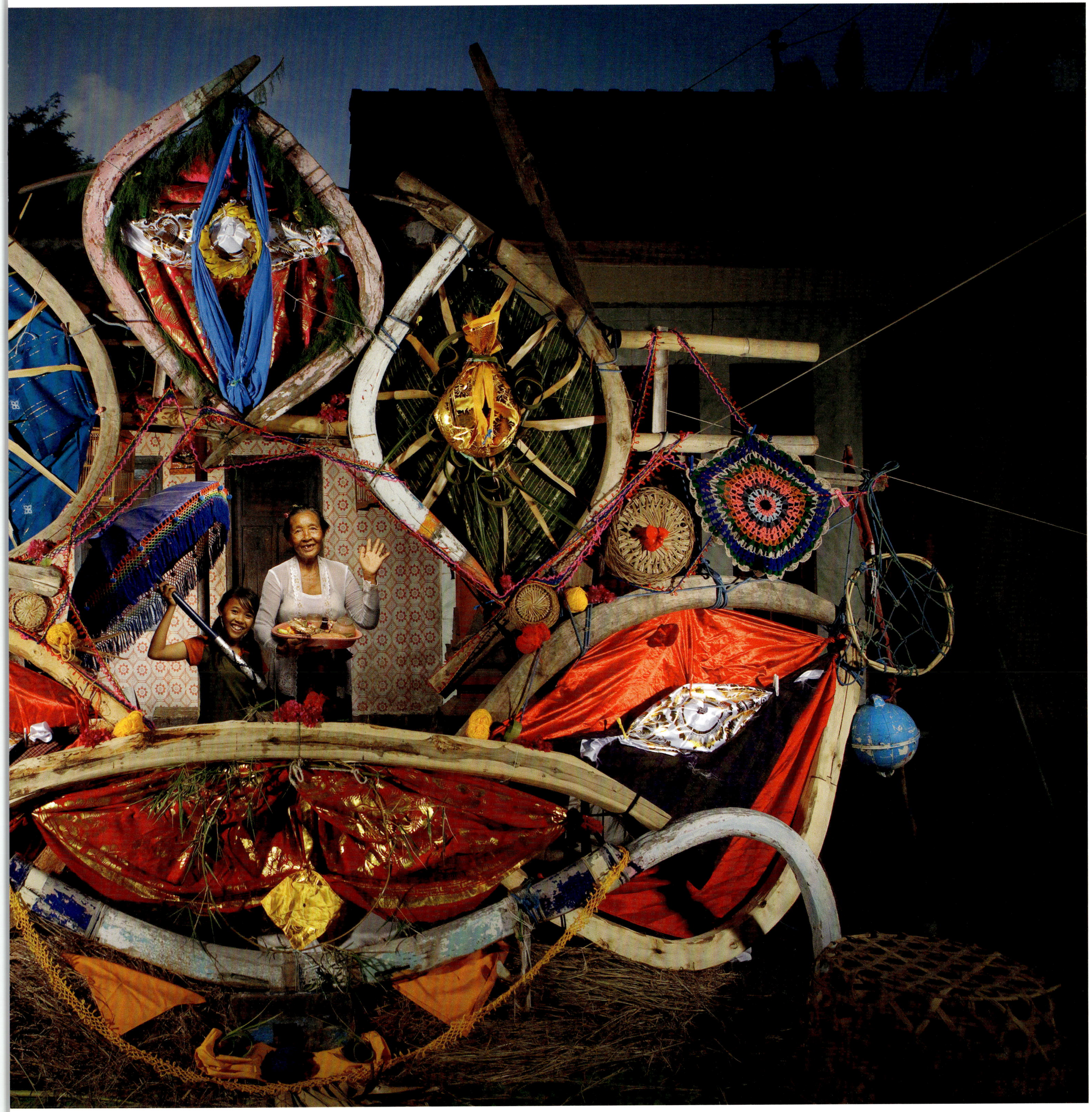

For several years when the night fell upon the sea we saw strange little lights flickering over the horizon. The more we saw them, the fewer langoustes we caught during the day. ¶ One evening, the young villagers went out to sea with rifles. They returned with a wooden and iron monster whose crew had to abandon ship and swim ashore. Three hundred men, equipped with ropes and logs spent all day dragging it onto the beach. That evening, for the first time, all that could be heard was the whisper of the wind. We barricaded access to our village with large dinghies, fearful that the army might come. ¶ These monstrous motorboats come into our fishing zone despite the bans. Thanks to the air compressors, their divers walk on the sea floor and empty our traps, depleting the langouste population. Soon we will have to leave our village and abandon our sailboats. ¶ We still laugh and love but a sense of fear has set in. We asked our children to draw this story in the pages of a book. The teacher wrote the text and we sent it to the government, in the hopes that they would free us from these monstrous motorboats.

THE CAPTAIN RAYMUNDO GERMANO DA CRUZ WITH TWO SAILBOATS, TWO LANGOUSTES, AND A MOTORBOAT, BRAZIL.

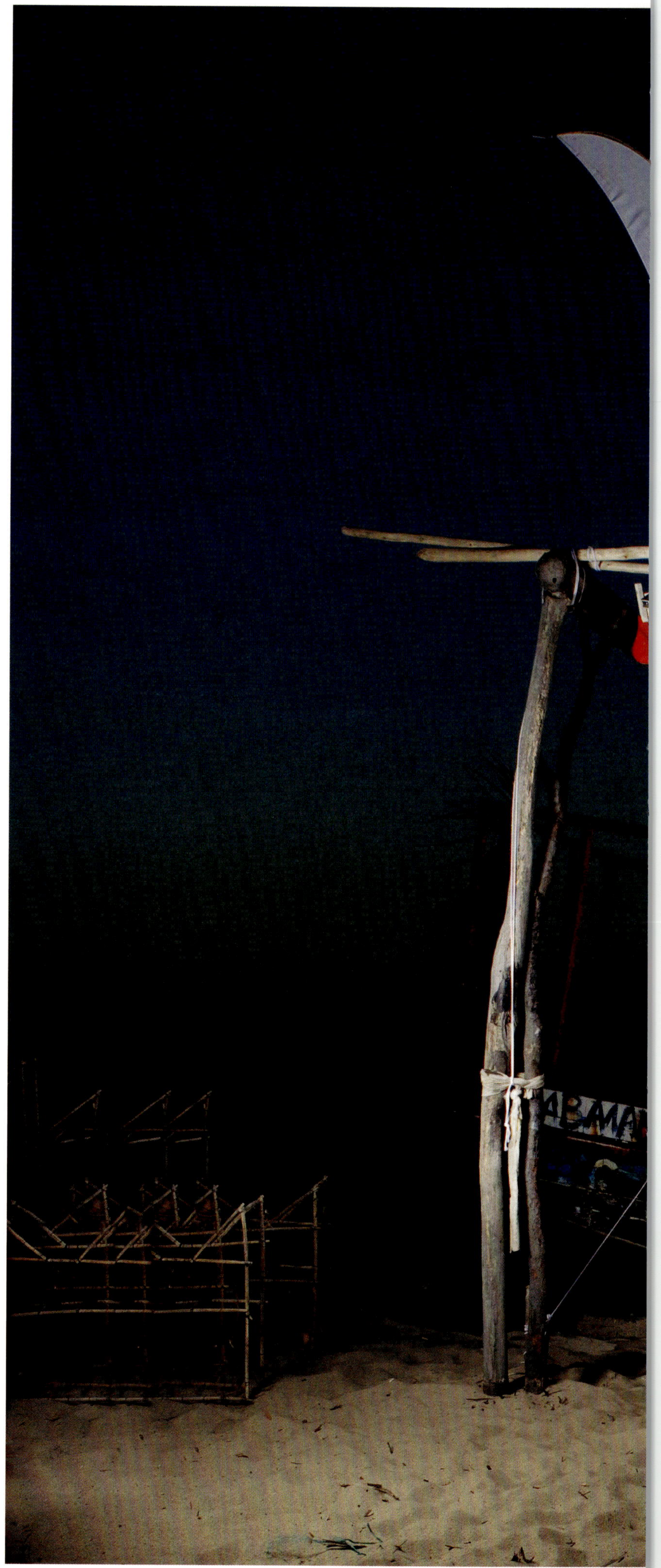

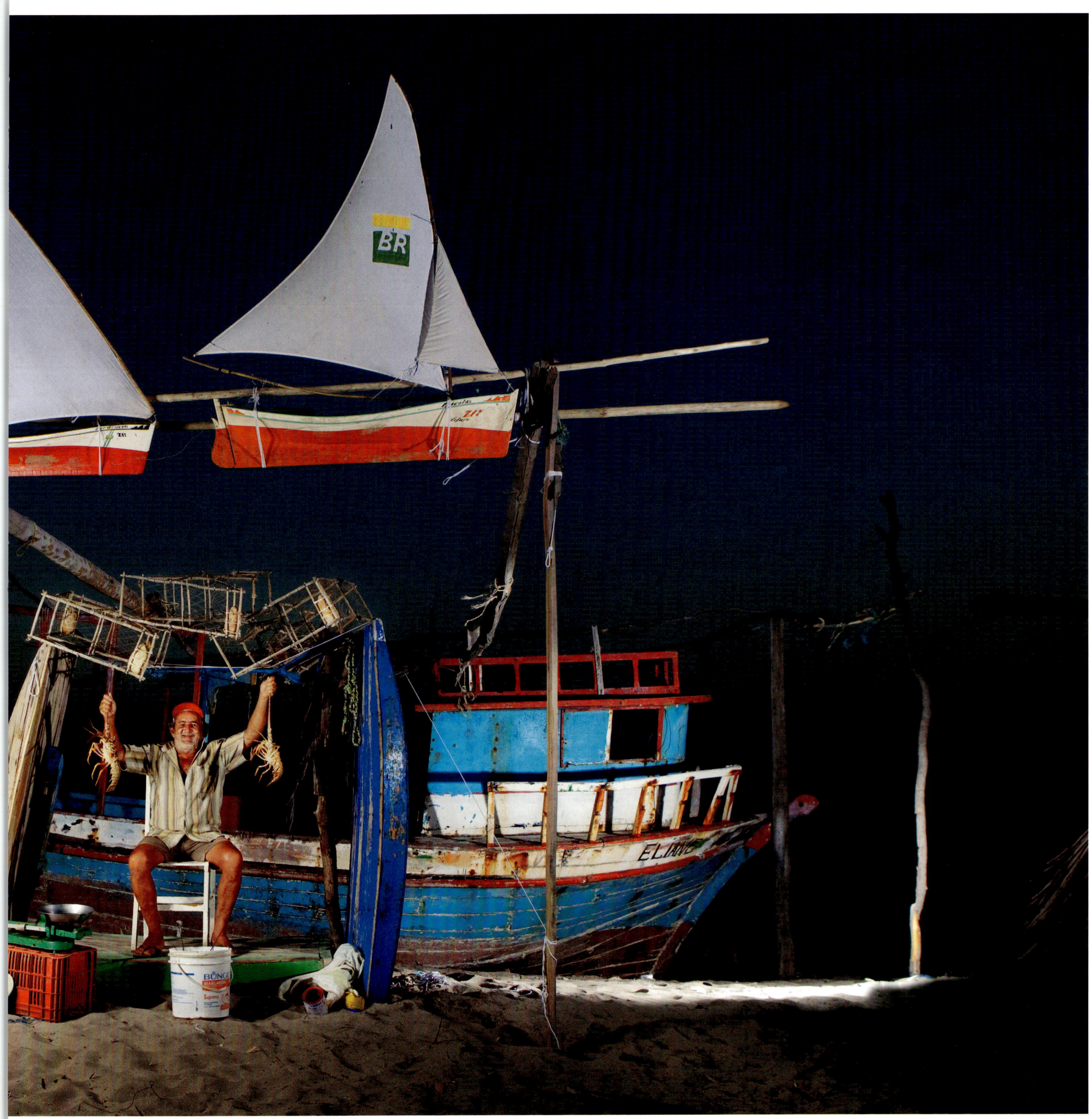
BR
BUNGE

My whole life has taken place on the sand of this beach, in the shadow of the tree that has no season and that cries its colored tears throughout the year. In my childhood, when the Japanese boats came, we ran and ran. I saw fire, explosions. I witnessed the death of my father. When the war came, the doors of the houses closed, and thus joy, rice and money became scarce. ¶ The ocean was once the territory of the sea gypsies who traveled from land to land. With the arrival of the white man, the borders were drawn and lives were changed. People invented new needs for themselves. Machines, producers of greed and money, brought riches to those who destroyed nature. Corruption led them to exploit the land until life's immutable balance was broken. For a new television we will plunder the seas and cut down huge trees. People no longer fix anything, they just throw stuff away. Tourists have come with their needs and their trash cans. Now that the beaches are covered in plastic the dolphins and manatees are on the verge of extinction. Today I no longer walk well. My grandson carries me on his back. The heat of his body gently warms the hope that will always keep my heart beating.

TAE LEAMAN, BENEATH THE PANKA TREE, KOH MUK ISLAND, THAILAND.

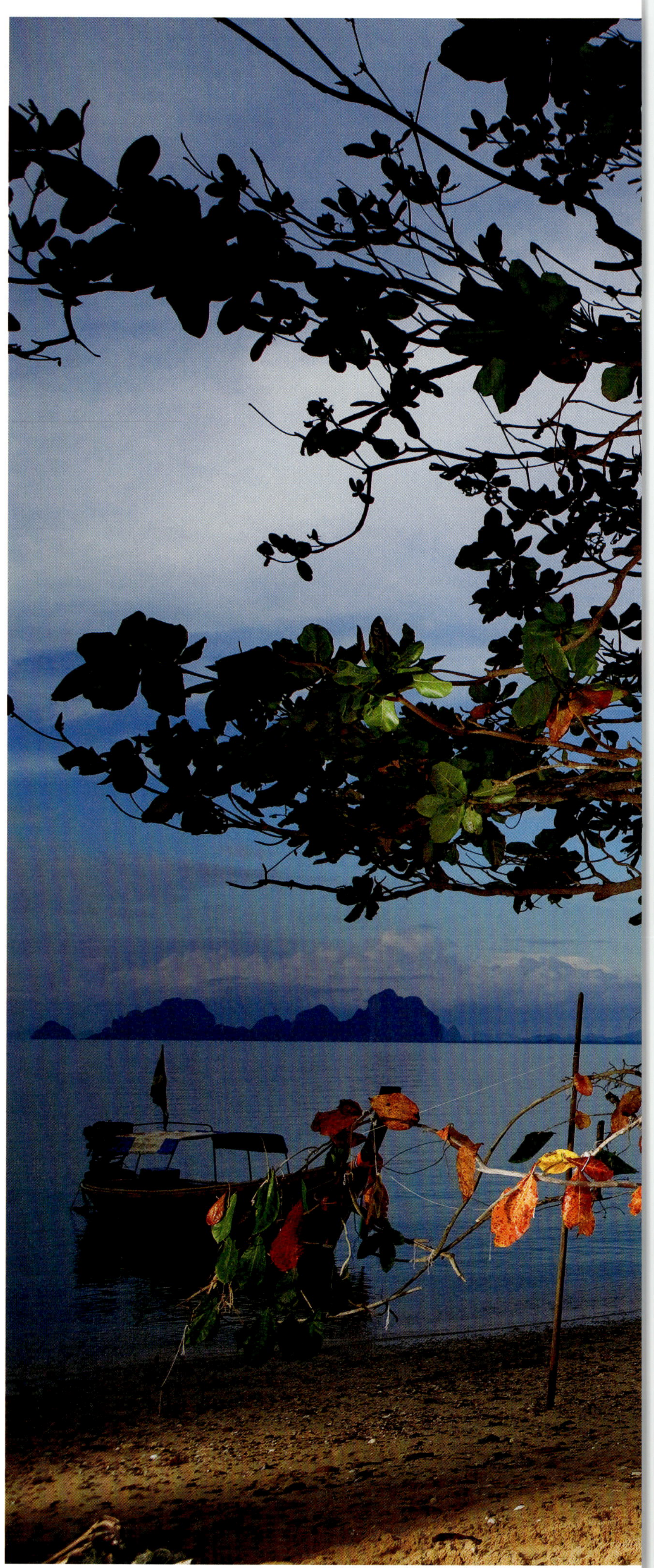

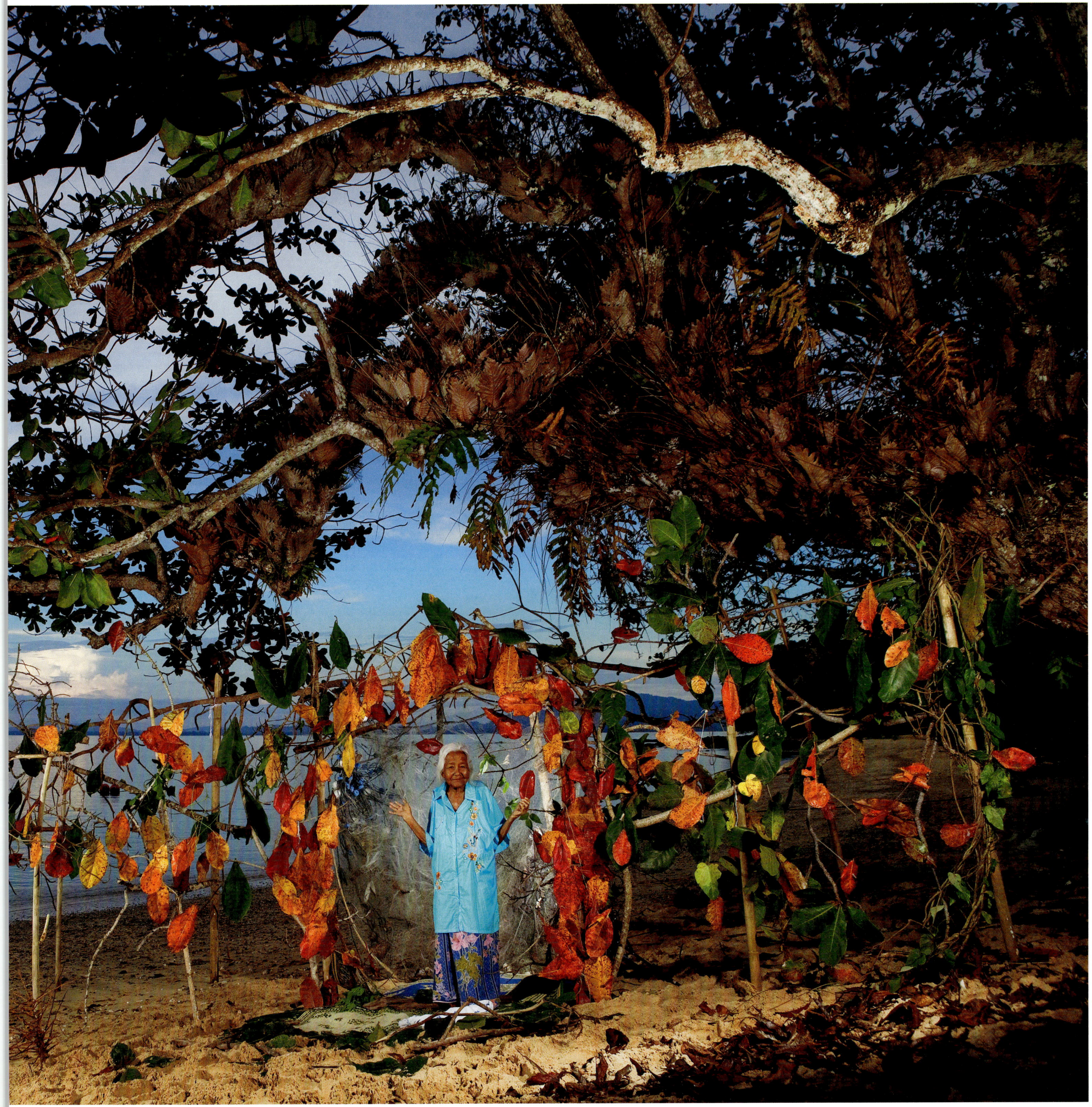

GEORGE TREVORROW ¶ ANNA REVA ¶ KARLO
MARIE-HÉLÈNE MILHOMME ¶ FADIMATA ¶
YI ¶ GEORGE TREVORROW ¶ ANNA REVA
SCHAFFERS ¶ MARIE-HÉLÈNE MILHOMME ¶ F
ZHENG YI ¶ GEORGE TREVORROW ¶ ANNA
JOE SCHAFFERS ¶ MARIE-HÉLÈNE MILHOM
BHAAT ¶ ZHENG YI ¶ GEORGE TREVORRO
LINDSAY ¶ JOE SCHAFFERS ¶ MARIE-HÉL
BHAGWAMDAS BHAAT ¶ ZHENG YI ¶ GEOR
ATAN ¶ RITA LINDSAY ¶ JOE SCHAFFERS
ROWHDA ¶ BHAGWAMDAS BHAAT ¶ ZHEN
KARLO HULI ATAN ¶ RITA LINDSAY ¶ JOE
FADIMATA ¶ ROWHDA ¶ BHAGWAMDAS B
ANNA REVA ¶ KARLO HULI ATAN ¶ RITA L
MILHOMME ¶ FADIMATA ¶ ROWHDA ¶ BHAGW
GEORGE TREVORROW ¶ ANNA REVA ¶ KAR
RITA LINDSAY ¶ JOE SCHAFFERS ¶ FADIN
ZHENG YI ¶ GEORGE TREVORROW ¶ ANNA R
SCHAFFERS ¶ MARIE-HÉLÈNE MILHOMME ¶ F

THE PLAYHOUSE
TO WHICH WE LOST THE KEY

Us "Abos" officially only became human beings in 1967. Before, we were thought of us as animals. Cook, who discovered Australia, considered himself to be the first man to live on our land. The white man brought us fear. They convinced our elders to stop practicing customs, which disrupted the cycle of handing down tradition. We shall no longer be able to pass along our legacy of knowledge to our children. ¶ They forbade us to speak our own language. They erased six thousand years of history. Today, we are still victims of racism. Our environment is disappearing. Dying. Our lakes are dry because all the water has been diverted to the big cities in the north. People buy this water, which puts our lives in peril and our tears cannot replace it. Salt kills everything. Nothing can survive here. The sea has now drowned the traditional camps that my children once knew. In our culture the land and water are like living beings. Like a body. The totem represents our responsibility to them. If they disappear, so shall we. With my grandson in my arms I sit beneath these rings that symbolize the ebb and flow of existence, in hoping that we can still be a part of it tomorrow.

GEORGE TREVORROW, GRANDFATHER OF KEVINA AND CHIEF OF THE ABORIGINE TRIBES OF THE COORONG REGION, AUSTRALIA.

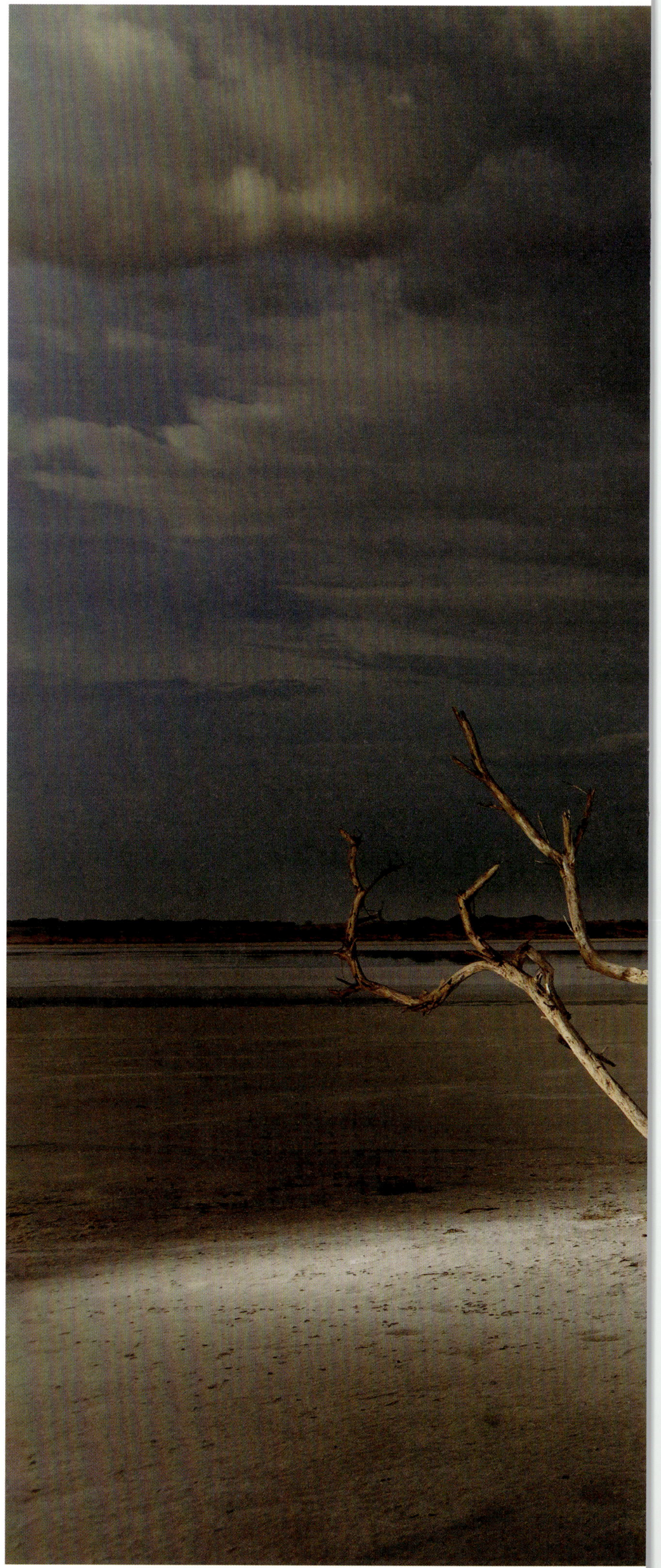

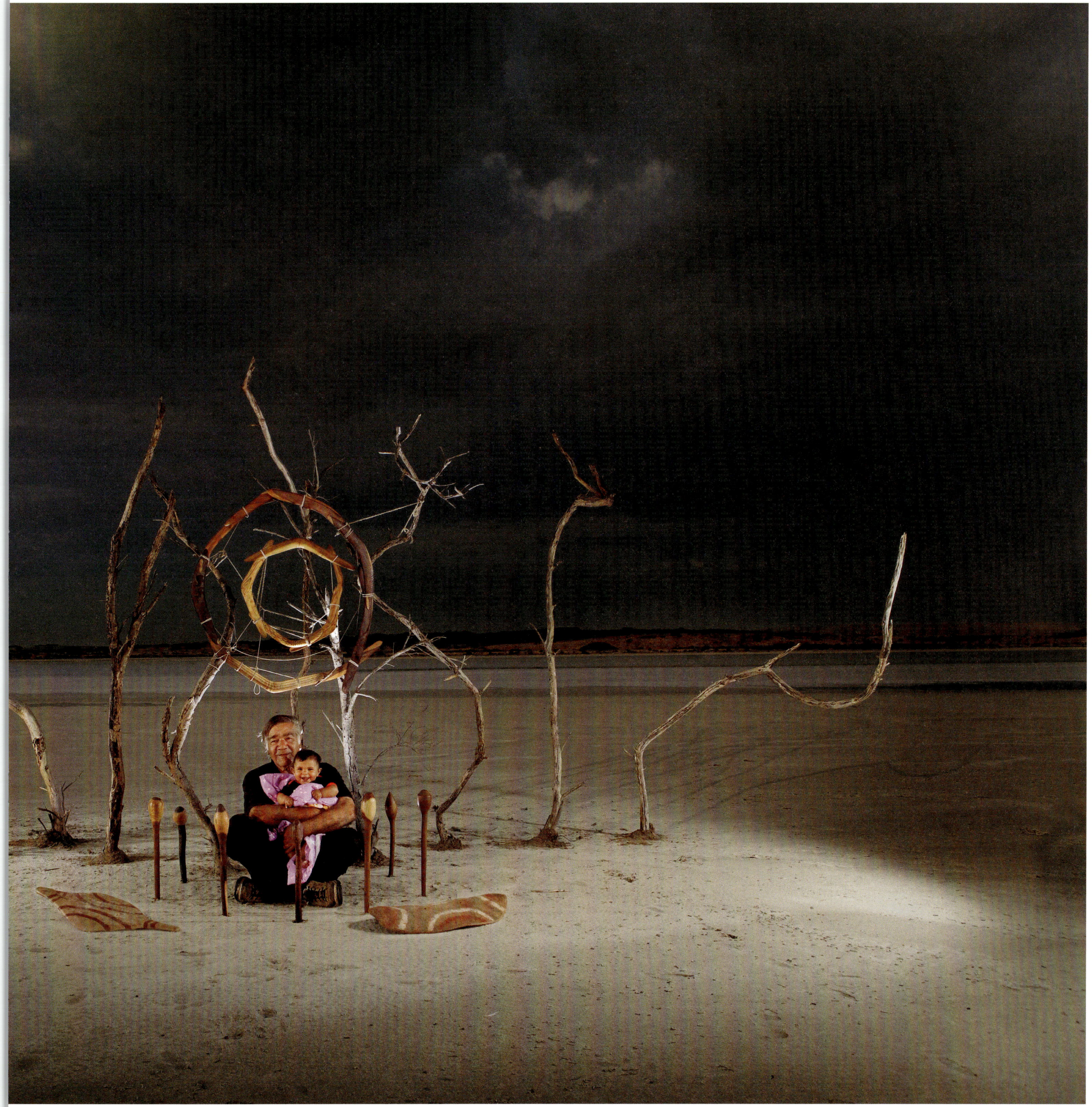

In 1967, I saw a television for the first time. Inside, there were American Indians being attacked by the whites who had rifles and wore large hats. I was both excited by this invention and angry because of what I saw inside. ¶ Back then we didn't wear clothes. We cut down bamboo to transport our water and make our shoes. We used the leaves to gather fruit from the gardens and protect us from the chill of the night. When plastic came we thought at first that it was natural, then we realized that it spoiled quickly, and wasn't biodegradable. It killed the fish and turtles in the sea. And, yet, we could no longer live without it. This is like cigarettes, which are too expensive for us and reduce our life span. One stormy day a large sailing vessel headed out of the bay. We had told the white man not to go out but he didn't listen to us and his boat was smashed against the black rocks. We never saw him again. To this day we find bits of sail throughout the village and plastic all the way up into the mountains.

ANNA REVA AND THE SAILS OF THE GREAT SHIP, PORT RESOLUTION, VANUATU

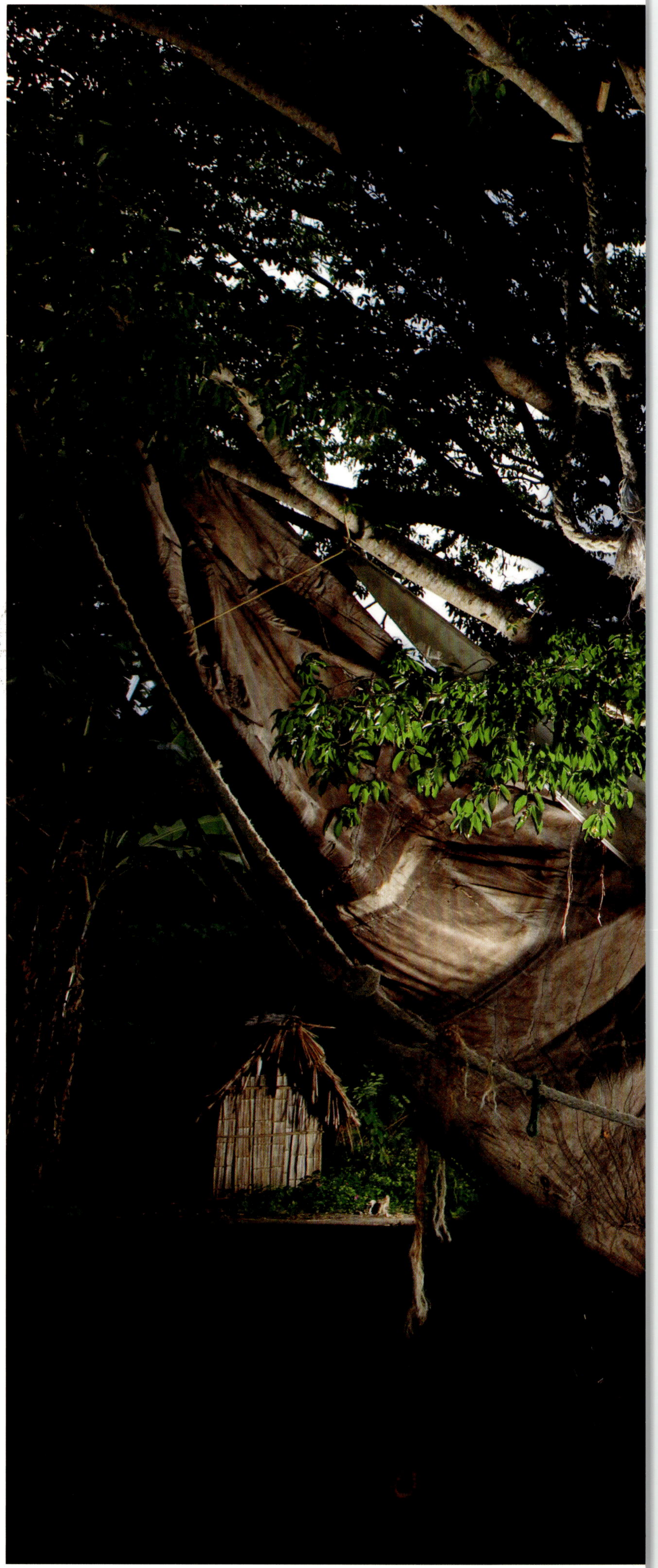

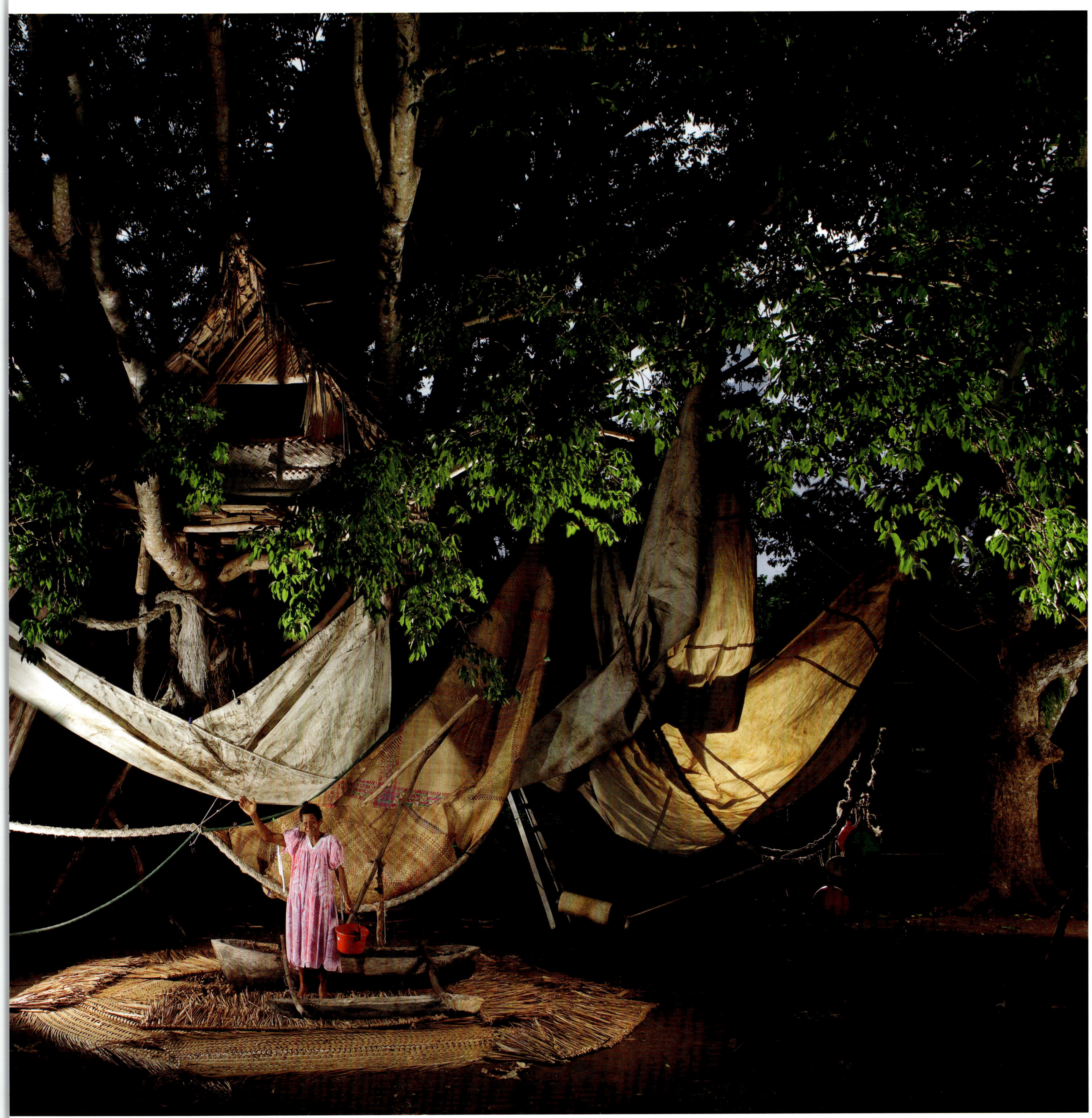

For me, nature is first and foremost man, not the ground nor the stones. Light is first clarity of things in your mind, choice and wisdom. It is spirituality that enables us to escape obscurity. ¶ I have brought objects from my culture, that of all the Polynesian islands, for important ceremonies. I came home, for I belong to the land of my ancestors. I built my house near the statue of Mohai, my grandfather. Even today, foreigners want to ban me from what they call our family's land, a 'natural park'. They build airports and hotels that expel us from their world and make us a minority. The shadows of the planes in the sky bring theft, violence and greed. They have caged us in and the Rapa Nui has almost disappeared. Our memory is still scarred by the arrival of the boats. ¶ I walk along my land. I look around me and try to understand who I am, where I come from and where I am going. On the horizon, I see the Pacific islands as the immense Oceania continent united in the common dream of the Maori nation.

KARLO HULIATAN AT HOME, IN THE EASTER ISLAND NATURE PARK, RAPA NUI, CHILE.

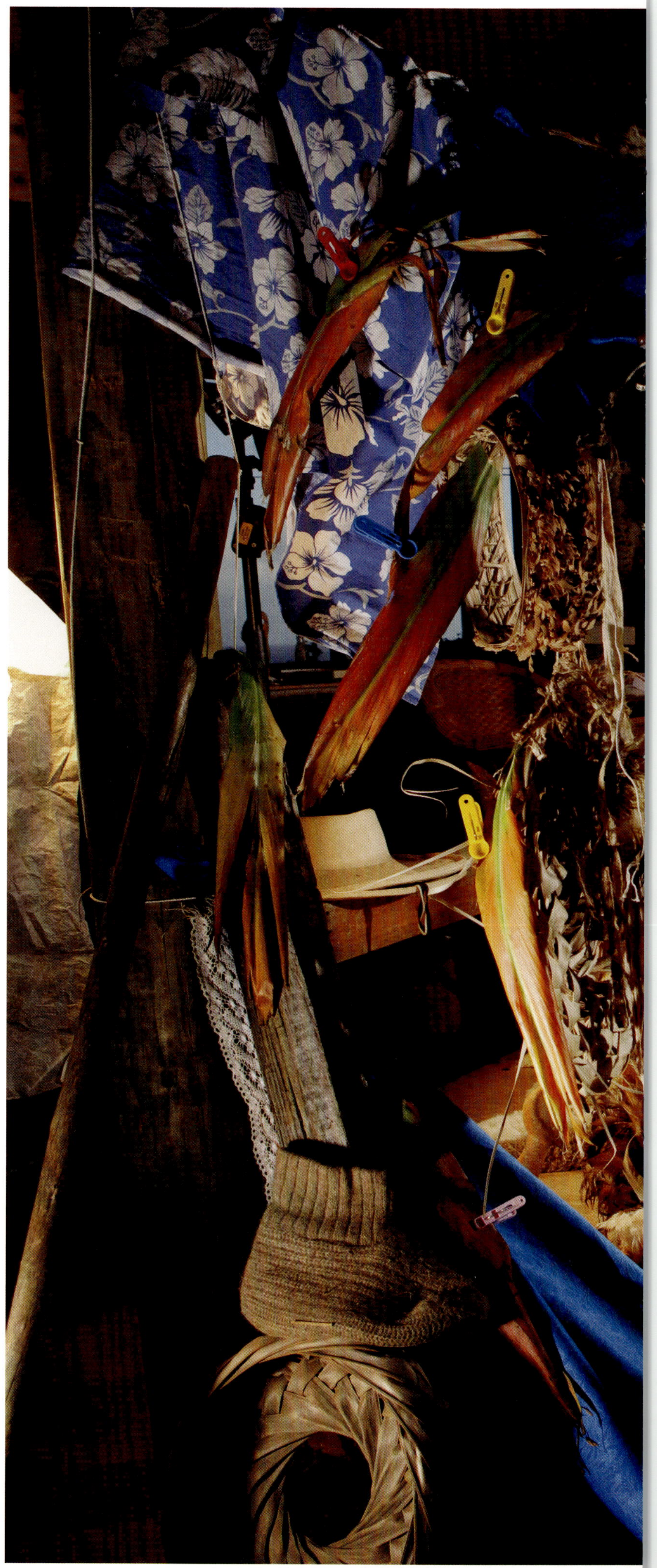

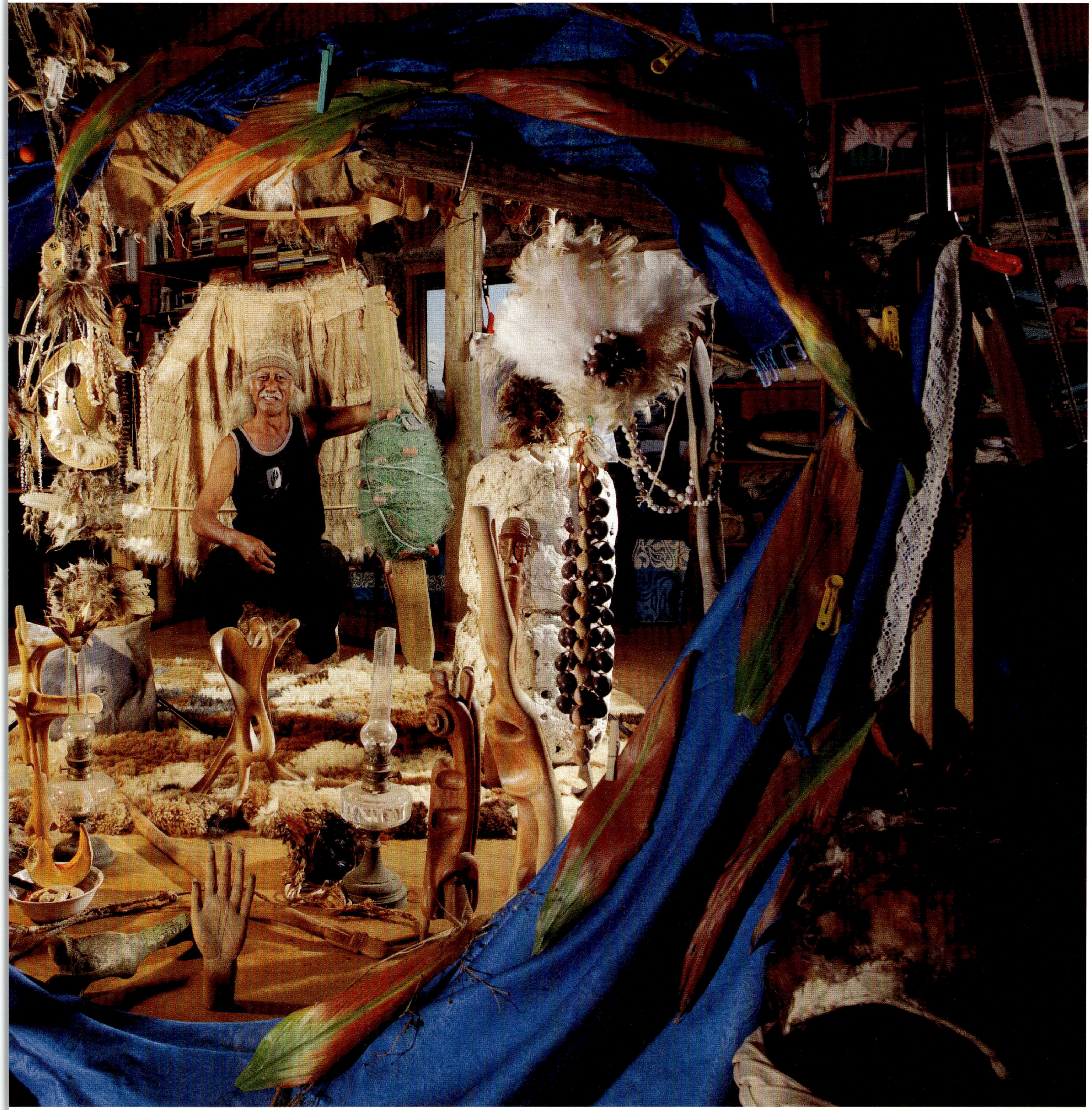

It was a long, long time ago. Two fishermen had caught so many fish that their boat had swollen sides. On their way home they came across a boat that hadn't been so lucky. So as to not have to share their catch, they said they barely had enough to feed their family and they continued on their way. Their boat was so heavy it nearly sank on several occasions. When they arrived at the shore the elder asked if they had enjoyed a good fishing trip and if they had met anyone. They spoke only about the fish that were too small and the nets that were too short. But the elder easily caught them in their lie; the spirit that they had seen had come to see the elder to speak of their greed. ¶ The white men are like those fishermen. They do not want to share their riches. They scoff at our sacred land and they push us into poorer places. They've taken everything, even our young. Thousands of children were kidnapped by the white man and raised by missionaries. We've only just begun to speak about this lost generation. Our duty is to forgive but we must not forget what has happened. ¶ These plume flowers were passed on to us by our ancestors. The sky above us is reflected in our pupils, like sunsets of times gone by, when campfires mirrored our understanding of the universe. I have made thousands of flowers to cultivate one hope: that man escapes the disasters begot by greed.

RITA LINDSAY AND HER PLUME FLOWERS, MENINGIE, AUSTRALIA.

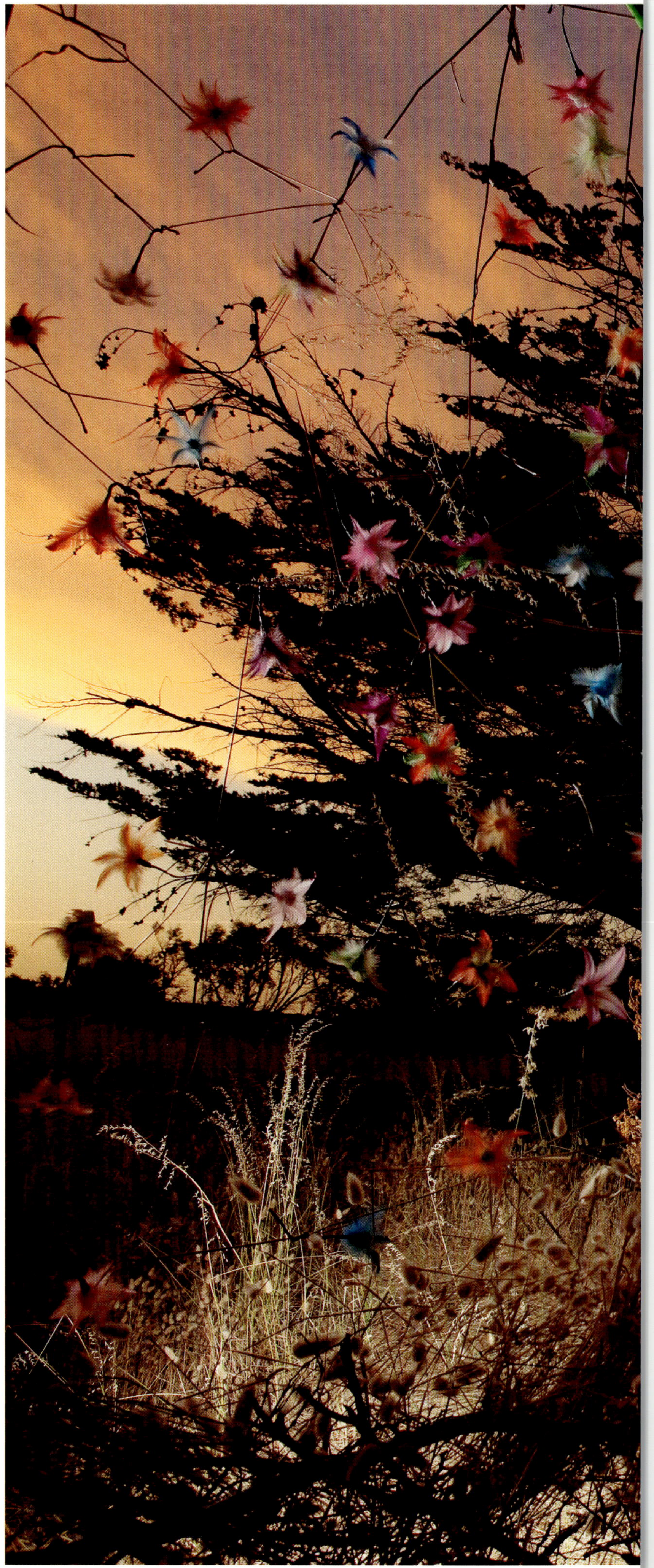

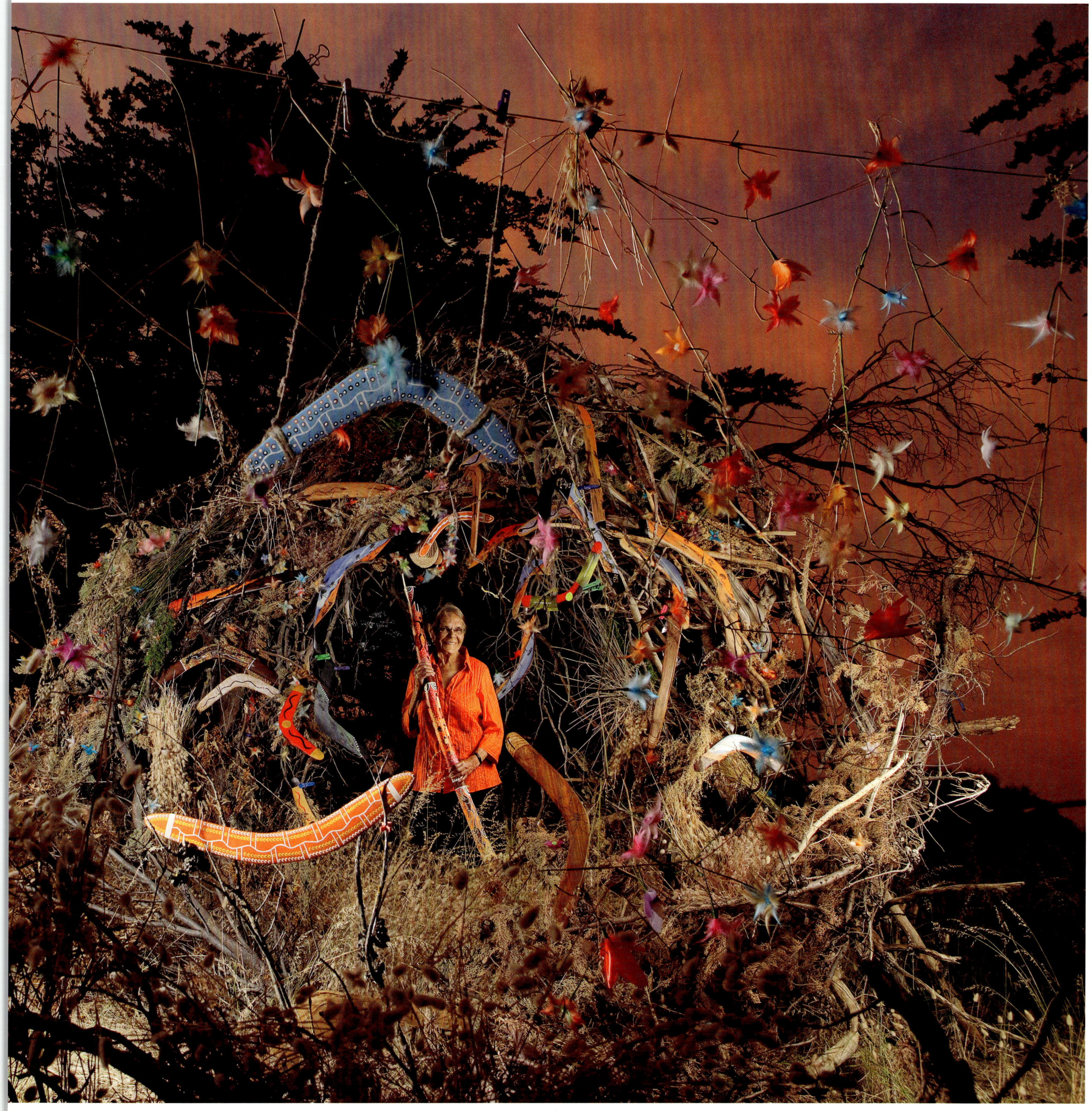

When I was 28 I lived in District 6. It was the only area of Cape Town where blacks lived. One day they declared it a 'white zone'. The bulldozers came, they destroyed everything and we had to leave for the shantytowns. If we fought for our rights we were in danger of being locked up and coming back roughed up. To resist, we only had our words. The whites, they had the police and the army. ¶ It all started with a small photography exhibition. Then, we felt the need for a bigger space to preserve our memory and the unity of the community. We found an old Methodist church. These street signs became the heart of our museum. We symbolically reconstructed the places where we had lived. All of the members of the community came to lay images and objects there. We all have the right to reclaim our land. Today we are asking for its restitution. ¶ The goal of this museum is to proclaim that Cape Town is a city inhabited by humans who are entirely of the same race. I am 'colored', a word that originated in the ideology of apartheid. When they segregated us into groups they didn't know about DNA. If we examine the genetic imprint of everyone it's obvious that races don't exist. ¶ I have a habit of saying that we are the only species to wear our ears as an ornament. We don't listen to others. However, we are Homo sapiens. We have intelligence. If we look on the positive side, I am sure that it is possible to live together.

JOE SCHAFFERS IN THE DISTRICT SIX MUSEUM, CAPE TOWN, SOUTH AFRICA.

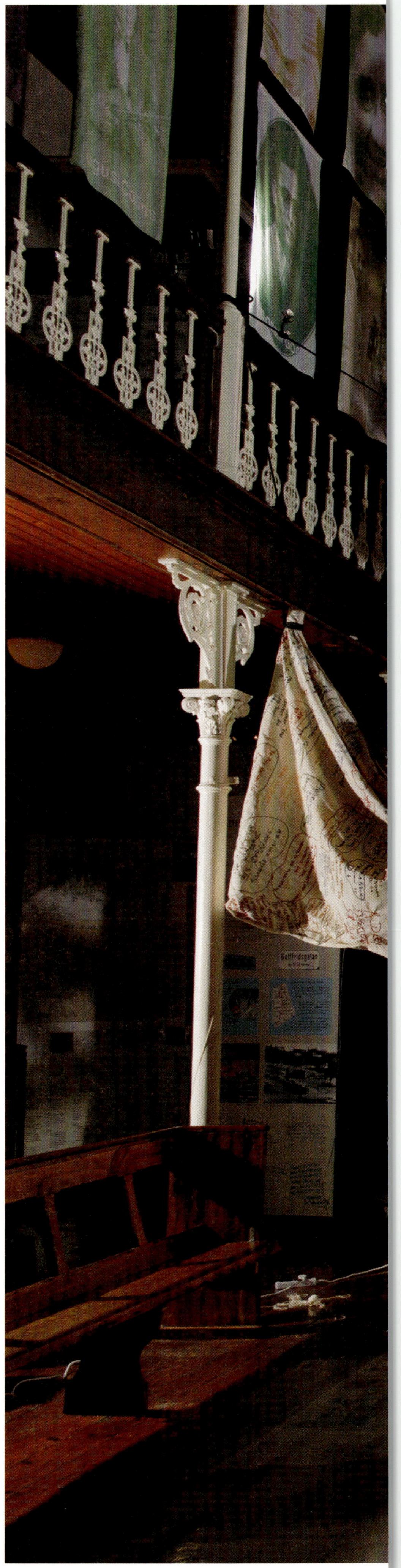

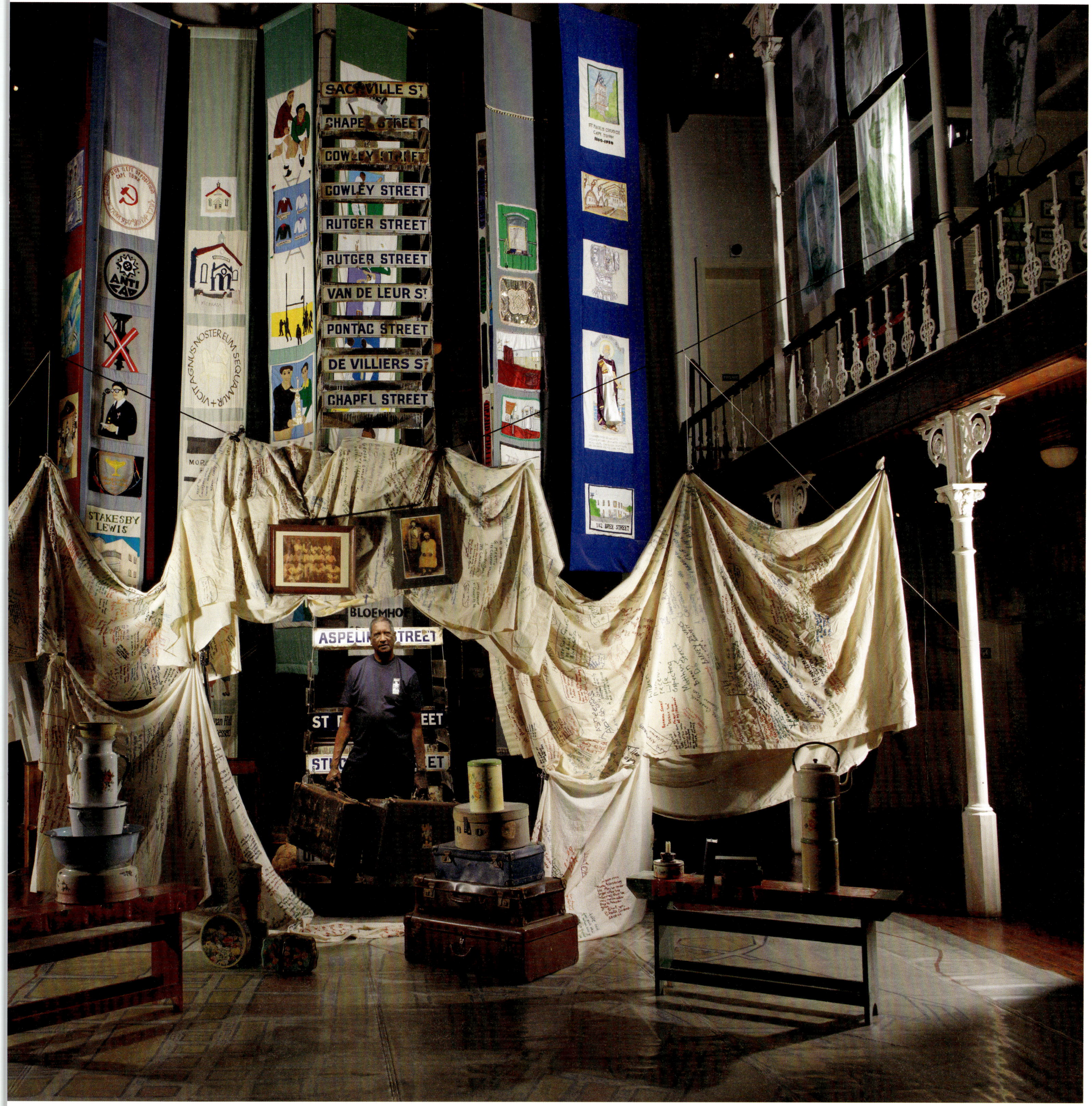
SACKVILLE ST
COWLEY STREET
RUTGER STREET
RUTGER STREET
VAN DE LEUR ST
PONTAC STREET
DE VILLIERS ST
CHAPEL STREET
STAKESBY LEWIS
BLOEMHOF
BREE STREET

My grandfather

sometimes talked about the time of slavery. It is a painful legacy and I think that even today we have a long road ahead of us. We are the richest country in the world but we see everything in the short-term: in reality, we have lots of poverty and too many boundaries between men. ¶ Here, we separate everything into classes, into types, whereas at the heart of it all few of us come from this land. Of course, there are many who really strive to free themselves from prejudice. Nevertheless, most of the poor people are colored. Yet, whatever our origin may be, we all love our children, we all have hearts, we all have emotions. The better we understand that, the less we will see others as objects and only then will we become better people. We can only live a meaningful life if we reach out and touch that of someone else.

MARIE-HÉLÈNE MILHOMME WITH HER FAMILY PHOTOS, AUSTIN, TEXAS, UNITED STATES.

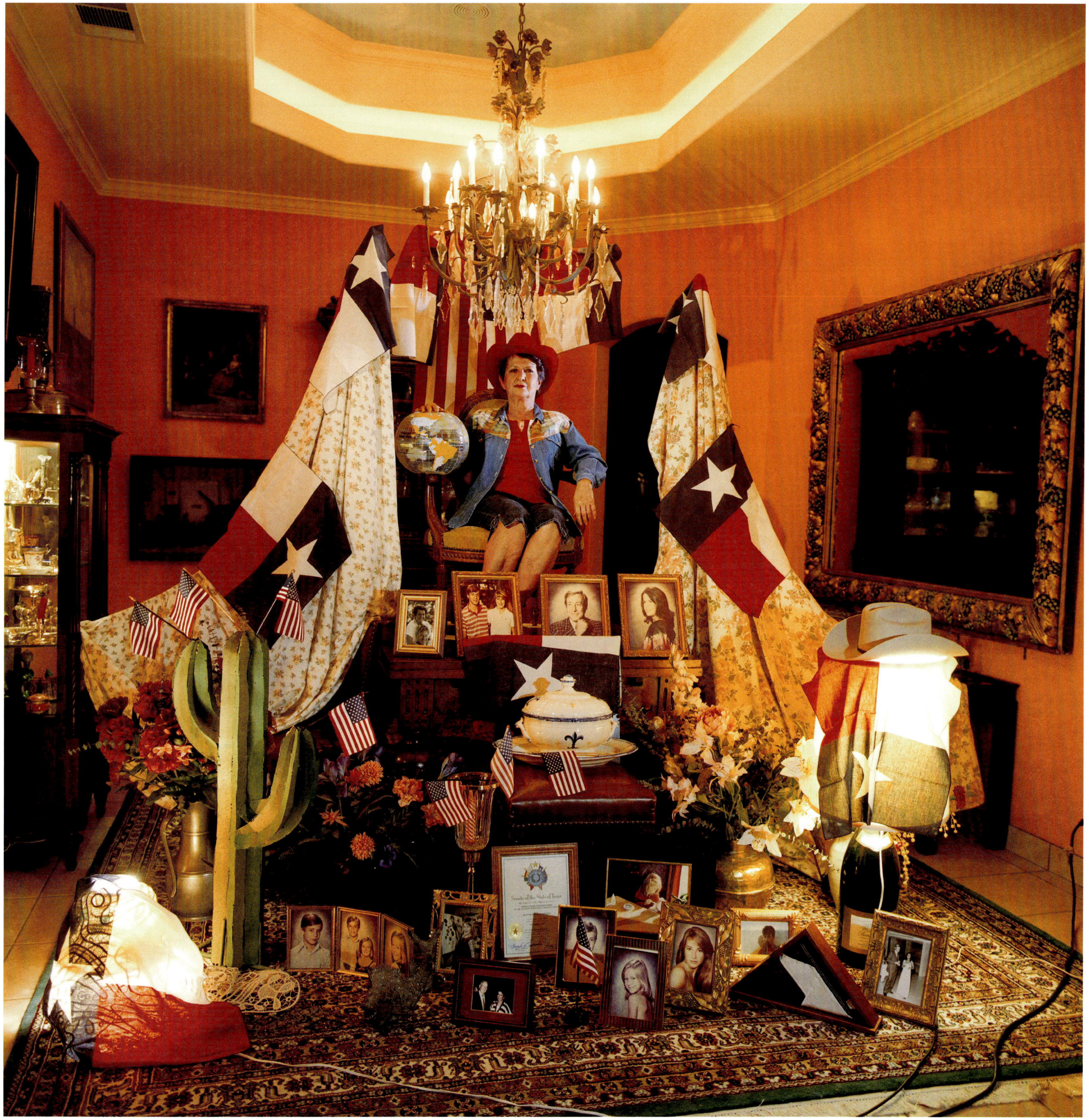

Borders are imaginary lines that only exist in man's mind. Our Earth needs to belong to everyone; she needs to be inhabited by men, without limits or barriers. She is large enough to hold us all, big enough to feed all of us. Man's greed is the only thing that creates these borders. Without this desire, they have no reason to exist. ¶ Our children must grow up with herds of animals, must be able to sell them to buy what is needed. When they come back to camp, to its bonfires and stories, we take the time to live and to love. ¶ I see it in my desert: before, there were many oases, we had grass, we had what we needed. Today this is disappearing, little by little. In our community, nature is all providing, and God is gradually starting to take back what he once granted us, as a result of of man's behavior.

FADIMATA WITH HER HERD, SETTING OUT INTO THE DESERT, MALI.

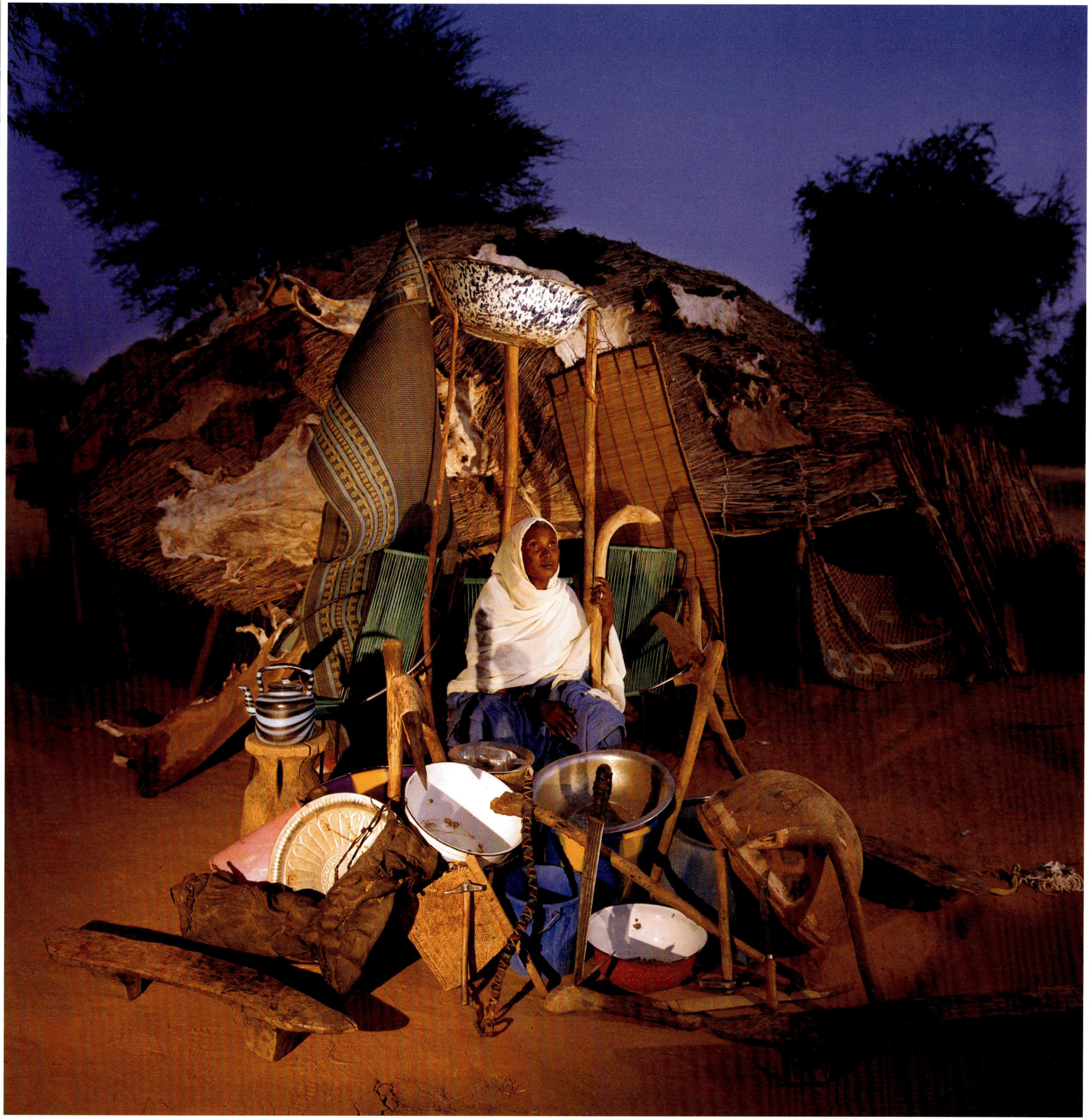

We live in the street. It's been 5 years. We squat on the half-built bridge in the center of Cape Town. The cops often come around and throw our clothes and bedding over the edge. My man, Gameit, with all of his tattoos, the symbols of his gang, spent 8 years in prison. One piece of advice, when you find a man, check him out first. Before shaking his hand, you need to check them first – given most men never wash their hands. I have 18 grandchildren. Most of my family members have stayed in townships where they have their routines. The mothers don't want to leave their kitchens and creature comforts. But me, I prefer to live out here. I find it safer. At least we are far from the gangs and violence. Here in Cape Town I can protect my children. Even if they can't go to school, I would like my oldest to become a lawyer. My daughter would like to become a flight attendant so that she can travel around the world but I'd prefer she dance. When you express yourself with your body it helps you forget everything. ¶ When I was little, I lived in nature. The baboons came to play with me. Today, on the street, dogs bite us. Yet, here, I find myself at peace and I feel like I am getting younger and younger, as though I were 40 again. ¶ In our neighborhood, they call me the "Mama". Those who come and those who go are, for me, all part of the same family.

ROWHDA, GAMEIT AND THEIR "CHILDREN" ON THE HALF-BUILT BRIDGE, CAPE TOWN, SOUTH AFRICA.

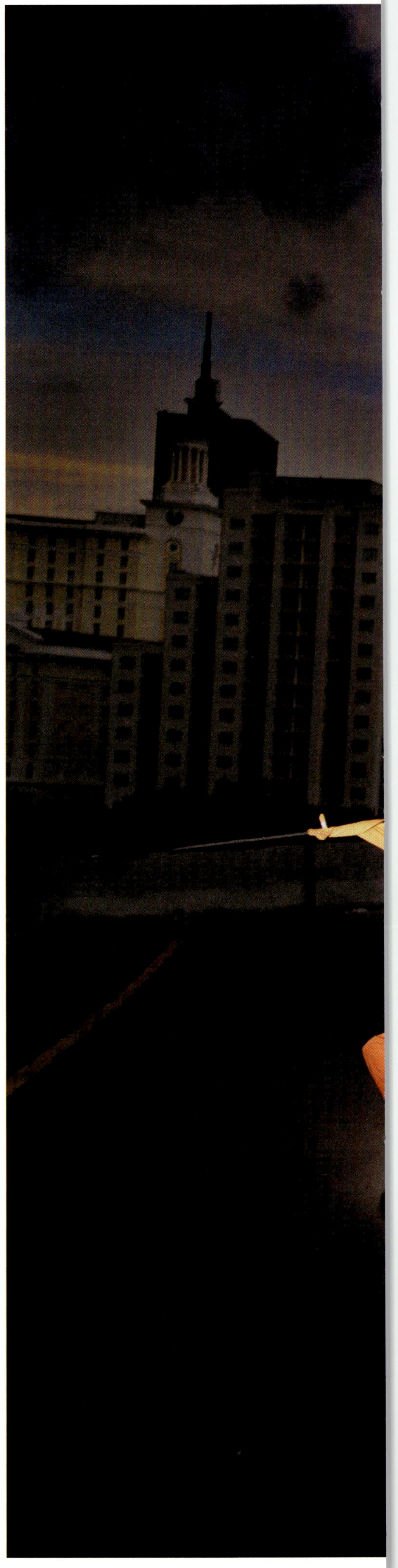

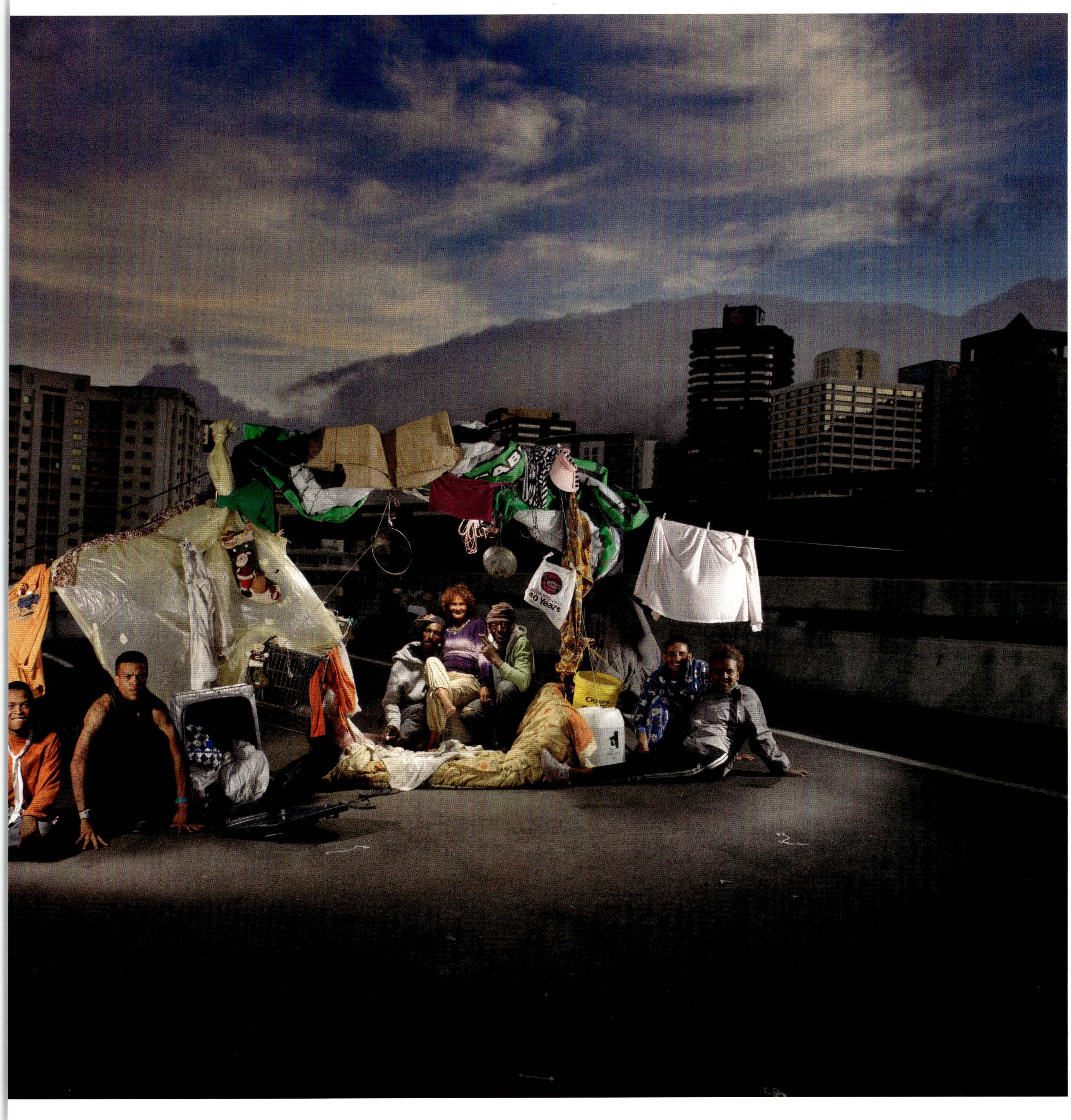
40 Years

As a child I would travel with my father, my grandfather, elephants, cows, camels, a harmonium and a band of puppets. From village to village, we'd spread the word of the kings of Rajasthan, to whom our community was close. Our puppets were the messengers of all the stories in the region. Then cinema and television came along and the nomads disappeared. We abandoned our tents for houses of stone and mud in the slums. The world today is as different from that of my youth as the sky is to the earth. ¶ In India, in the shadow of each building, there is a slum, a shantytown. It's not a 5-star hotel but here, we'll always give you a smile. This is where life is. Here, there are over 20 different castes and over a thousand artists. Before, we could feed our family with 10 rupees. Today, 10,000 isn't near enough. There's no longer any respect for our art. Our children want trendy clothes so they can look like everyone else. They like the slums, but they prefer no one knows that's where they come from. ¶ It is art that allowed me to travel the world and I would like for my children to follow this same path. They like to express themselves as well, through hip-hop, their music, with their words. The life of an artist is hard, but when you get out on the road it's like a dream. When you come back nothing has changed, yet nothing is the same. But we have something to share.

BHAGWAMDAS BHAAT AND HIS FAMILY AT A GIANT PUPPET FESTIVAL, KATHPUTLI, DELHI, INDIA.

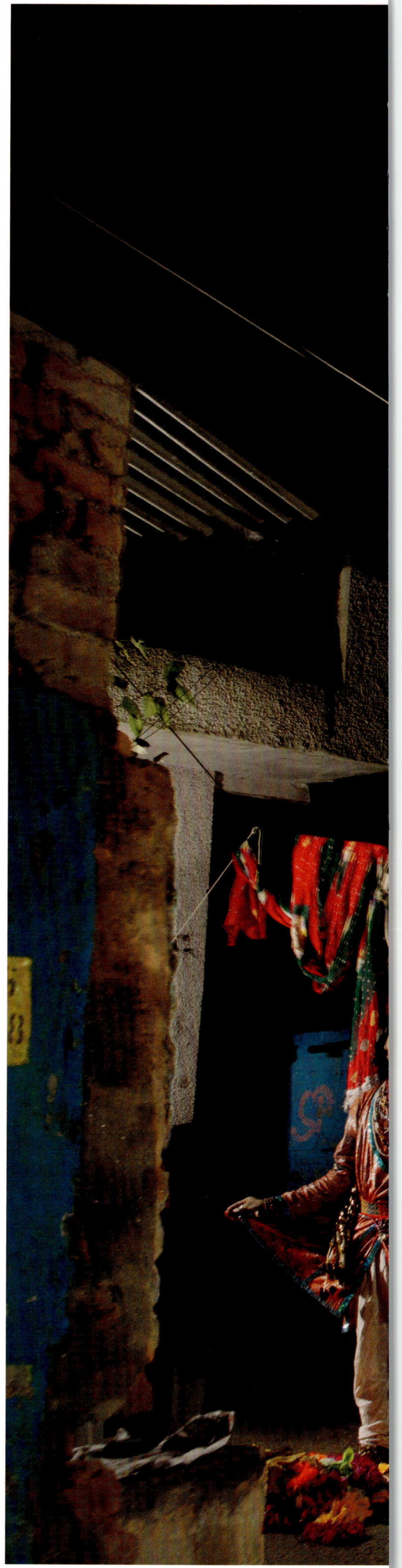

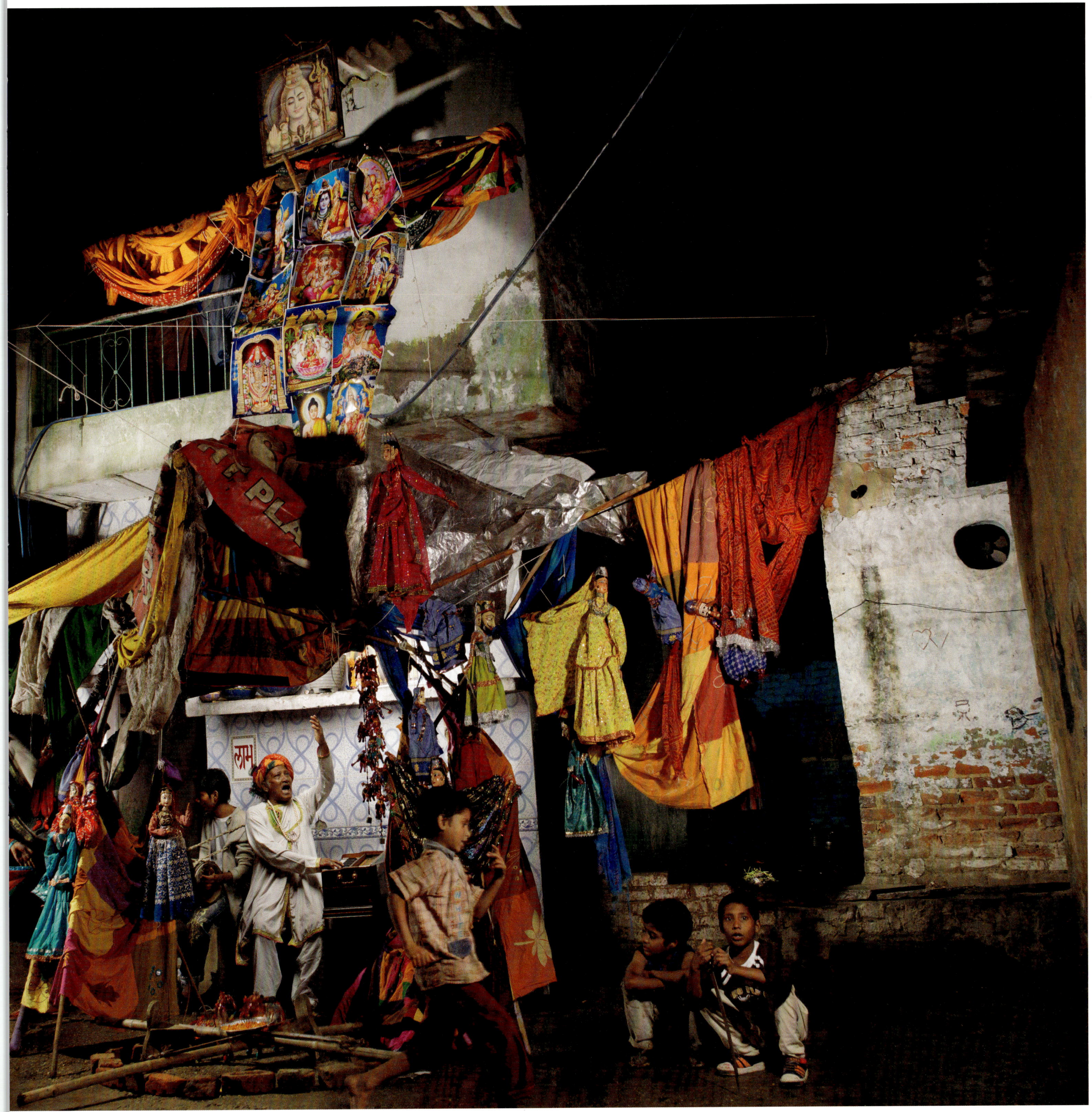

Everywhere around us there were little houses, real houses like in children's drawings. The light of the morning would fall just across my bed. The wind and the sun would call to me and I could follow the course of time and the seasons. It becomes harder and harder to see the shapes and forms we used to imagine depicting other lives in the clouds. In the place of what we knew before they want to build enormous buildings. ¶ Our house is nothing but ruins. The bulldozers came to destroy it. The roof of my grandchildren's old school has been opened to the sky. All that remains is a few toys, with which I built a little colored house, of wood. This is where I'd like to live. ¶ The house in which we once lived was built entirely by the hands of my father and his father. Each nook and cranny was full of history and memories. But as for the work of my children, all that shall remain is imagination and absence.

ZHENG YI AND HIS TOY HOUSE IN THE FORMER NURSERY SCHOOL OF HIS GRANDCHILDREN, SHANGHAI, CHINA.

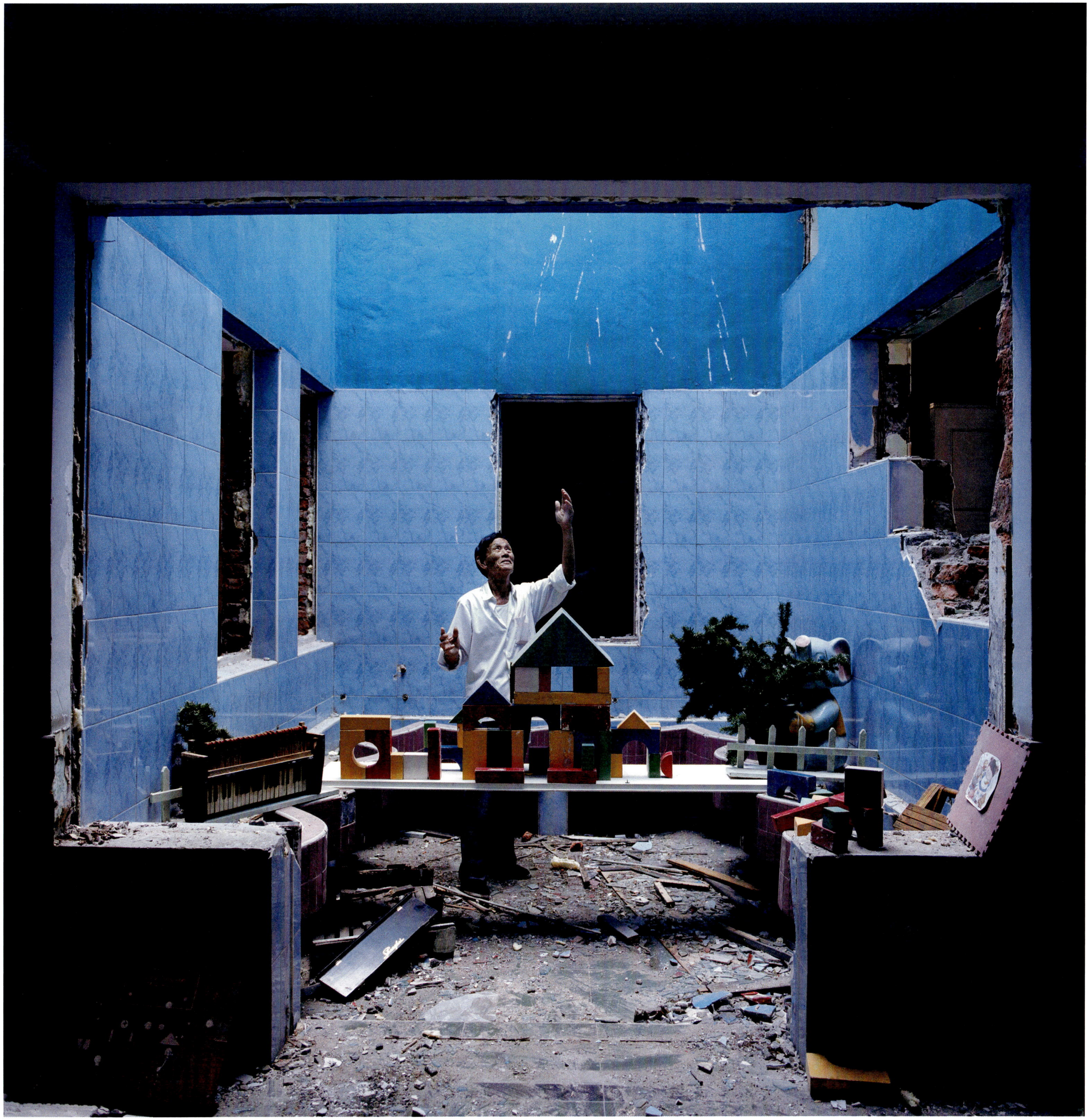

IRINA OLIVIA CASTRO BUSTOS ¶ FRANCISCO
DA SILVA RELVA ¶ SOPHIE SCHWARTZ ¶ RICK
KAFA JAMIL SALAMEH KAWALDEH ¶ ELLEN T
BHUQA ¶ MEENAKSHI GHOSH ¶ IRINA OLIVIA
NAOMI ABETA ¶ ANGLE MARÍA DA SILVA RELV
PARIYAR ¶ MIRIAMA MAOUNI ¶ KAFA JAMIL
MAMGEMA XAKAMA ET NOPIKAPA BHUQA ¶
BUSTOS ¶ FRANCISCO ET RAIMUNDA ¶ NAOMI
SCHWARTZ ¶ RICK ¶ SANÉ ET POMPA PARIY
KAWALDEH ¶ ELLEN TREVORROW ¶ MAMGEM
GHOSH ¶ IRINA OLIVIA CASTRO BUSTOS ¶ FRA
MARÍA DA SILVA RELVA ¶ SOPHIE SCHWART
MAOUNI ¶ KAFA JAMIL SALAMEH KAWALDE
ET NOPIKAPA BHUQA ¶ MEENAKSHI GHOSH ¶
RAIMUNDA ¶ NAOMI ABETA ¶ ANGLE MARÍA DA
PARIYAR ¶ MIRIAMA MAOUNI ¶ KAFA JAMIL SA
TREVORROW ¶ MAMGEMA XAKAMA ET NOPIKA
CASTRO BUSTOS ¶ FRANCISCO ET RAIMUN
RELVA ¶ SOPHIE SCHWARTZ ¶ RICK ¶ SANÉ

THE PLAYHOUSE
IN THE ARMS OF THE LOVEBIRD

From one end to the other, along our coasts, there are clusters of buildings rising from the earth. Each day, the population grows. Traditional fishing has practically disappeared and the sound of motors has replaced the ripples from our little boats on the water. The youths of our village today dress like the American rappers they discover by watching television. ¶ The Oceano Pacifica hacienda has been our land, passed from generation to generation. Our horses take shade in the great trees whose roots are over a thousand years old. The plants and flowers that we grow give color to the buildings that crowd our beaches. They perhaps help us forget the sad state of our mangroves, full of plastic bottles. ¶ The dream of the bird resembles love. In one word, in one look, it fulfills all life. Even one little thing is enough to rediscover the tenderness and affection, which is essential nourishment. Even as our world changes, we shall continue to foster this hope. We will always find love when it is least expected.

IRINA OLIVIA CASTRO BUSTOS IN THE ARMS OF THE LOVE BIRD, ECUADOR.

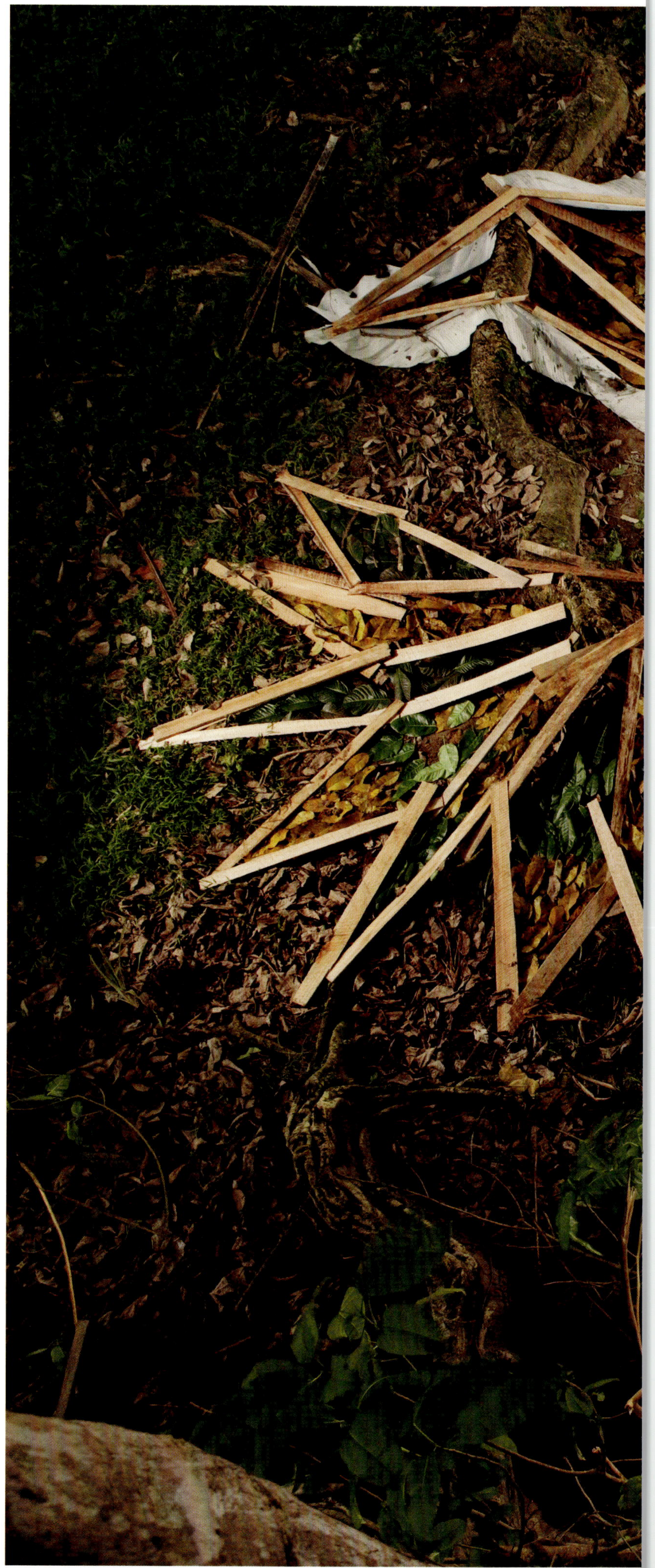

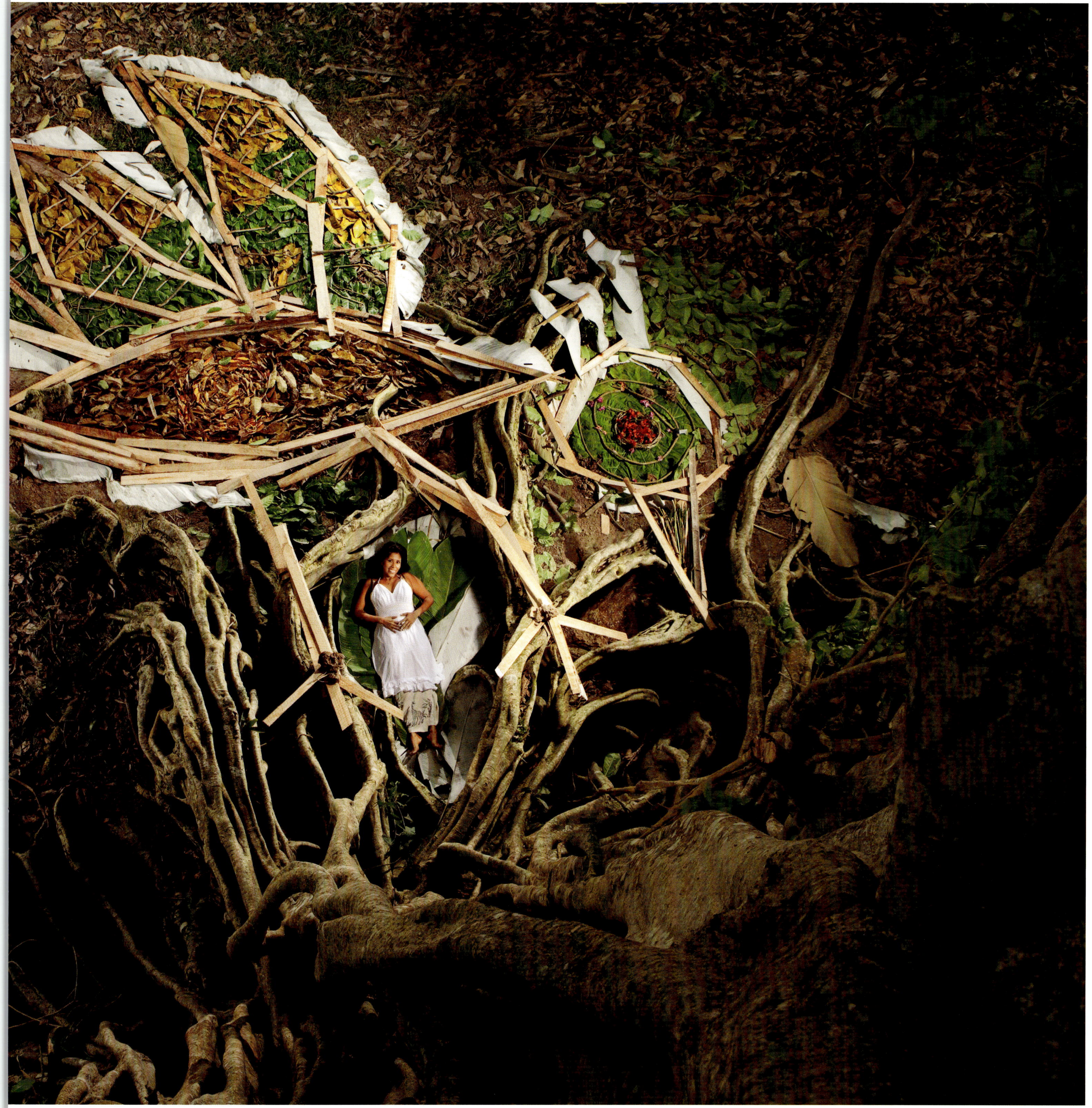

Francisco: What makes me angry is that we don't have enough energy to squander like rich countries. It's our duty to find a different path that will serve as an example, if not, the planet will waste away. When I was a child we didn't need useless things to make us happy. ¶ Raimunda: I'd like to be able to dive into the television. We'd dance in Bollywood. I'd travel the world always in a different dress, but each evening, I'd come back to my kitchen to prepare the fish, langoustes and shrimp that you love so much. ¶ Francisco: Because you love your son you always want to buy new things, but when we were his age, it was nature that gave us everything we needed. ¶ Raimunda: Feelings are the most difficult, the way you react to them and what you hope for. But when you grow old, the images of happiness are still there. ¶ Francisco: The most beautiful moment of my life was when I saw the birth of our son Itamar. Women are an extraordinary mystery to men!

FRANCISCO AND RAIMUNDA CHATTERING AMOROUSLY IN FRONT OF THEIR SON ITAMAR, REDONDO, BRAZIL.

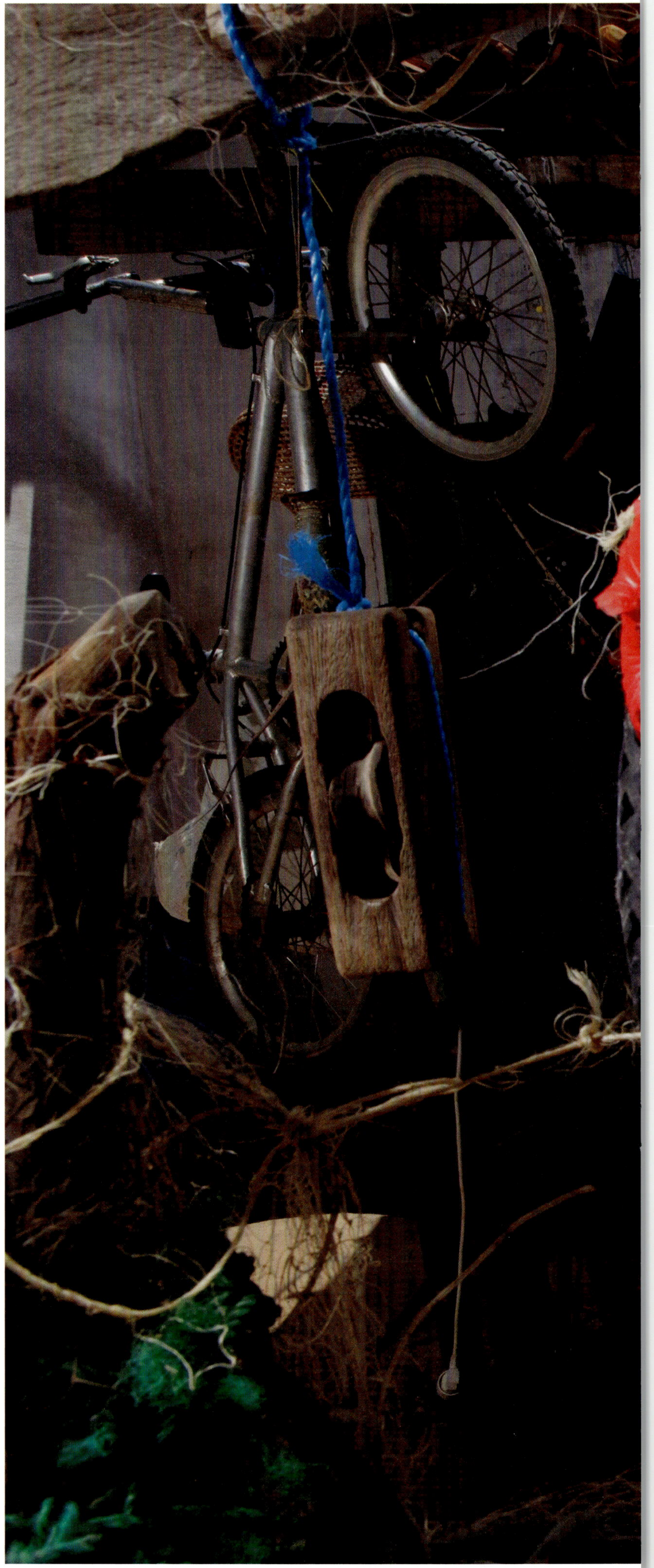

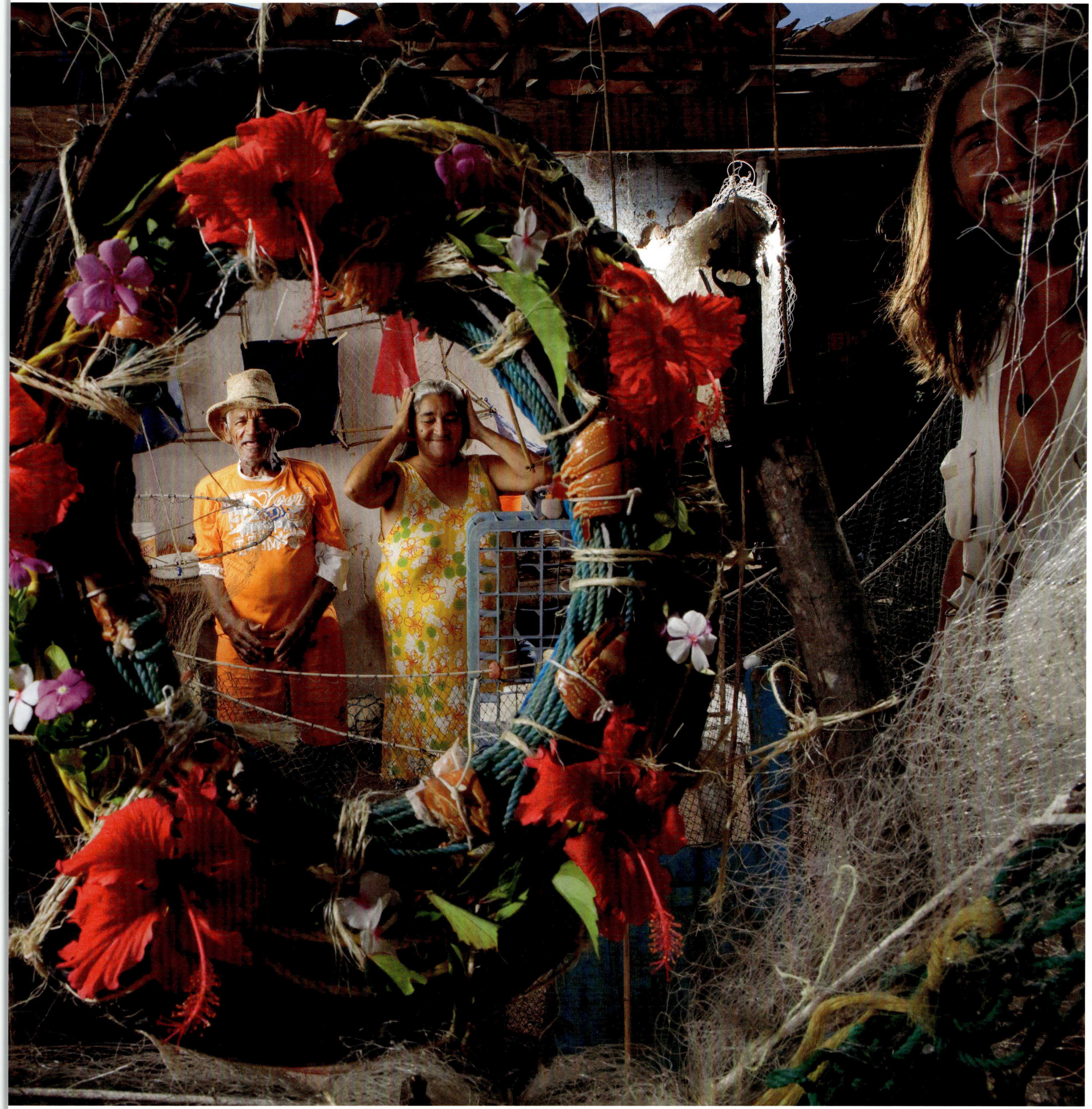

I like the invisible lines that run through space like the lines of a child's drawing or those traced by planes flying through the sky. These are things that make me happy. ¶ Drawing helps young disabled people in communicating with the world and allows them to grow up, to free themselves from their confinement. That's why teaching has become my work. Without dance and children, I think I would have gone mad. I danced a lot in Japan and Bali. Being able to express yourself, by drawing one's own lines, and crossing those of others is a blessing. Our society is very faithful to its traditions. In the countryside, a woman's place is in the home. There, I tended my secret garden, my universe in which no one was allowed. It was difficult to talk to my husband. Dance allowed me to free myself, to communicate in my own way to those around me. Thanks to this outlet, I gradually learned to be more natural in my relationships. ¶ Tsuchinoko is a little fellow who lives in nature. If you find him and if you catch him, you will be rich. He is an imaginary animal but everyone talks about him. If you look carefully at my photo, you will see that he is hidden somewhere.

NAOMI ABETA AND THE TSUCHINOKO, IN THE GARDEN WHERE THE KIMONO PHOTOS GROW, JAPAN.

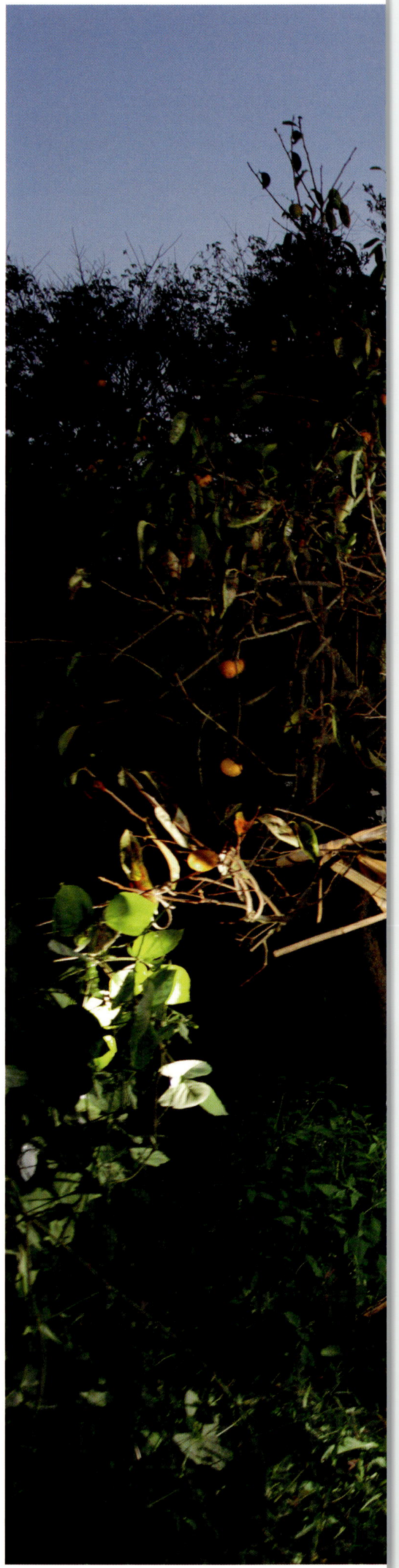

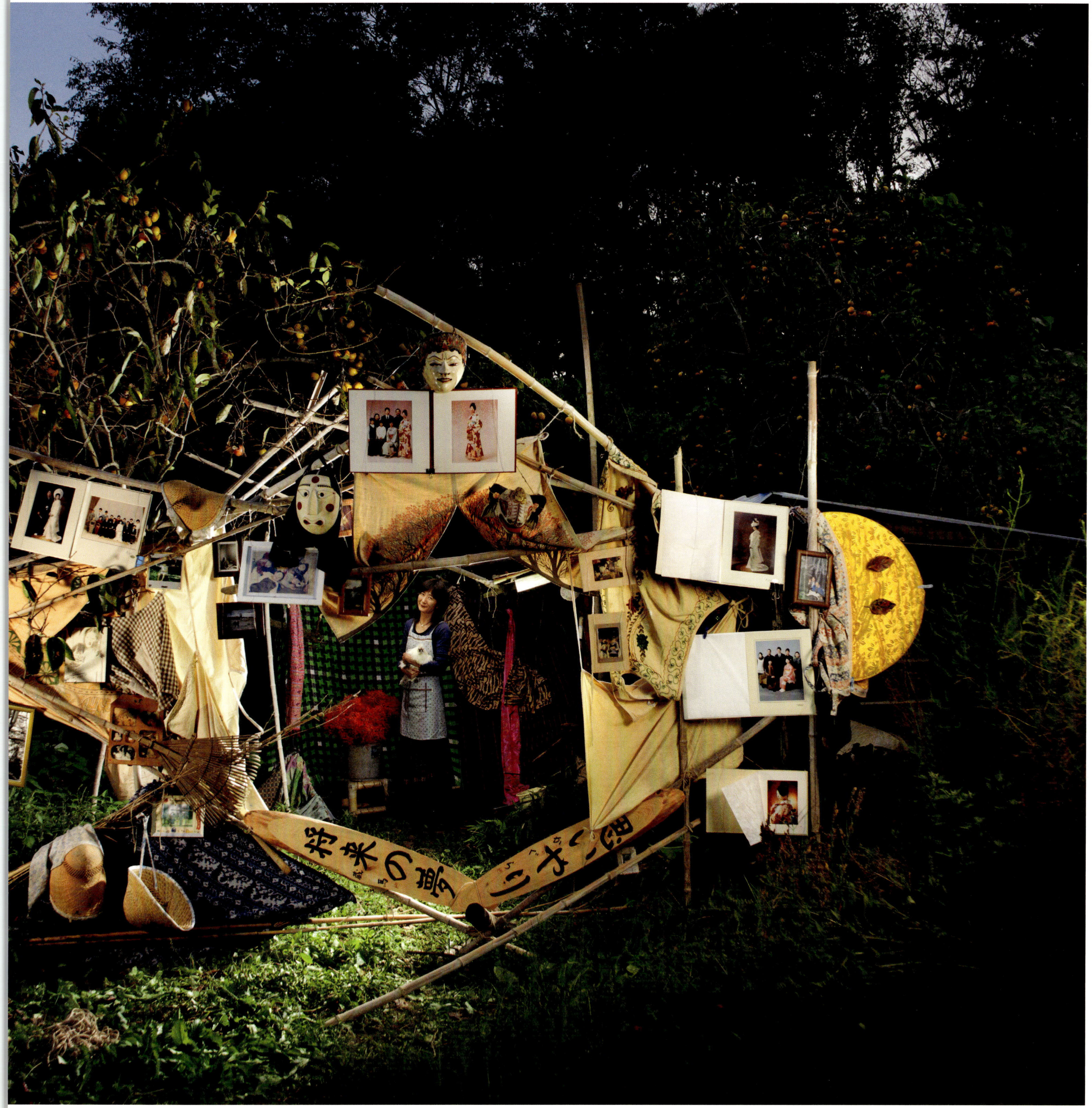
将来の夢
思いやり

I was born into a very traditional family. My husband was my first love. We were so young at the time… but life drifts by, and love with it. When we separated, it was very hard but we always respected each other. Out of respect for our children, we never said bad things about one another. And, years later, we found each other again. Today, we are good friends. We even bought a house together. Everyone we love was reunited, even our new spouses and the children from our new marriages. We have big parties that everybody comes to. The children laugh together and splash in the pool while we chat on the terrace. ¶ With the end of the dictatorship, this is what we won: freedom. Now we can live and love freely. And there is contraception, which makes things much easier. I advise my children to have more experiences and as many girlfriends as possible. Why deprive yourself? I want them to steer their ship as they feel fit. ¶ Talking is great, but living is better, that's what I say. People today talk about everything, all the time, especially when they don't know anything. That's when people start to come apart, usually for silly reasons. As for me, I prefer to live as I like and let others do the same. That's what I consider my liberty to be.

ANGLE MARíA DA SILVA RELVA, THE SWIMMING POOL AND COLORED CUSHIONS, SAO TEOTONIO, PORTUGAL.

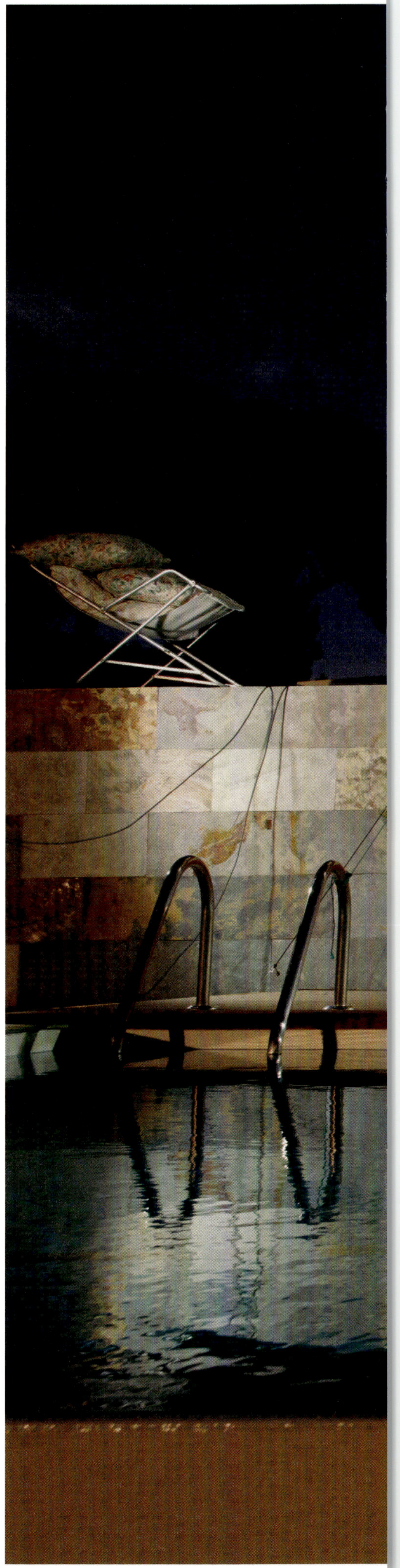

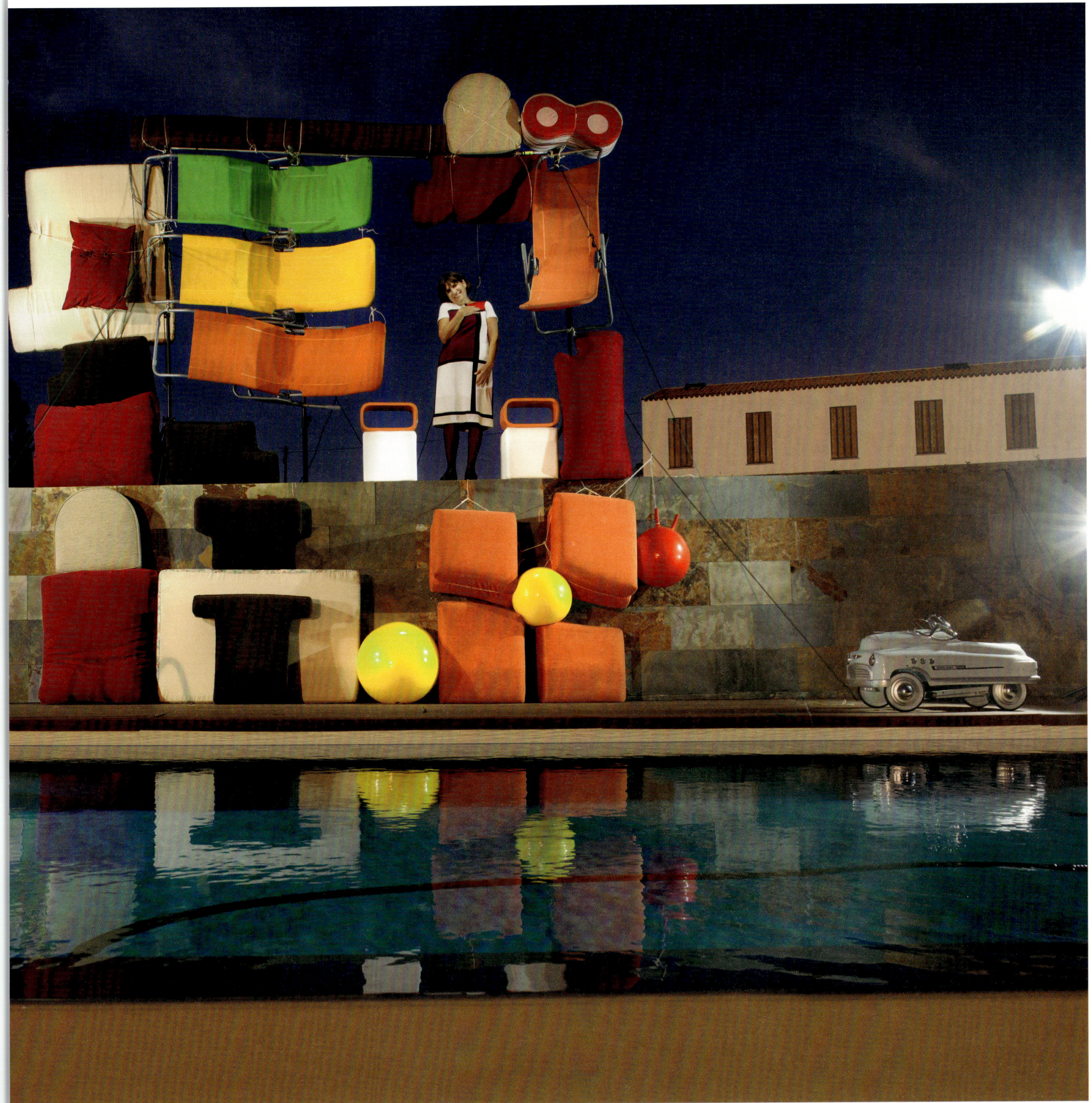

I have spent my life with my head in the clouds, floating through the sky. When you are lighter than air you have the feeling that the whole world belongs to you. You are carried by the winds, succumbing to their will; you come across changing forms in which you imagine a horse galloping or a bloodthirsty monster. ¶ During traditional Brazilian celebrations we send large paper balloons into the air. When they fall to the ground the first person to find them gets to keep them. When my husband and I introduced the first hot-air balloons to Brazil, people had never seen such things. We bought alien masks to frighten anyone who was envious and wanted to take them from us. ¶ Our travels across South America led us to the canopy of the great forest, where we landed and encountered unknown tribes. The Indians watched us descend from the sky like figments of their imagination. We built hundreds of hot-air balloons, in a whole array of colors. Some were shaped like imaginary beings. ¶ What I like is that everything is changing around me. Sometimes, when my husband comes home from work, I've re-arranged and changed the color of all of the furniture in the house. I believe that in life we must always choose the path of adventure, emotion and joy. If you are able to have this courage, this consistency in your choices, destiny will reward you.

SOPHIE SCHWARTZ AND THE UMBRELLAS SHE MAKES, RIO DE JANEIRO, BRAZIL.

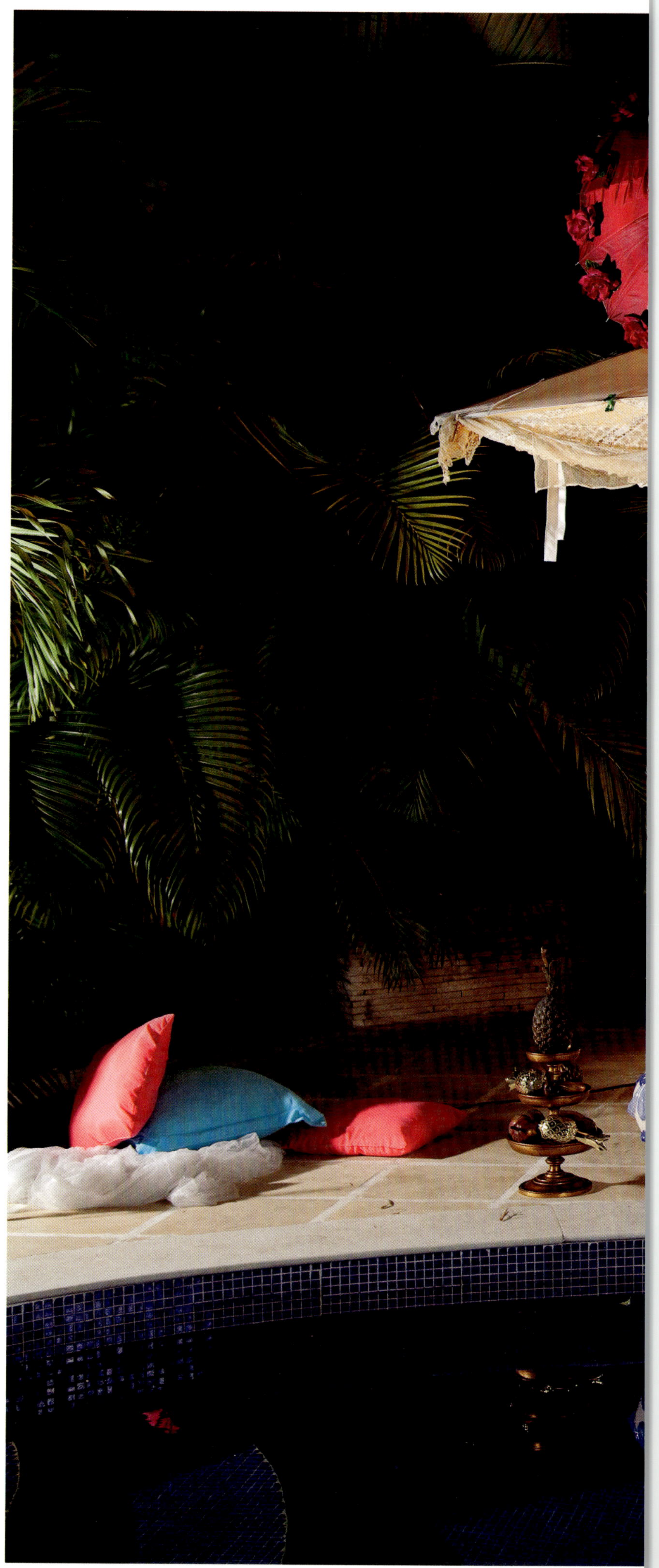

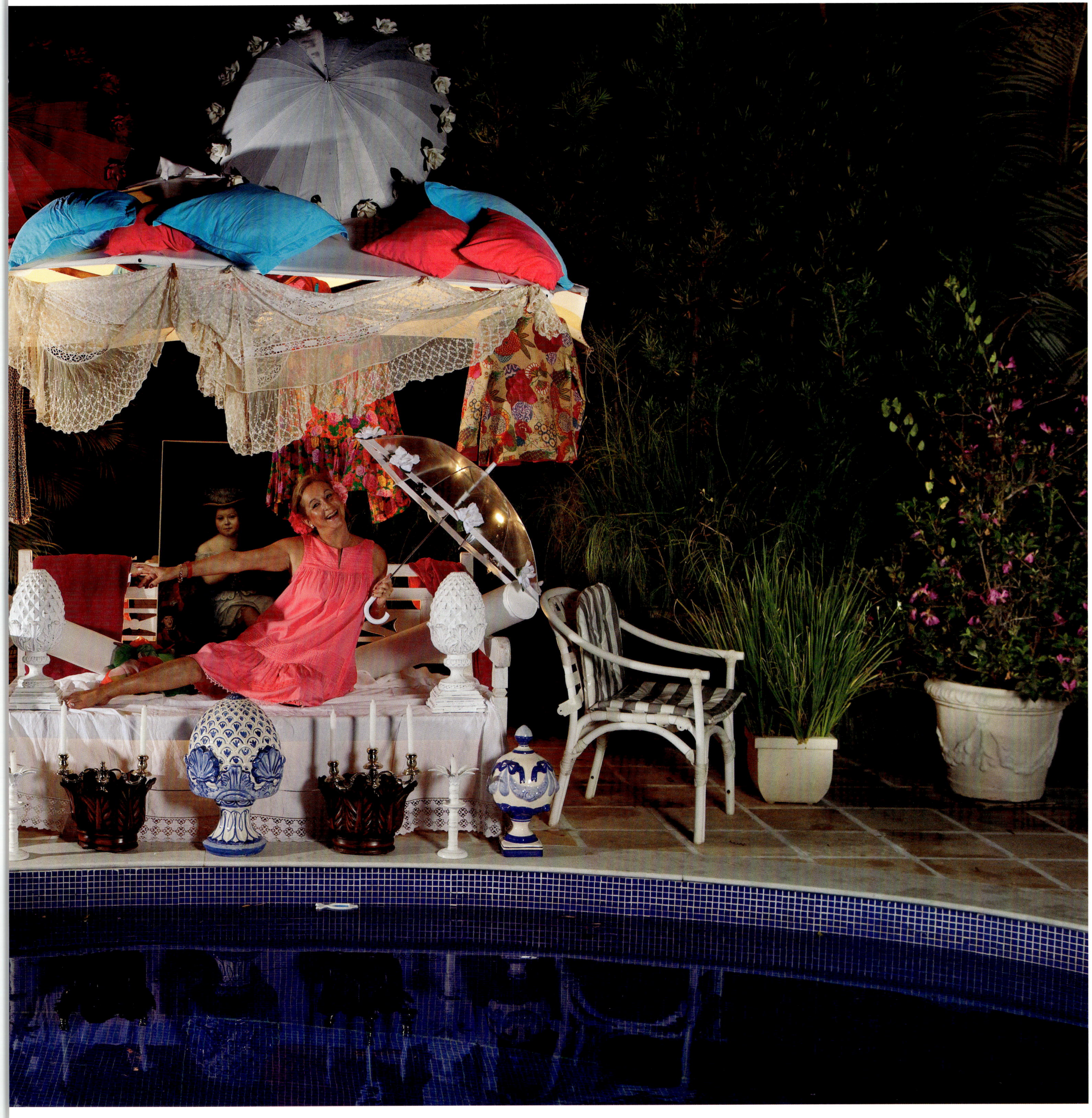

Around here we drink Lion Red, the beer of rugby. Rugby is our national sport. Today I am sharing a drink with the imbecile who messed up my garden and then expected me to smile for a photo! ¶ The way I take care of my grandchildren is to send them outside. They can climb trees, run, fish, ride motorbikes… whatever they want as long as they're not in front of the television. ¶ I was raised with a love for nature, not to waste time with meaningless struggles. The duty for us, the elders, is to pass along the art of working fabric and a sense of creativity. I work with kauris, the giant trees that are over 3,500 years old. They fall in the storms. This wood, we can turn and polish it for days at a time. My grandfather did the same thing. Passing along customs like this from generation to generation is in our genes. That is what keeps the heart strong.

RICK, HIS CHAINSAW AND THE WOODCUTTERS' PUPPET, DARGAVILLE, NEW ZEALAND.

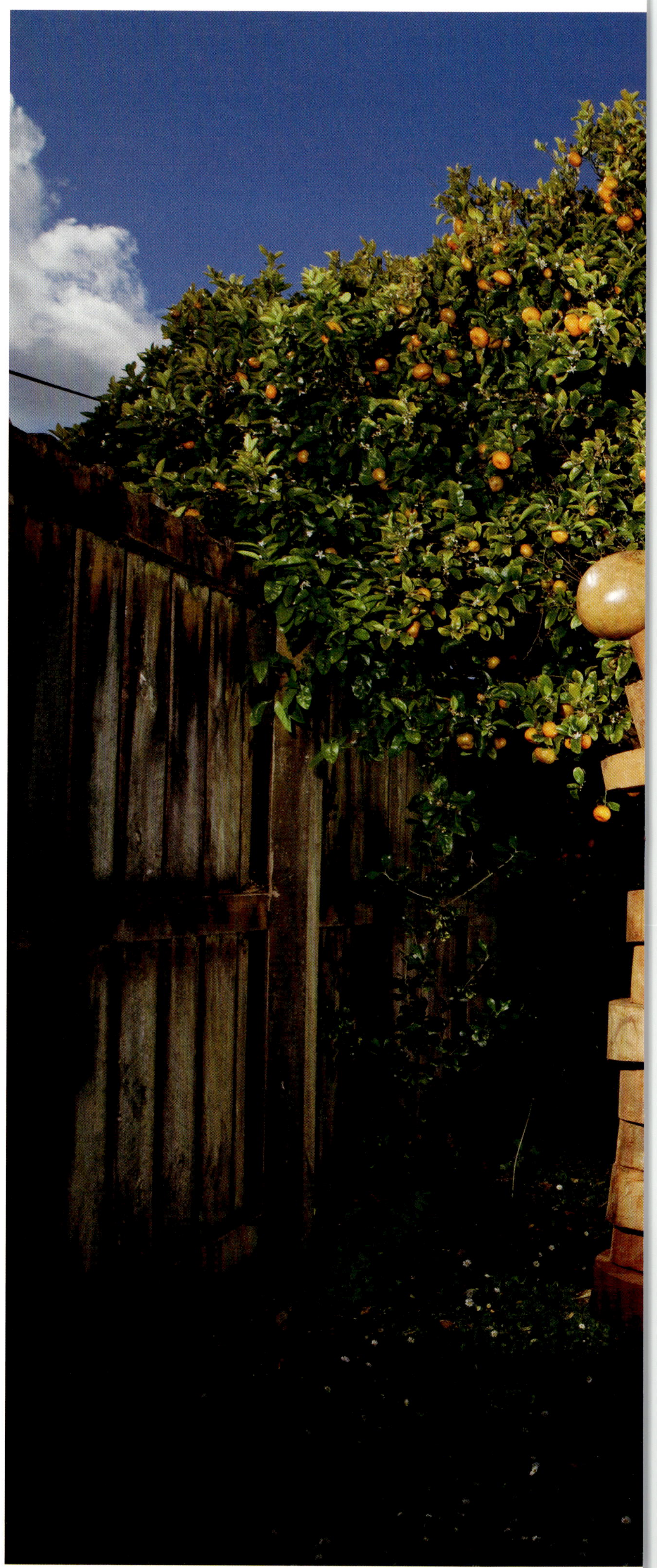

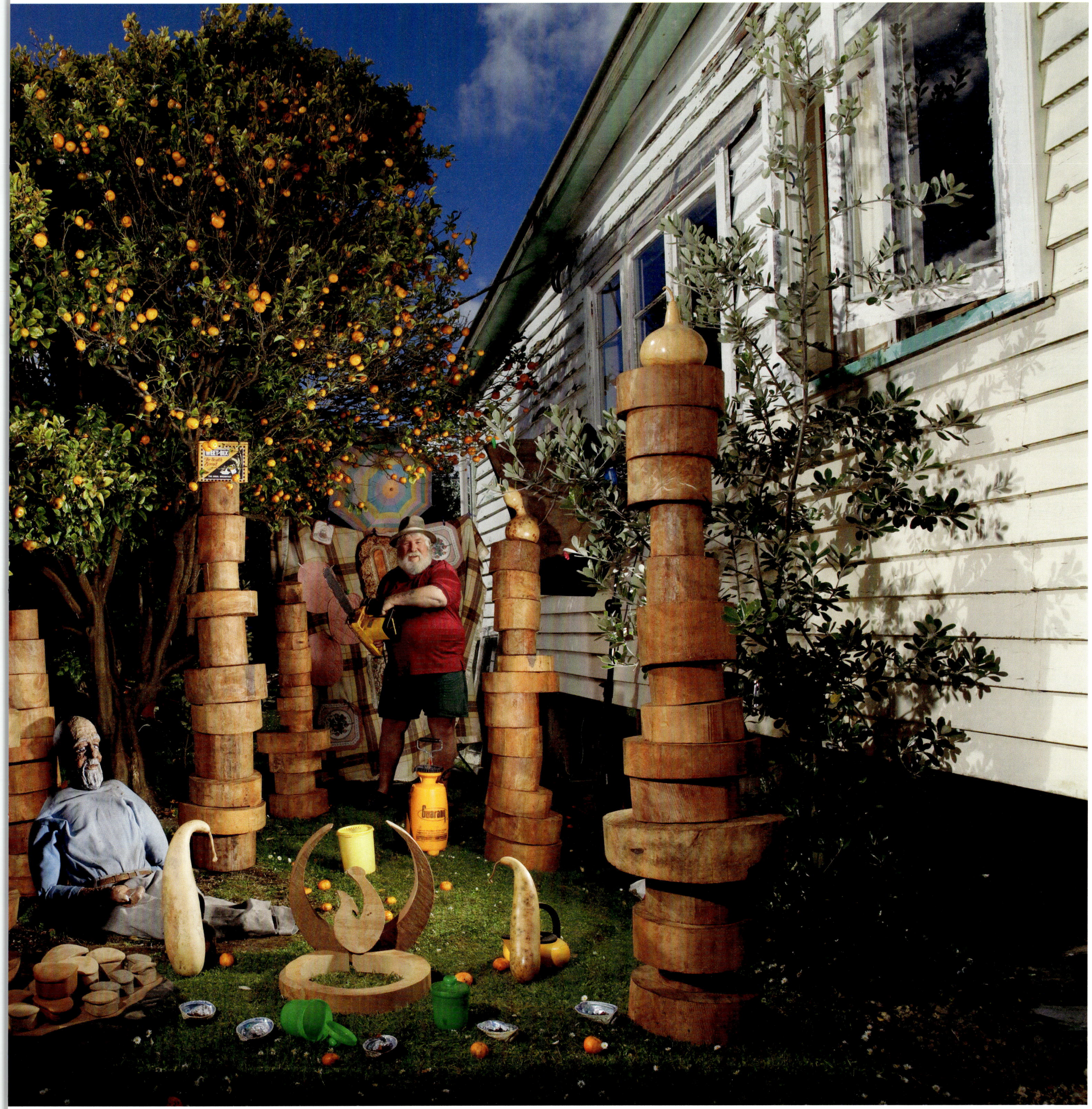

WEET-BIX
Guarany

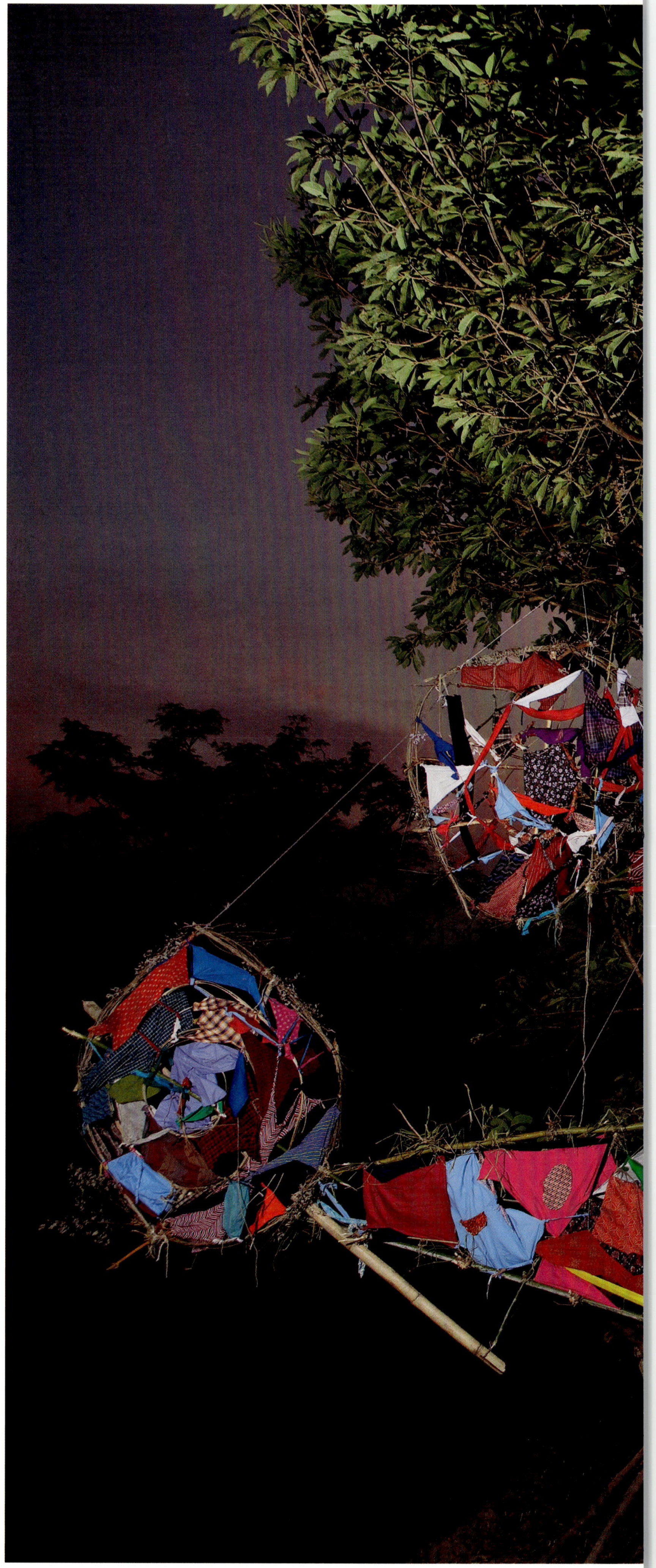

All of these colored fabrics are made from the leftover clothes of our community. They tell our story. When someone asks me to make them a piece of clothing, it's the time I pass in thinking about it that gives it beauty. Today, our great tree is evidence of our years of labor and friendship and the whole village has come to help me celebrate them. ¶ The most beautiful gowns I made were for my wife so that she could blend with the colors of the sky. When we were married I was 11 and she was 6. It was our families that chose us. After several years we fell in love and, the more children we had, the easier our life became. ¶ Back then I didn't have a mustache. To have a good mustache is important. It gives you an alluring pride. Young people think that as long as you don't have one, you're not a man. I tend to think you become a man when you know how to exhange something with another, brightening his life.

SANE AND POMPA PARIYAR WITH ALL THE FABRICS FROM THEIR WORKSHOPS, NEPAL.

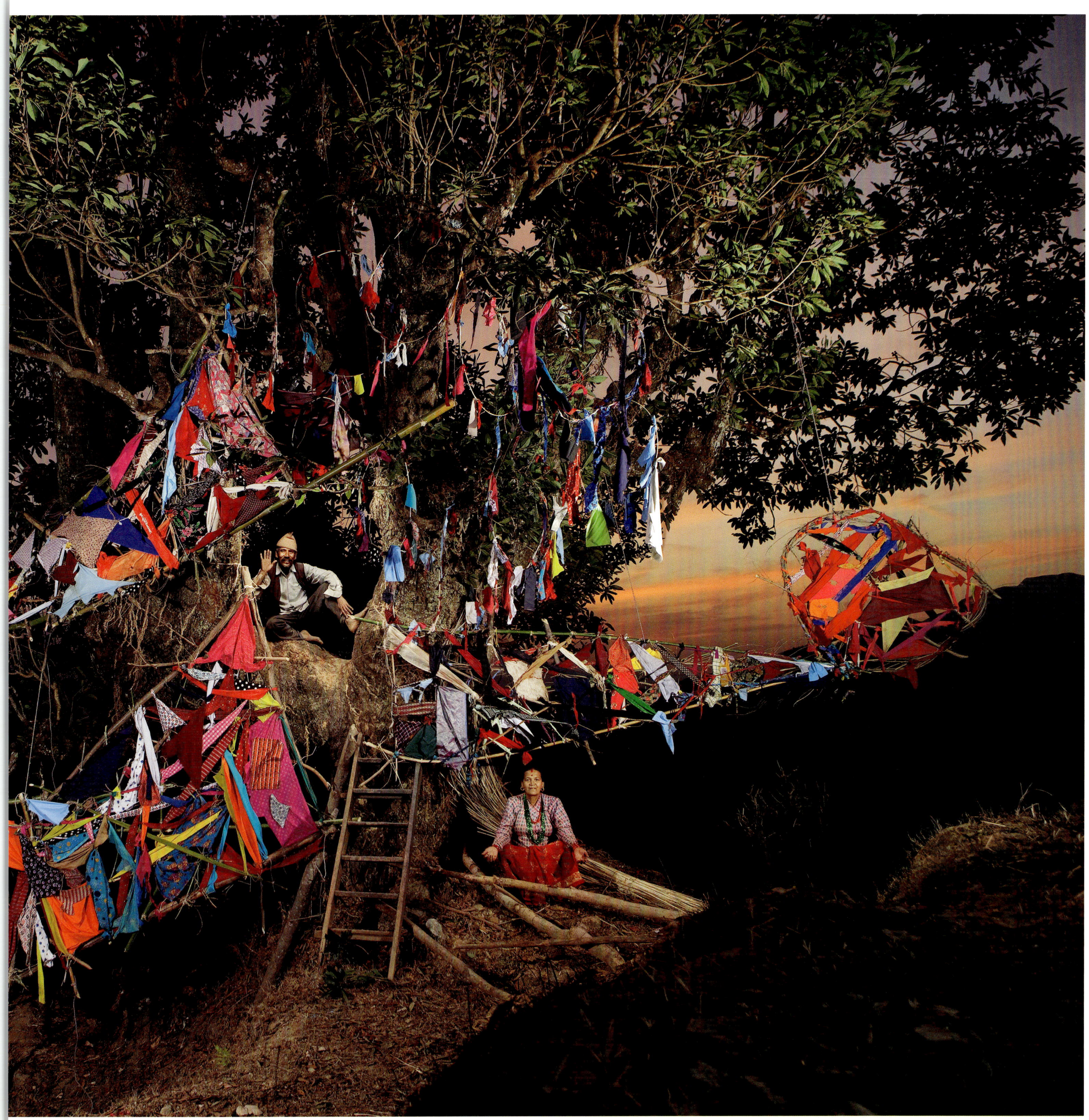

When you have your first child, it transforms your whole life. It's a magnificent gift. When you become a grandmother, it's even better. You can laugh to yourself as you watch the vanilla entangled with a tree's trunk and branches. Once you are a great-grandmother, it is the tears that express your joy and when you sneeze, you know God is thinking of you. In life, the older you get, the more intense your emotions get. ¶ If I had all of my children and grandchildren together, I wouldn't be able to count them. Every day the house is full of their laughter and even if I have to yell a lot, it's the greatest happiness in my life. And so I make monoi with coconut and red ginger and I gather fruit: pumpkins, mangos and star apples. ¶ On Sundays and for village festivities I wear colored dresses. I choose one of the hats I have woven with my own hands. These hats dress up every season, and accompany our prayers in the perfume of the flowers.

MIRIAMA MAOUNI, SURROUNDED BY HER HANDMADE HATS, MOOREA, FRENCH POLYNESIA.

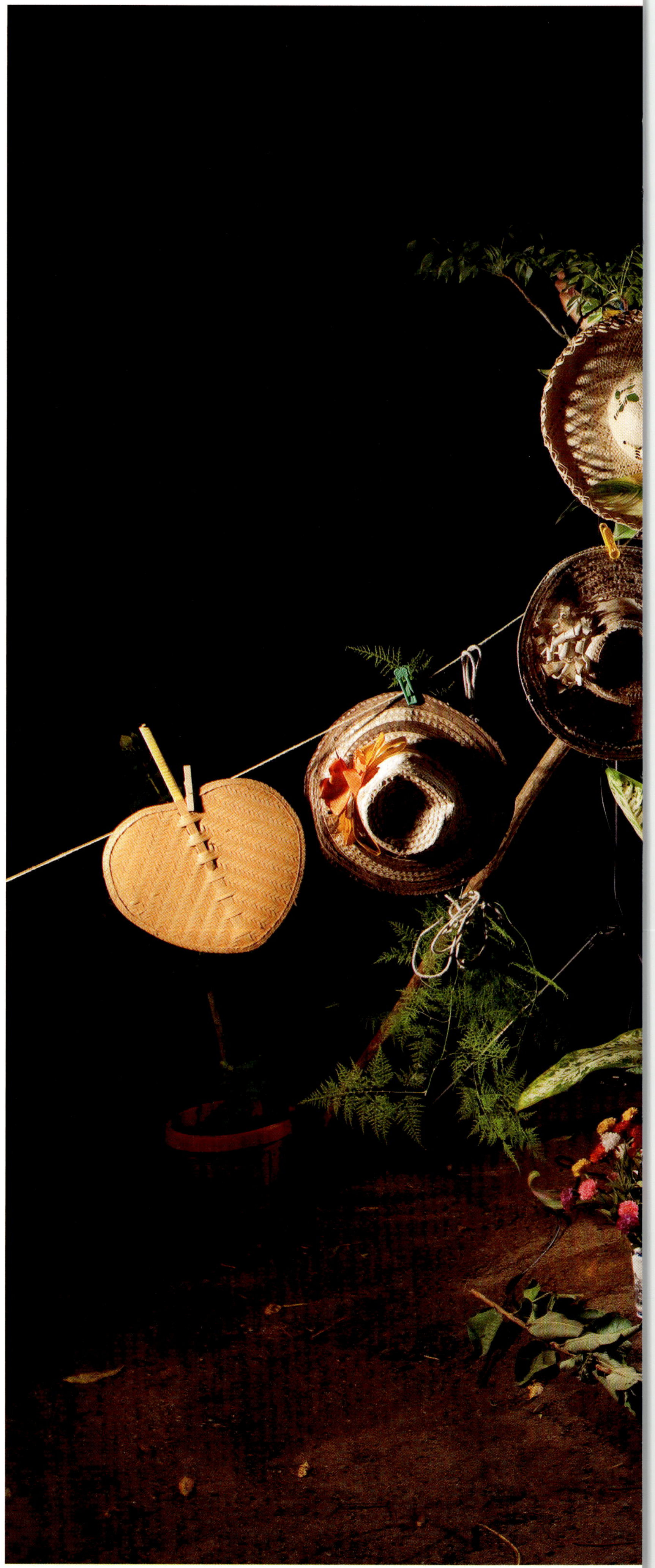

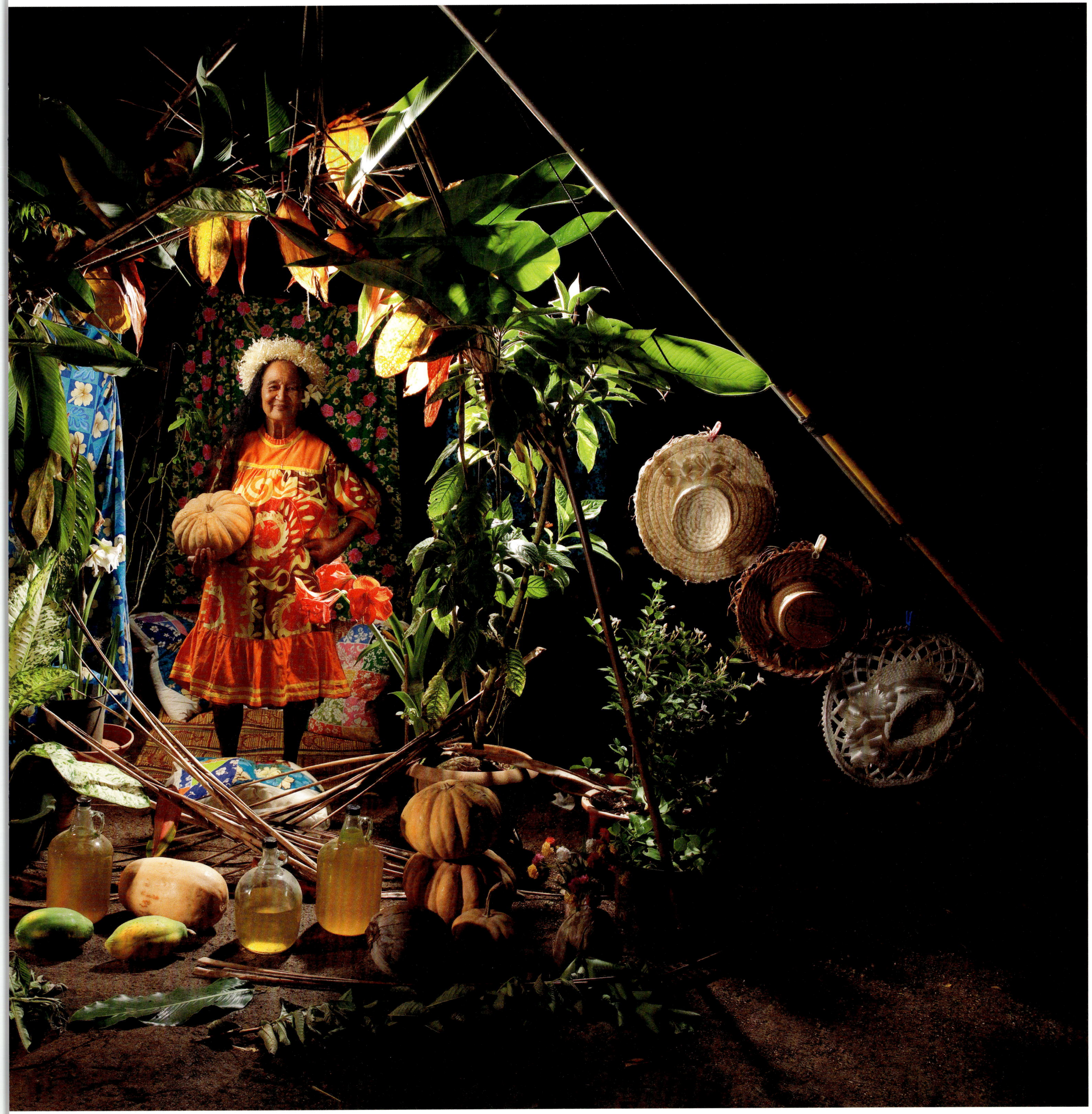

Our two fathers were brothers. Our families have known each other for a long time. Before, we married within the bloodlines and thus our whole village formed one big family. The writings of the Koran guide me in life, teaching me hospitality and prayers we offer to all. That fosters the love and respect that we share, my husband and I. ¶ For us Bedouin women, what is important is to cook well and take care of our children. At any given moment, our house is full of life and even now that our children have grown, there is never a moment of solitude. ¶ As children, we lived in a tent with our herds. We made ovens of mud at the entrance of caves. We burned dried goat's dung and made the best bread that one could imagine. Summer was too hot for camels so our lives followed the seasons, that of the plains and that of the mountains. We used to go draw water from wells and gather dead wood. ¶ When my grandfather left for Mecca, he spent 3 months crossing the desert on his camel. He saw the stone that turns all of us towards one another. That is my greatest pride.

KAFA JAMIL SALAMEH KAWALDEH, SERVING TEA IN HER SITTING ROOM, AL-QUASIDI, JORDAN.

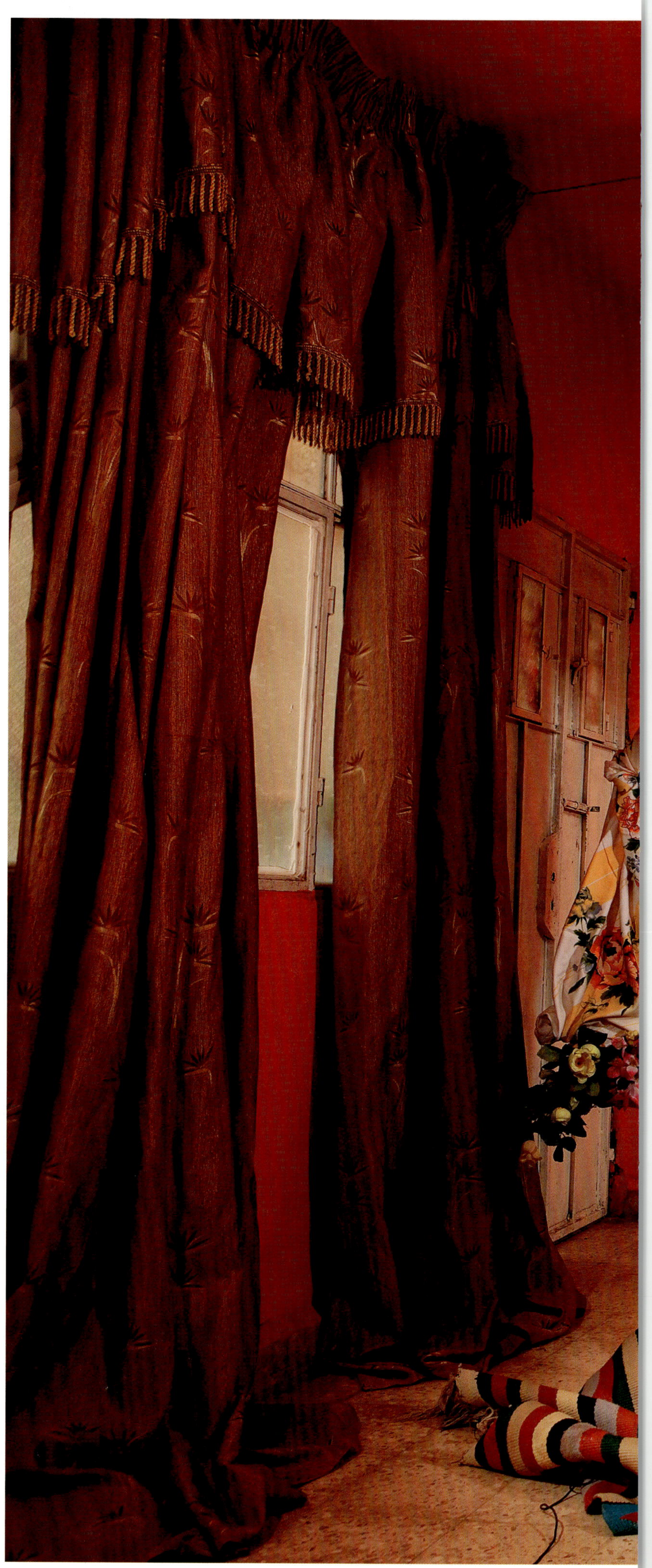

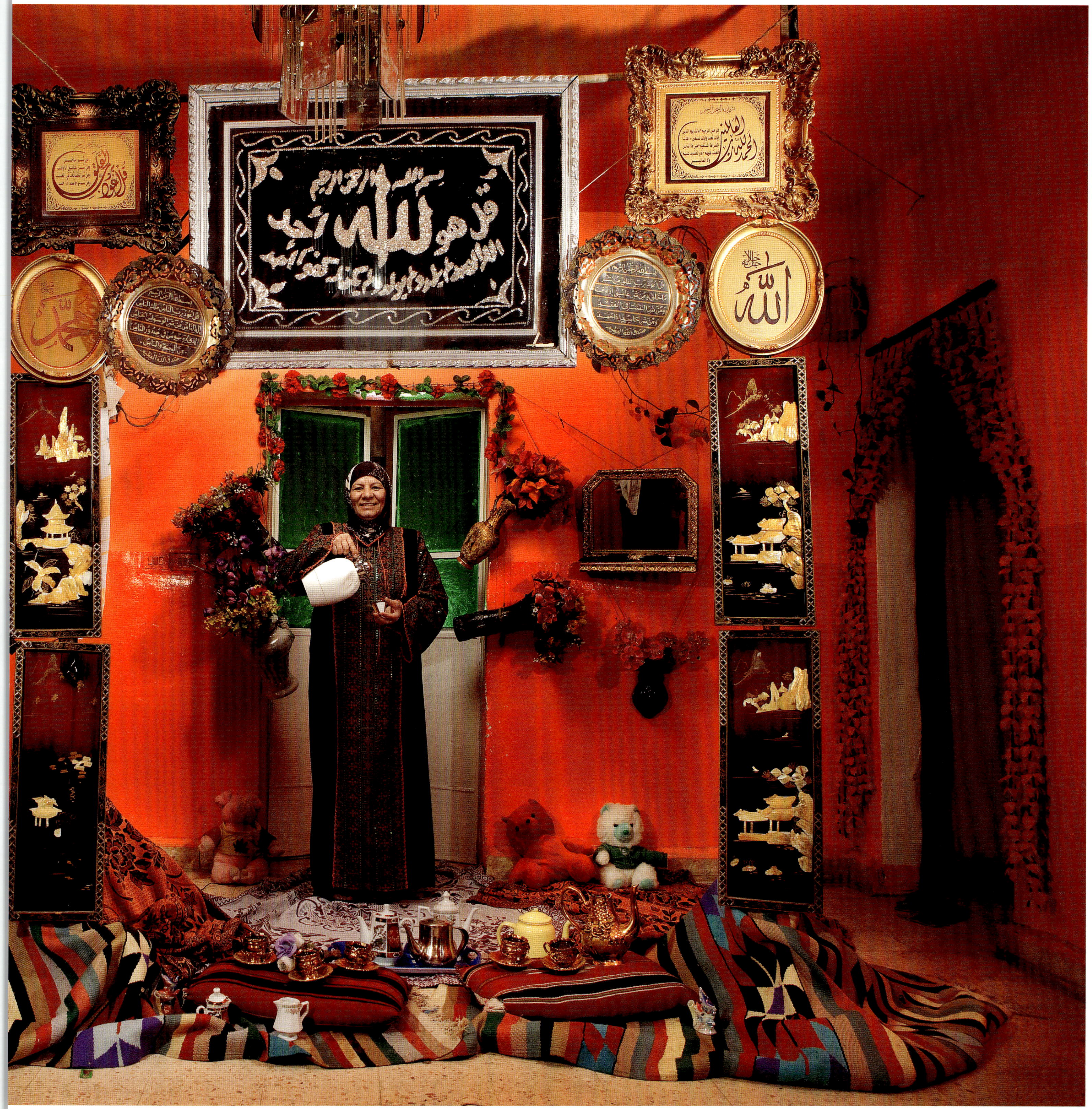
قل هو الله أحد
الله
محمد

The Ngarri is my land, born where the waters of the river meet those of the sea. We have always found sea grass along its banks. The art of weaving has developed from season to season through the exchanges and gifts between communities. ¶ Every moment of my life gives birth to a new form. My thoughts are tied to the links that weave my story. The fruits of nature come together to recount birth, love and death. The circle symbolizes the beginning of each thing, the creation, the generations and time as it goes by. It is the beginning of life, and its end. ¶ I belong to the pathways of my childhood. My daughter and my six sons have learned to think for themselves and find new beginnings through the patience of basketry. Today, grass is scarce. In certain areas, the water is as thick as milk. How to explain to my children that, once upon a time, we drank this water in our camps in the middle of the wild?

ELLEN TREVORROW, GATHERING THE GRASSES OF LIFE, MENINGIE, AUSTRALIA.

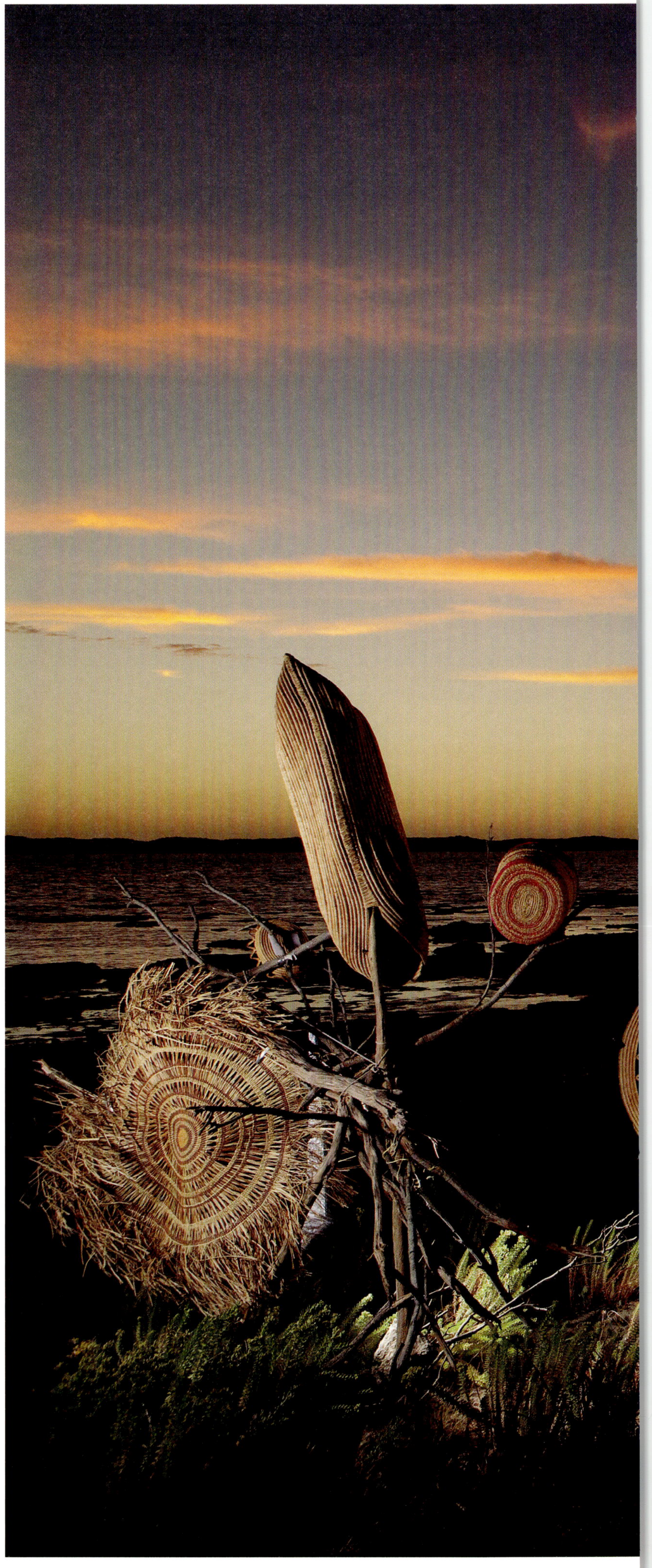

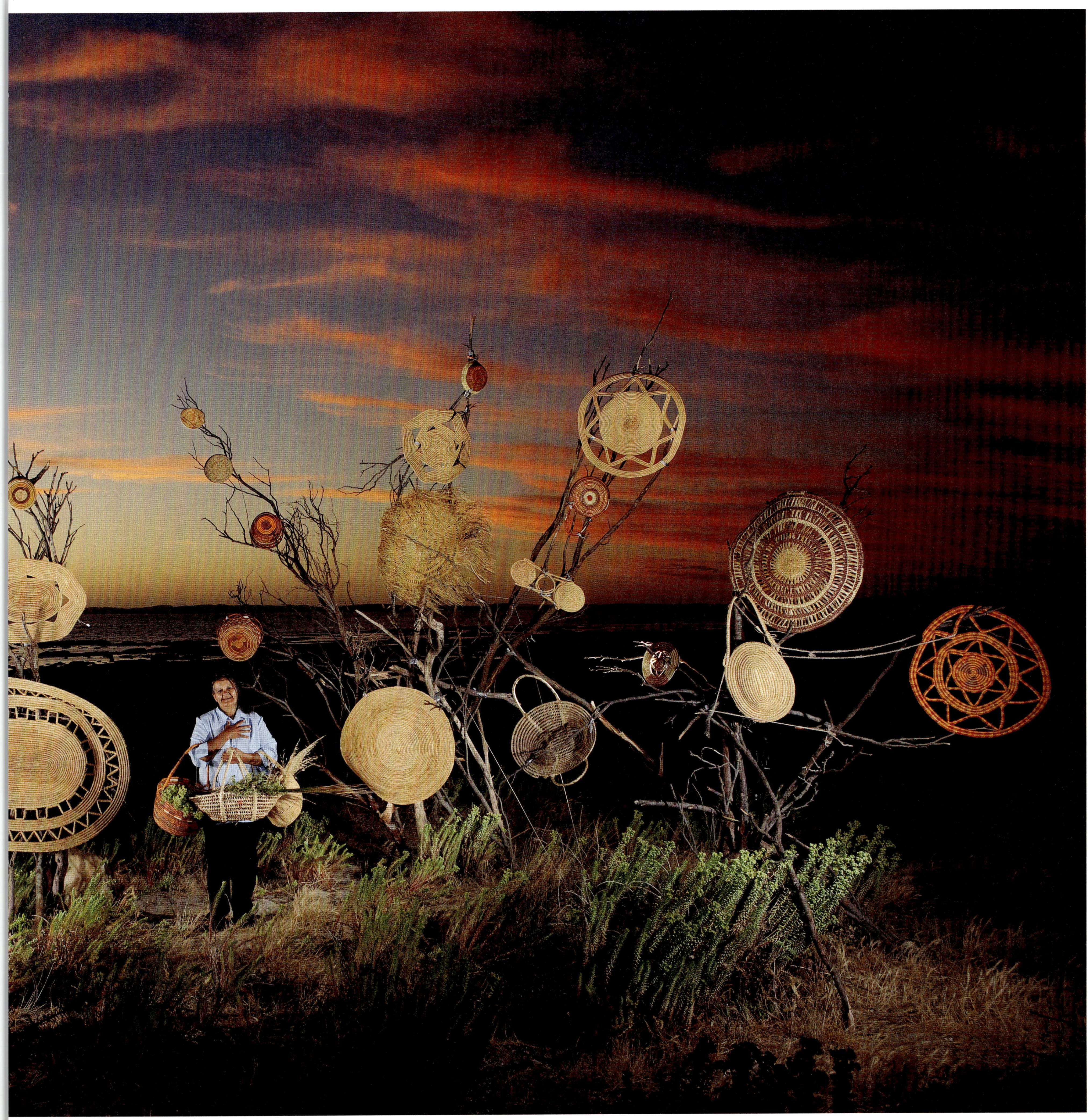

When I was born,

the sun had set in the middle of the day. Today we call this an eclipse. I don't how old I am but, when I was a child, we had no clothes or electricity. Instead of going to school, we ran naked after our parents' cows. ¶ One day, our house was burned down from the lightning of a storm. We left for the Cape to earn money in the hopes of rebuilding what had gone up in smoke. In the big city, I lived happily but I encountered danger, theft, disease and violence. It was very hard between the black communities. And, with the whites, there was a barrier of fear that no one could overcome. When Mandela gave freedom to our country, things changed in the townships. We could retire. ¶ When I saw your car coming I started to run after it. We don't see this often around here! I ran and ran, hiding myself so as not to seem too silly. I was completely out of breath but I didn't want to miss anything, not even a second. Then, I saw that you were going to Nopikapa's. I was curious but much too timid to come see you. So, I went home and when you came, everyone came to see what you were like. I must say, it was well worth it. Together, we laughed quite a bit. ¶ I prefer being a grandmother in the townships, rather than in the countryside. There is less solitude. Even if we only have one tap for 7 or 8 families, even if we are always scared of getting chased from this land. Here, at least, we are close to our children. We can protect them from the witches who steal parts of your body for their crazy magic. Now that we are old, Nopikapa's dream, and mine, is to be buried in the village, in the shade of the trees, near the tombs of our husbands.

MAMGEMA XAKAMA AND NOPIKAPA BHUQA, DANCING BENEATH THE TRUCK THAT WILL TAKE THEM TO THE EASTERN CAPE, ENKANINI, SOUTH AFRICA.

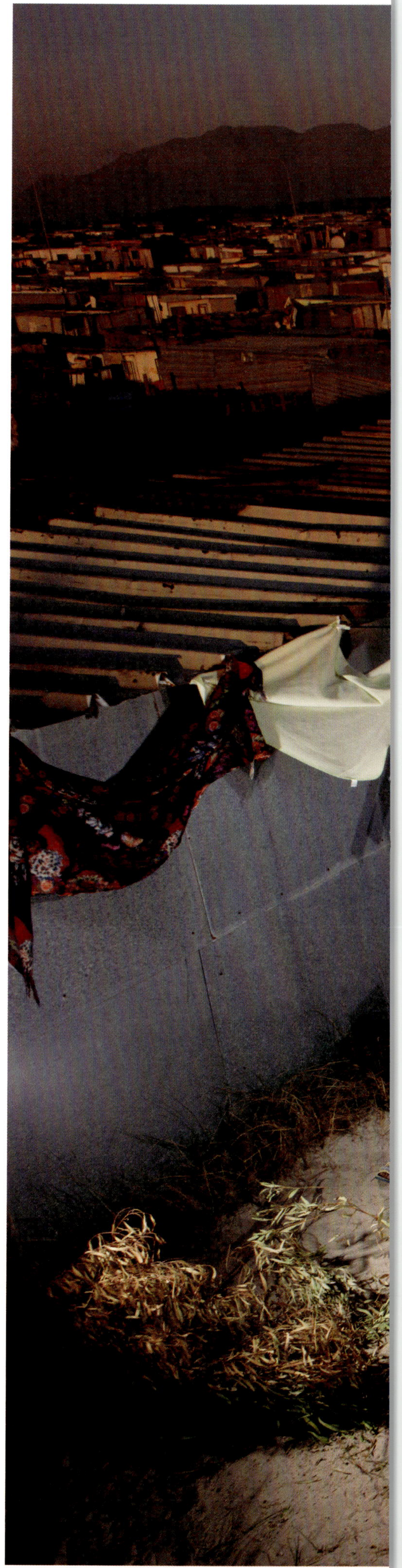

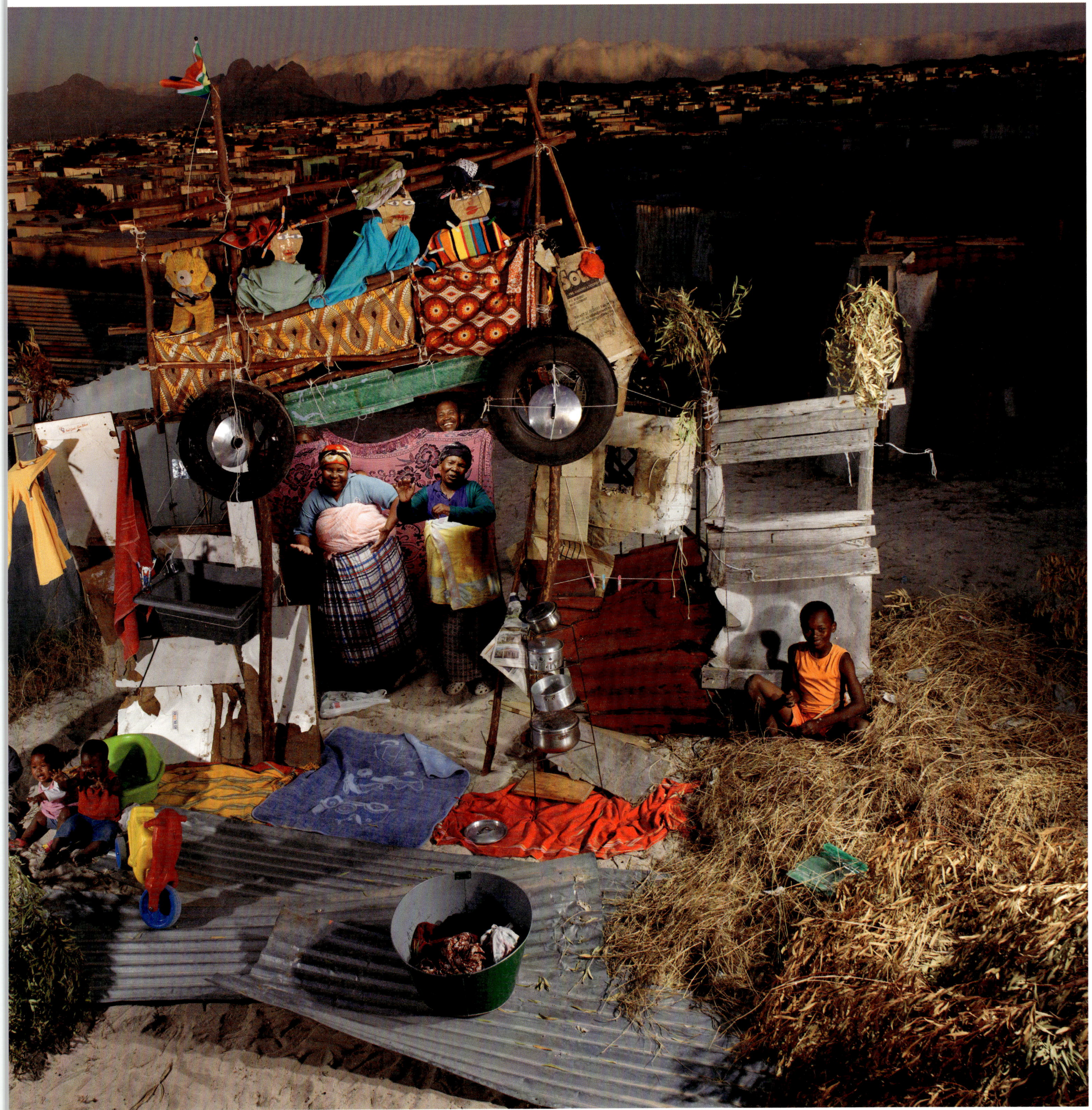

When you live in a hut, you want a cabin. When you live in a cabin, you want one made of slate, then one of stone. To make progress, I don't know, maybe things shoudn't move too fast. ¶ Take a tree that grows, for example. When a fruit falls, it grows in turn, following the way of the big tree. It's a bit like that in my family. If you find a fishing boat, or an ox, or a bit of land and a cart, well, you can watch nature grow, you can remember your wedding, the first time that you laid eyes on your husband, swimming as a child in the pools of water as the monsoon arrives. You can go to temple and share your rice with a hundred people. And even if you only have a glass of milk, you can make at least five people happy.

MEENAKSHI GHOSH IN HER SHANTYTOWN ACROSS FROM THE CINEMAS, DELHI, INDIA.

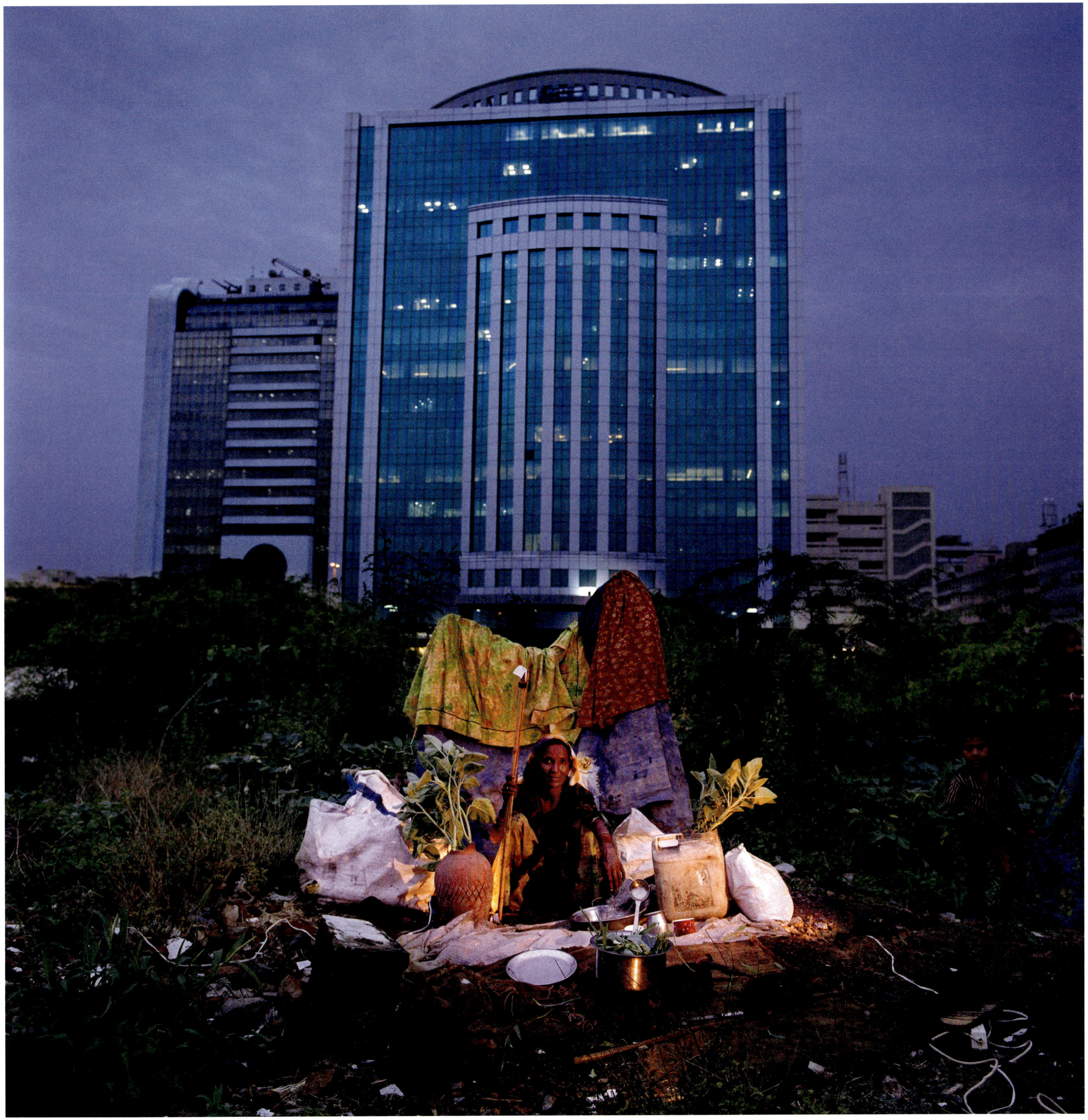

DYMPHAN VAN RYSBERGEN ¶ ESPEL AISIN
ORLANDO ¶ GERALDINE JOHNSON ¶ MARIA
SANTOS ¶ ETZUKO NUMAZAWA ¶ DYMPHA
SOMPOCH ¶ MASAE UMEZU ¶ JOSÉ ORLANDO ¶
GOLDBERG ¶ MESSIA DOS SANTOS ¶ ETZUK
ESPEL AISING ¶ LA-OR SOMPOCH ¶ MASAE UM
MARIA ANGELA ¶ CARIN GOLDBERG ¶ MESSIA
VAN RYSBERGEN ¶ ESPEL AISING ¶ LA-OR S
GERALDINE JOHNSON ¶ MARIA ANGELA ¶ CAR
NUMAZAWA ¶ DYMPHAN VAN RYSBERGEN
UMEZU ¶ JOSÉ ORLANDO ¶ GERALDINE JOH
MESSIA DOS SANTOS ¶ ETZUKO NUMAZAWA
LA-OR SOMPOCH ¶ MASAE UMEZU ¶ JOSÉ
ANGELA ¶ CARIN GOLDBERG ¶ MESSIA DOS
VAN RYSBERGEN ¶ ESPEL AISING ¶ LA-OR S
JOSÉ ORLANDO ¶ GERALDINE JOHNSON ¶ MAR
GOLDBERG ¶ MESSIA DOS SANTOS ¶ ETZUKO N
AISING ¶ LA-OR SOMPOCH ¶ MASAE UMEZU ¶
ANGELA ¶ CARIN GOLDBERG ¶ MESSIA DOS

THE PLAYHOUSE
WHERE WE LEARN TO LAUGH

When I'm at church with my family, I always take the microphone so I can sing. I don't hold back, I just grab it and that makes me happy. "One day at a time, sweet Jesus!" ¶ My little theater is as beautiful as a rainbow. All my dolls are here. I love them so; they are like my own daughters. There is also an eagle who brings me joy when he takes me flying with him up above. My dream is to be able to stay, even after death, in my "super paradise". ¶ They call me Mother Theresa because I have given so much to others. When I was a little girl I favored playing catch as opposed to playing cards! One day I put goat's dung and anise flowers in a charming little box and gave it to a friend. I laughed so hard! The poor girl, she's still alive… ¶ I have raised four children and I know that the heart has infinite resources. The importance for me is to make others laugh. Now you have met me and tonight you're going to have sweet dreams.

DYMPHAN VAN RYSBERGEN IN THE THEATER BENEATH THE VERANDA, ADELAIDE, AUSTRALIA.

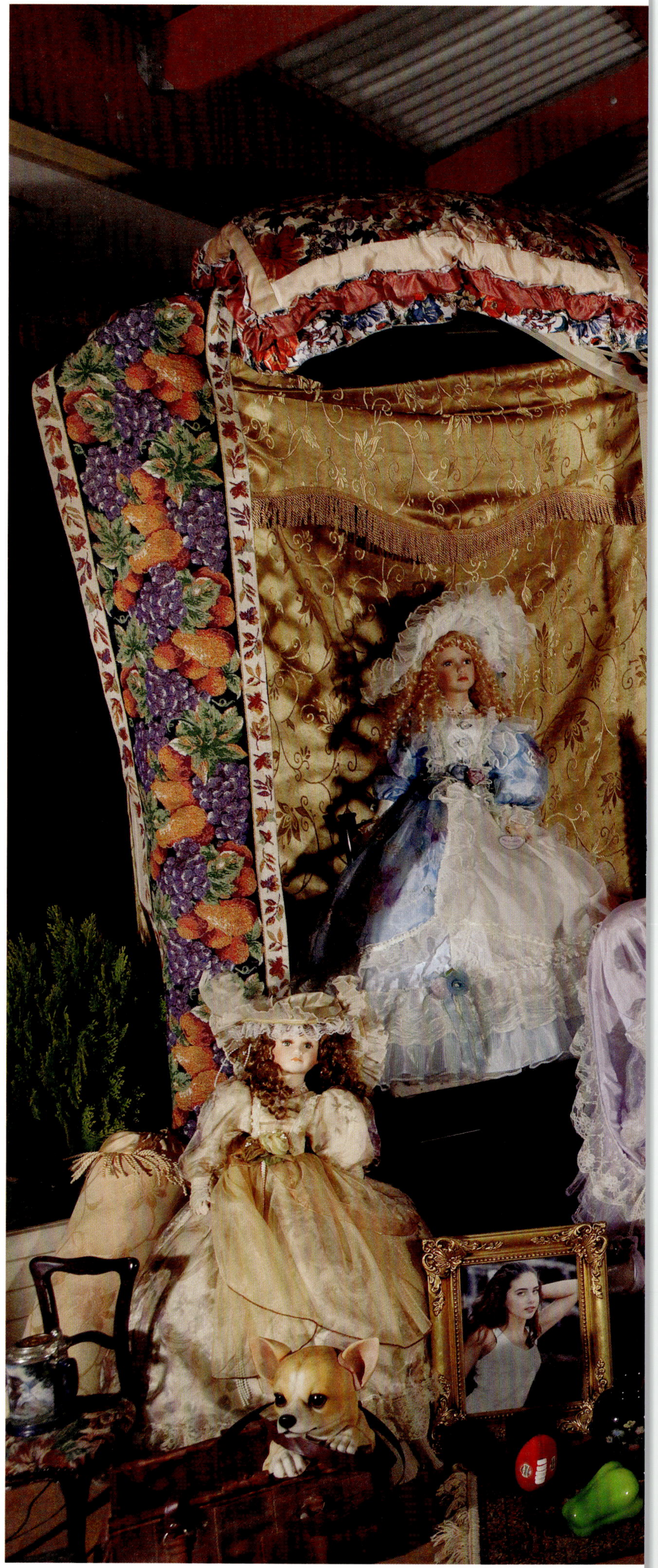

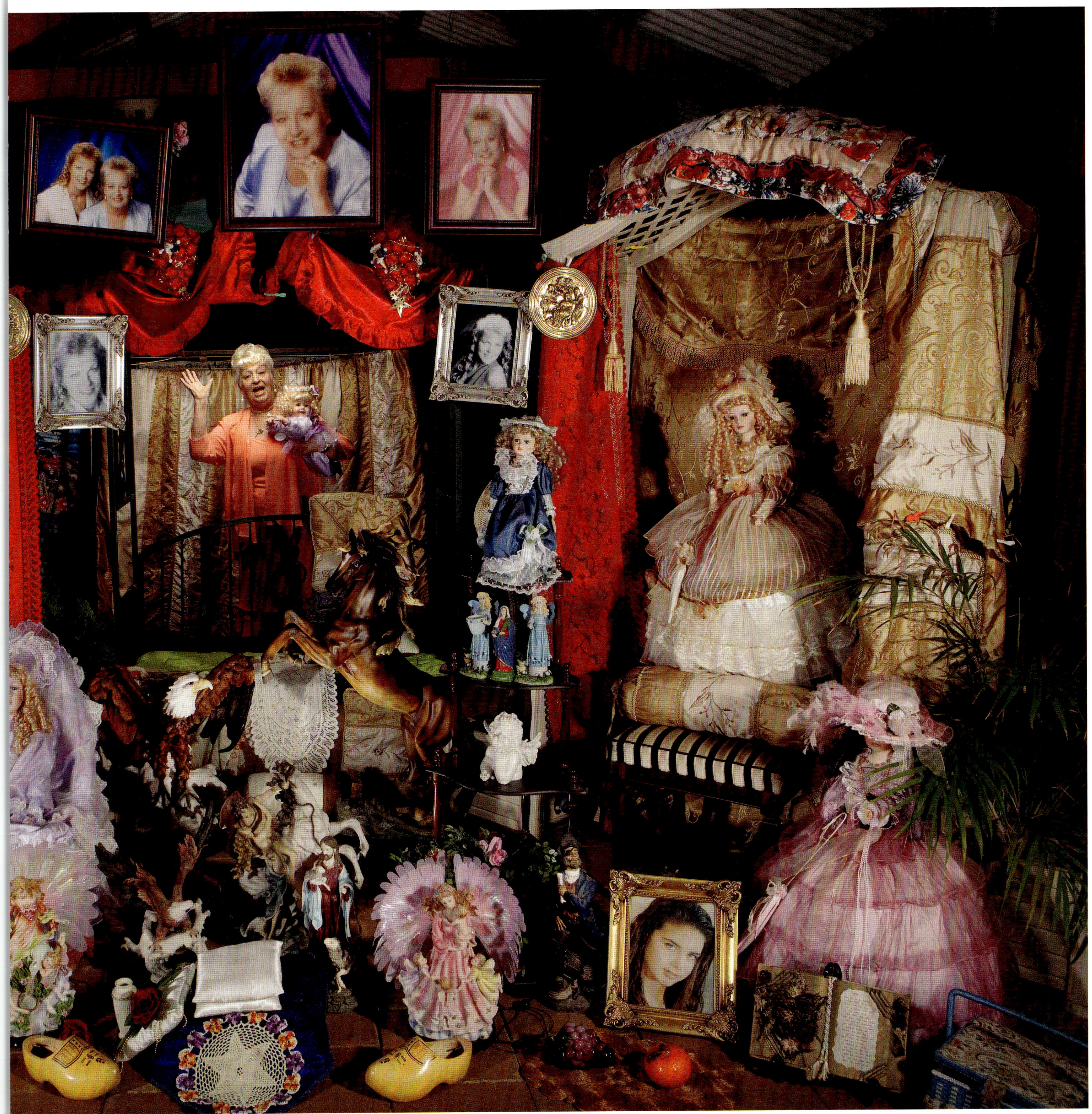

Around here, if you do not laugh, people will think you are sick or that someone you love has been taken by death. We have to reach out to children and show them the joy around them, shake them and make them dance. They often sleep in my arms and the moon accompanies the songs and nursery rhymes I whisper in their ears. ¶ It is easier to have several children, for the big sisters can take care of the little ones. To make them happy you make them "laplap": grated vegetables mixed with coconut milk, wrapped in banana leaves and placed on hot stones. When the tom-tom sounds on the split trunk we put on colourful dresses and gather at mass. The young play reggae and our community resounds with religious songs. ¶ I am afraid my children will go afar and that we won't see them anymore. Going to school is good, but our young must spread our message throughout the world.

ESPEL AISING IN HER COURTYARD WITH HER FABRICS, MATS, AND KITCHENWARE, VINTUA, VANUATU.

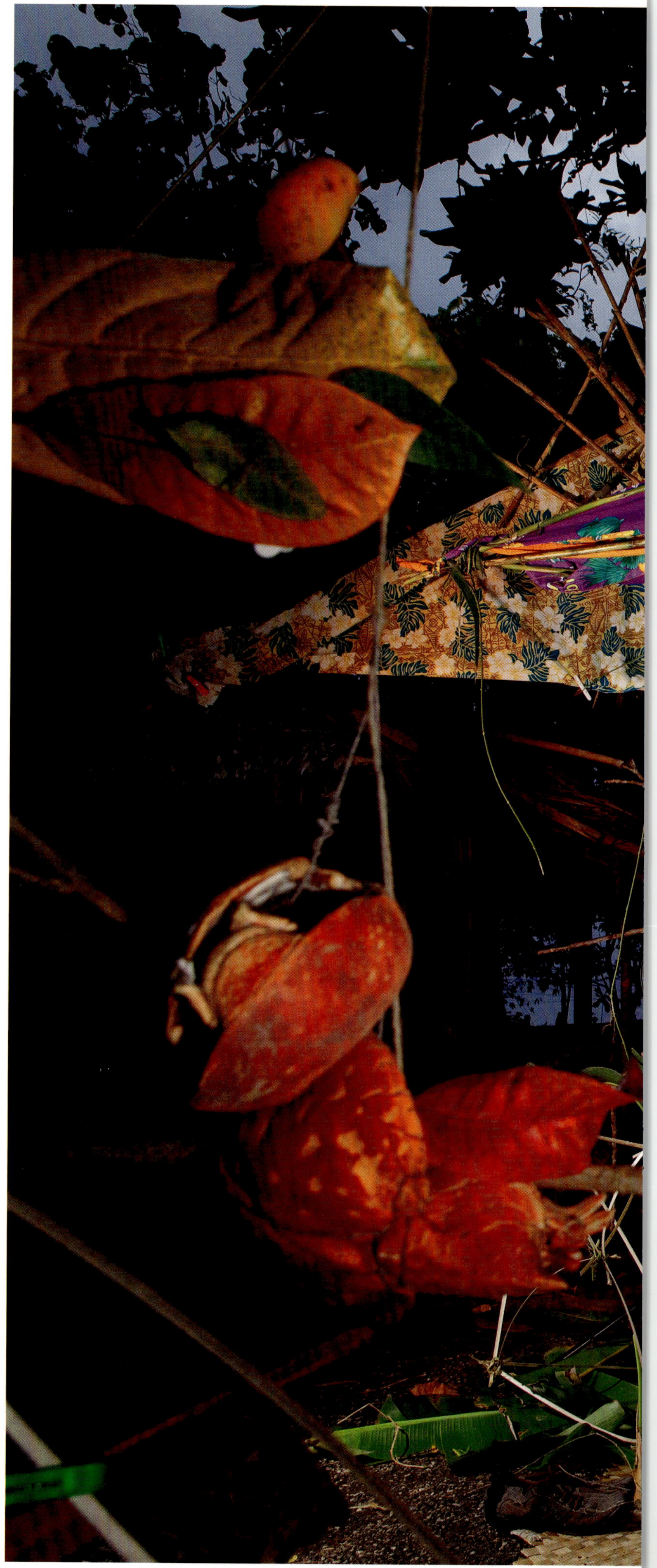

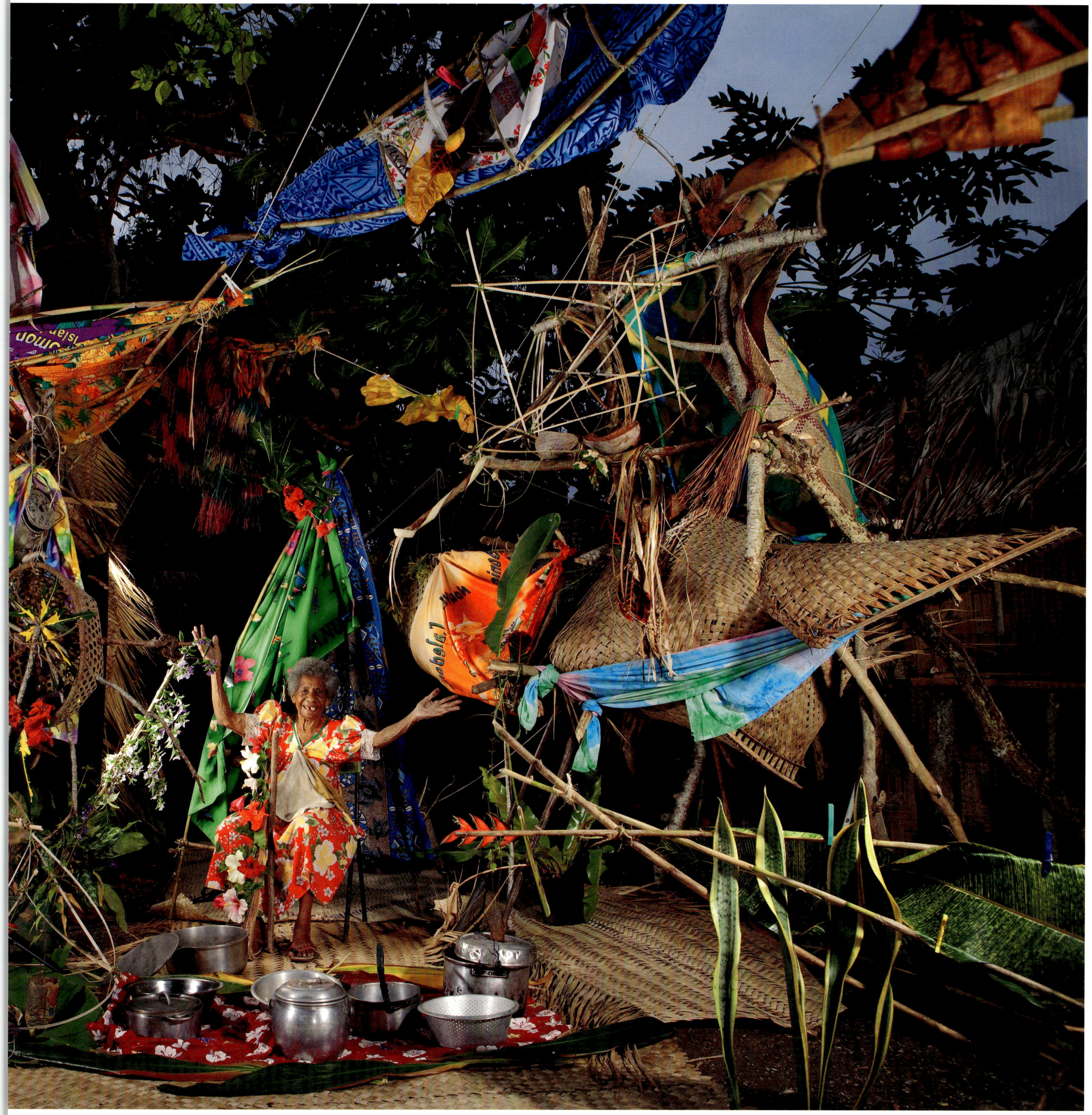

Thailand is a country of laughter and smiles. When you laugh it lights up the old age on your face. In our house, three generations live together. When I find myself alone with my cousins and other grandmas, we laugh when we talk about the children and grandchildren who have left for work or school. ¶ When I was young, I wanted to be the prettiest and have all the men chasing after me. But I got married and I stayed with the same man for 50 years. The most important thing is, when one is angry, the other must stay calm. I was elated whenever I had a chance to dance, when the kids put on music, at the New Year or at coming-of-age commemorations. It is the looks people give you that warm the heart and set the beauty in motion. Thanks to the king and queen, we have good land and we are in good health. Before, we made everything with our hands, even our clothes, with cotton and weaving looms. Now, many things come from afar. Our children no longer listen to their mothers and grandmothers and their good sense. They only believe in the Internet and the television.

LA-OR SOMPOCH AND THE WORD "THAILAND" WRITTEN IN RICE, RIVER KWAI BRIDGE, THAILAND.

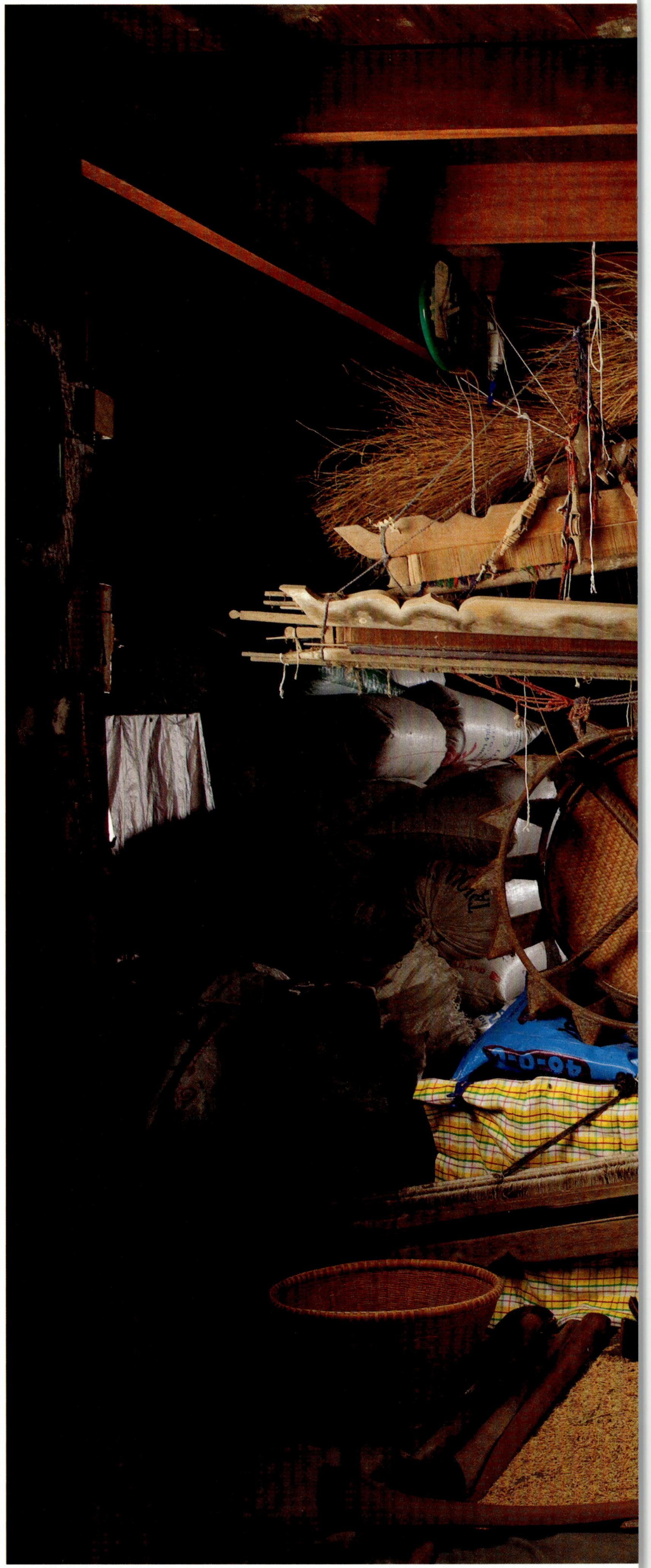

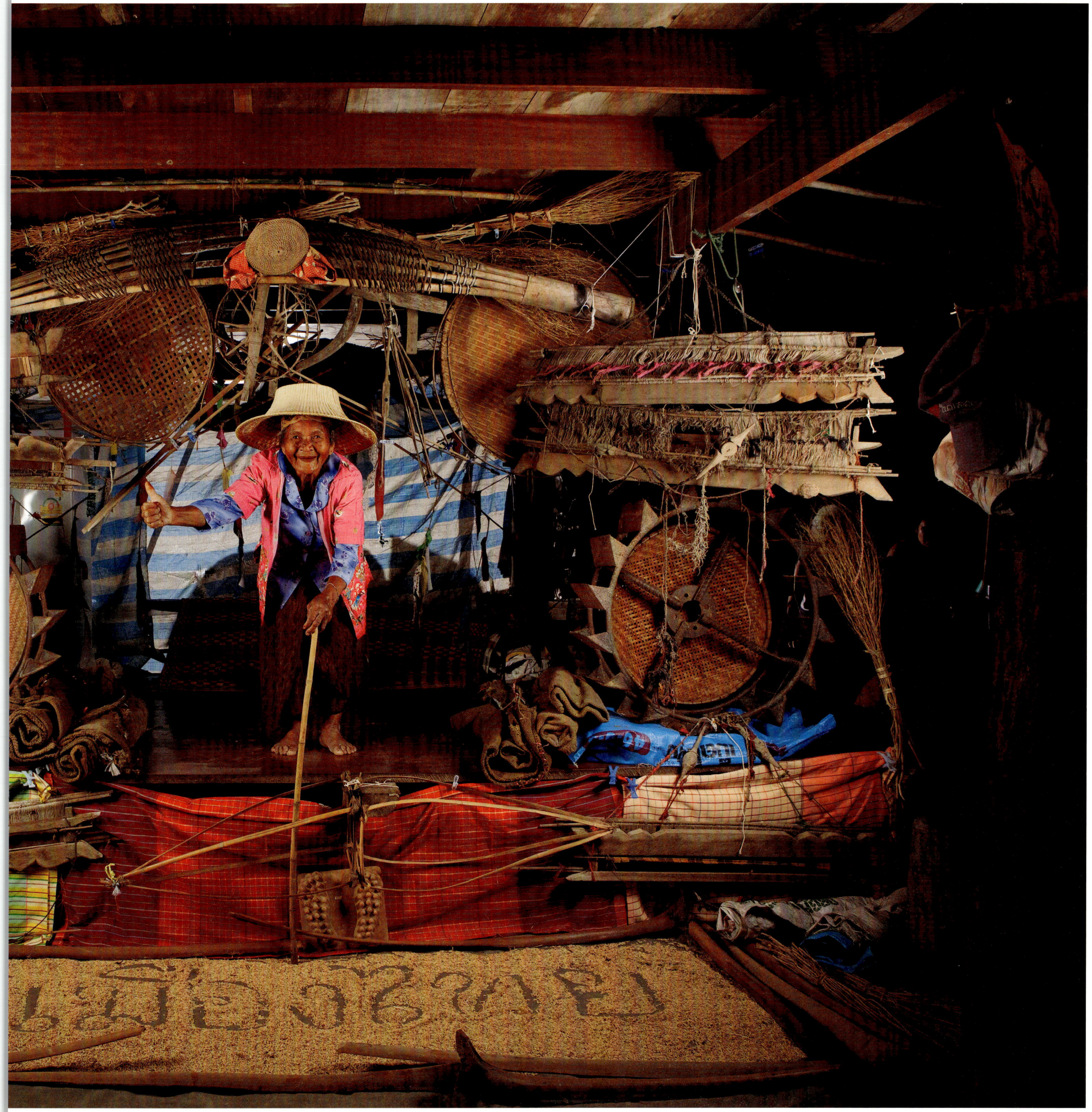

I am the lady of the temple. In its center there is the garden and the lake. They protect us from fire, for here, everything is made of wood. The incense and the candles give life to the spirits. ¶ I am very happy living in the temple. It is the guardian of the dead and we of memory, that of the whole community. We hold many ceremonies to celebrate our good fortune of being able to live amongst our ancestors. I like that the temple stays open to everyone and that, despite its spiritual character, it emits warmth. ¶ To help people understand religion, I teach them songs. Every day, I am surrounded by laughter. Teaching others to laugh is one of the hardest things in the world to do. ¶ Nature is the backdrop of my life. We eat the fruit of every season. I have been near the mountains since my childhood. However, I sometimes have a dark vision of our future. There is less and less snow and the red leaves that once brightened our autumns are ever more scarce. If nature loses its beauty, what will happen to man?

MASAE UMEZU AND HER REFLECTION IN THE TEMPLE'S GARDEN, YAMAGATA, JAPAN.

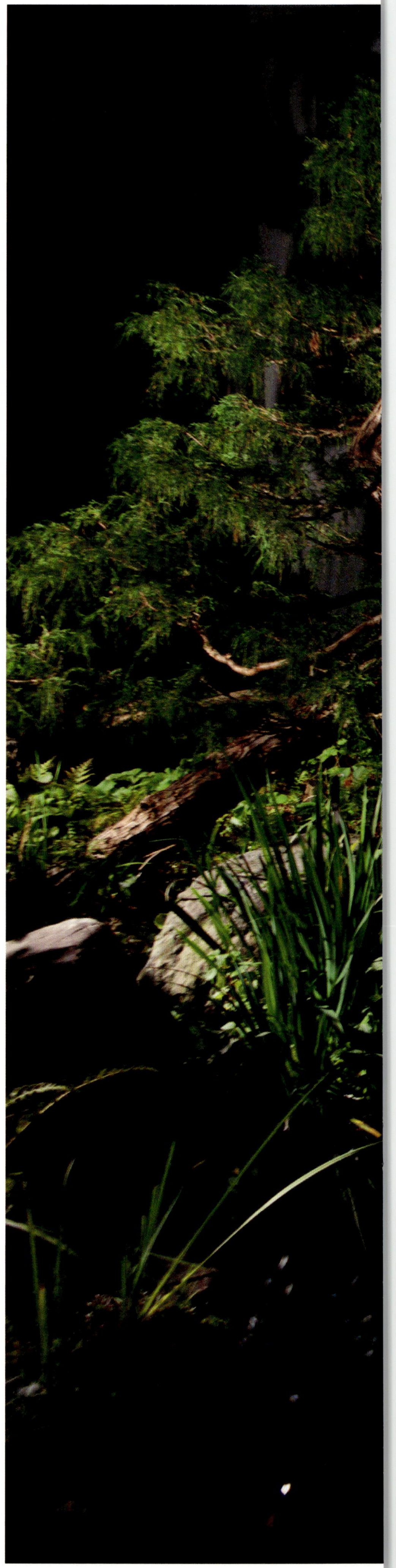

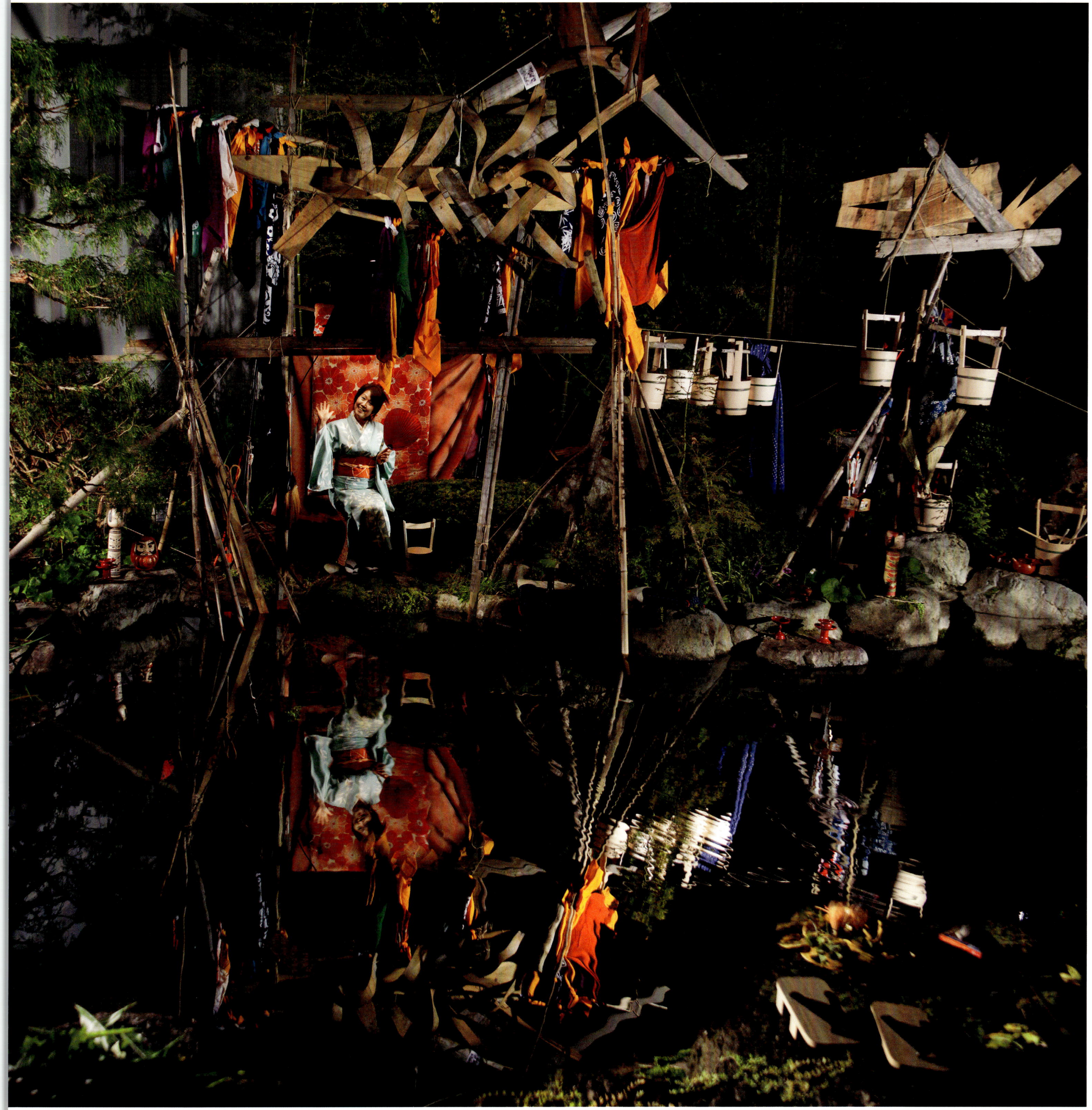

My bliss is our family. Our mule, Gazolina, is a member in her own right. Every morning she wakes us up with her joyful call. Her name changes according to the time of the year. During celebrations, when she leads me to the carnival, I call her the Queen of the town. A quick swig of cachaça from the gourd and we're singing amid the crowd. ¶ My wife and daughter each have a child of the same age. They are like two sisters who might have given birth the same day. Our house is filled with their laughter. Around the fruit trees, they've made circles out of plastic bottles that have been cut into the shape of flowers. They cultivate colors and birds. With them, life flows peacefully as the millet and feijoa seasons come and go. ¶ The first garment you wear is your garden, so I am teaching my son to pay attention to the cycle of the seasons. My father's garden was nourished with his care and his secrets will be my son's happiness. We grow with our children. This love is like friendship: it is only by giving it that we can hope to receive it.

JOSÉ ORLANDO, HIS SON AND GAZOLINA, BENEATH THE CASHEW TREE IN THEIR GARDEN, REDONDA, BRAZIL.

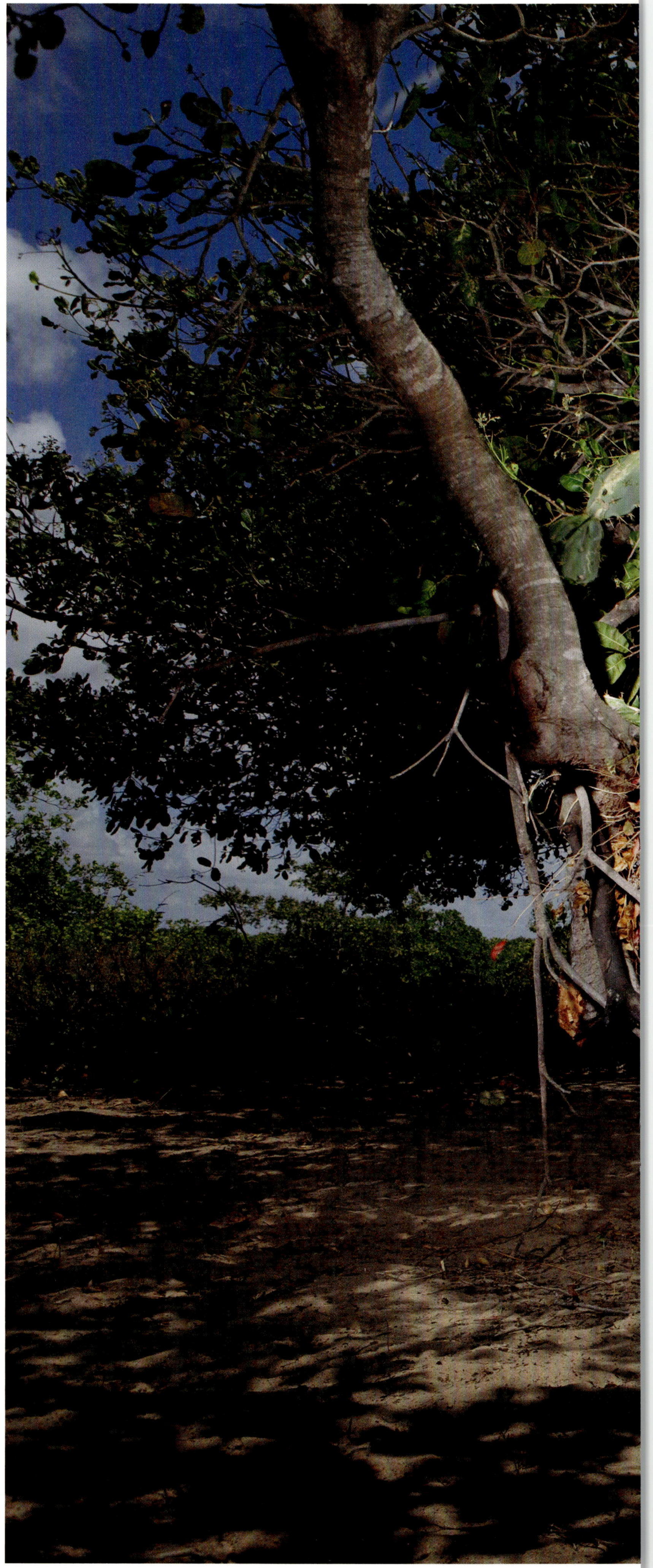

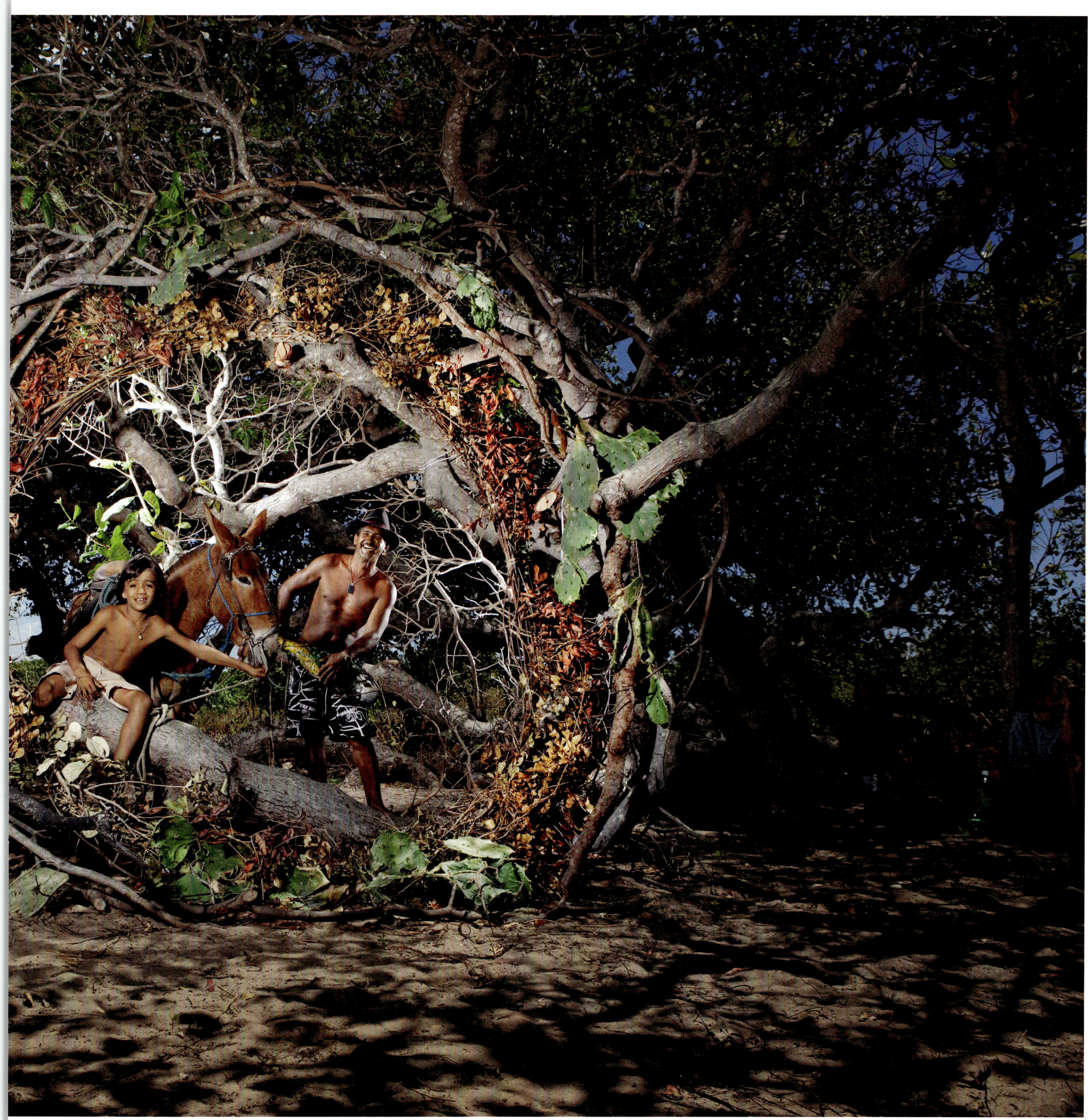

I am a nurse and I am Welsh. I come from the United Kingdom but I have lived here for forty years. I love my job. It allows me to mingle with people from all different origins with respect and dialogue. Because I am white but married to an aborigine, I have become a link between these two communities that have such a hard time understanding each other. ¶ The whites speak too quickly. They are always impatient. They don't let time just go by, at its own rhythm. Even today, tensions remain strong. Not long ago, an "abo" was putting his life at risk if he simply stole a sheep. Even to speak to whites was dangerous. They brought alcohol, sugar and fat. Now many aborigines have serious diabetes. Marijuana has ruined their brains and drink is killing part of the population. ¶ My four children live in the region. Being of mixed race didn't prevent them from getting a good education or from working. They understand the two cultures and feel free to leave without getting too homesick. ¶ As I grow older I am discovering my creativity through the love I have for the desert and its lights. Now I paint cartwheels and old tires, which decorate my garden. What makes people beautiful is not their wealth or color, but their ability to change.

GERALDINE JOHNSON IN THE GARDEN OF HER CREATIONS, NEPABAUNNA, AUSTRALIA.

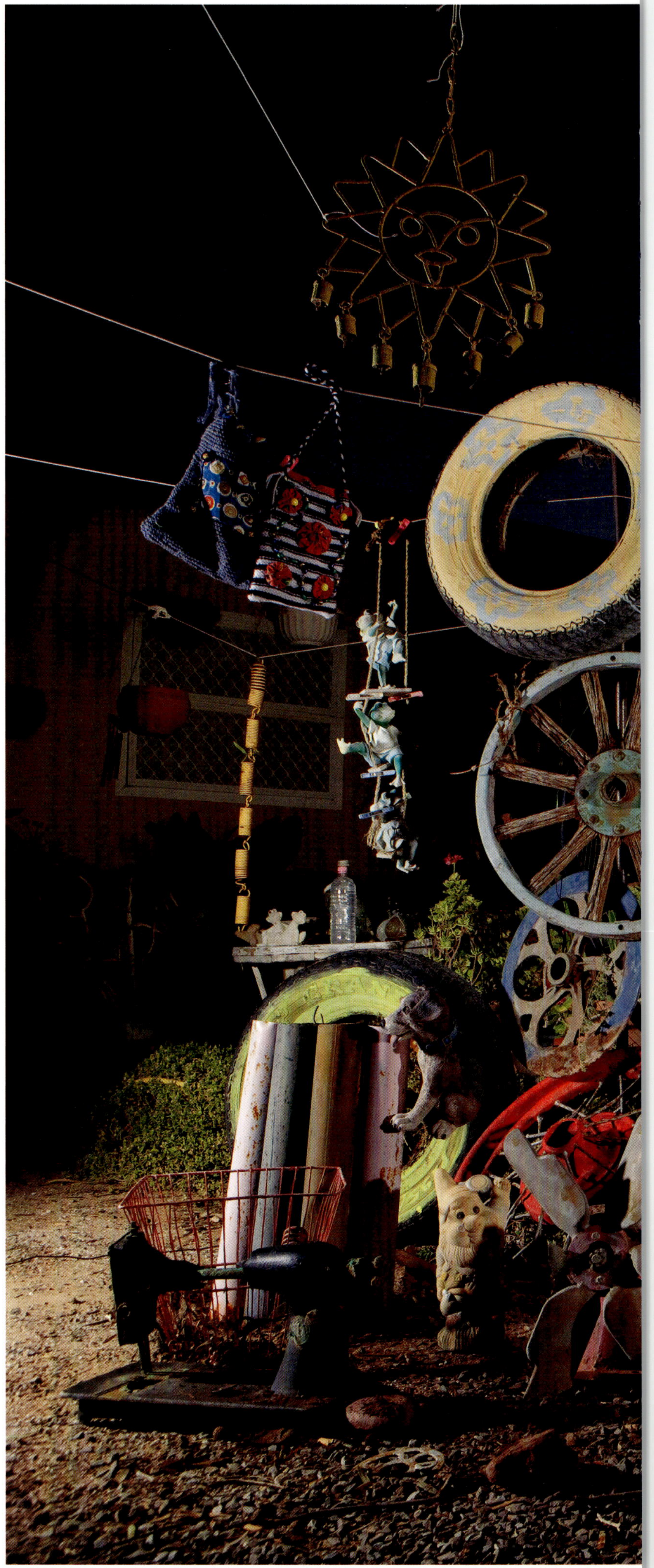

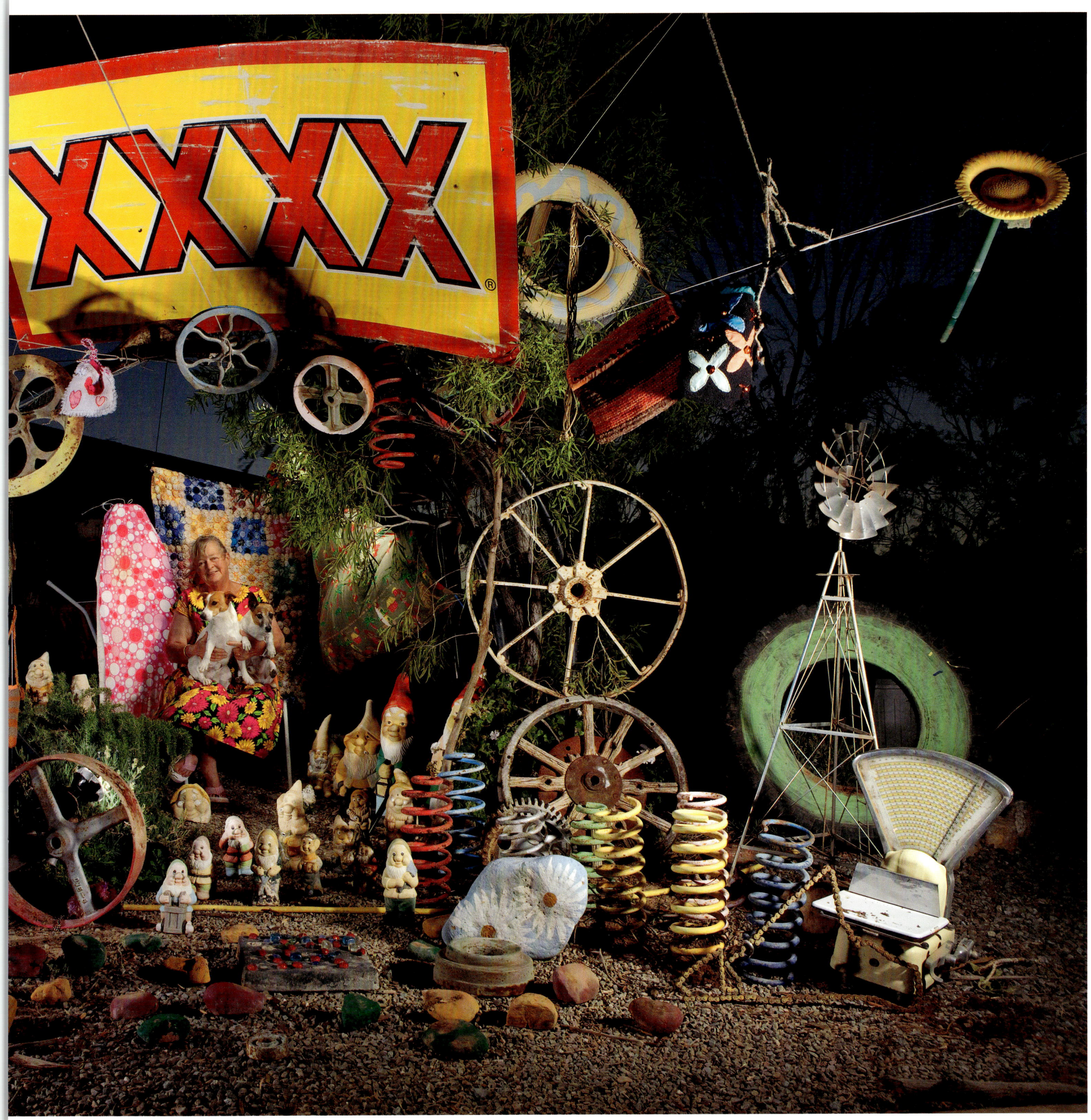
XXXX

When I was a little girl, I remember standing in the middle of a large crowd, crying. It was a parade. Queen Elizabeth herself comforted me, taking me in her arms and kissing me. My tears dried in that strange silence, enveloped by the gaze of the crowd. ¶ As a teenager, I was a member of the champion Brazilian volleyball team. My mother sent me to dance classes as she thought I was a tomboy. I became lead ballerina and, later, a ballet teacher in Petropolis. The stage gave me the most beautiful moments of my life, offering me the costumes and adventures of princesses. ¶ After we met at a dinner at the automobile club, my future husband came to see me dance. When he saw me in my costume, he fell in love with me and asked me right away to marry him. I was 21. We've been happy all of our lives. We've been nourished by family love and by literature. After raising my children I went to art school. Engraving has allowed me to capture the beauty of a moment and to express the emotions that live in my memory.

MARIA ANGELA, GRANDMOTHER AND GRANDDAUGHTER, IN THE LIBRARY OF HER APARTMENT IN RIO, BRAZIL.

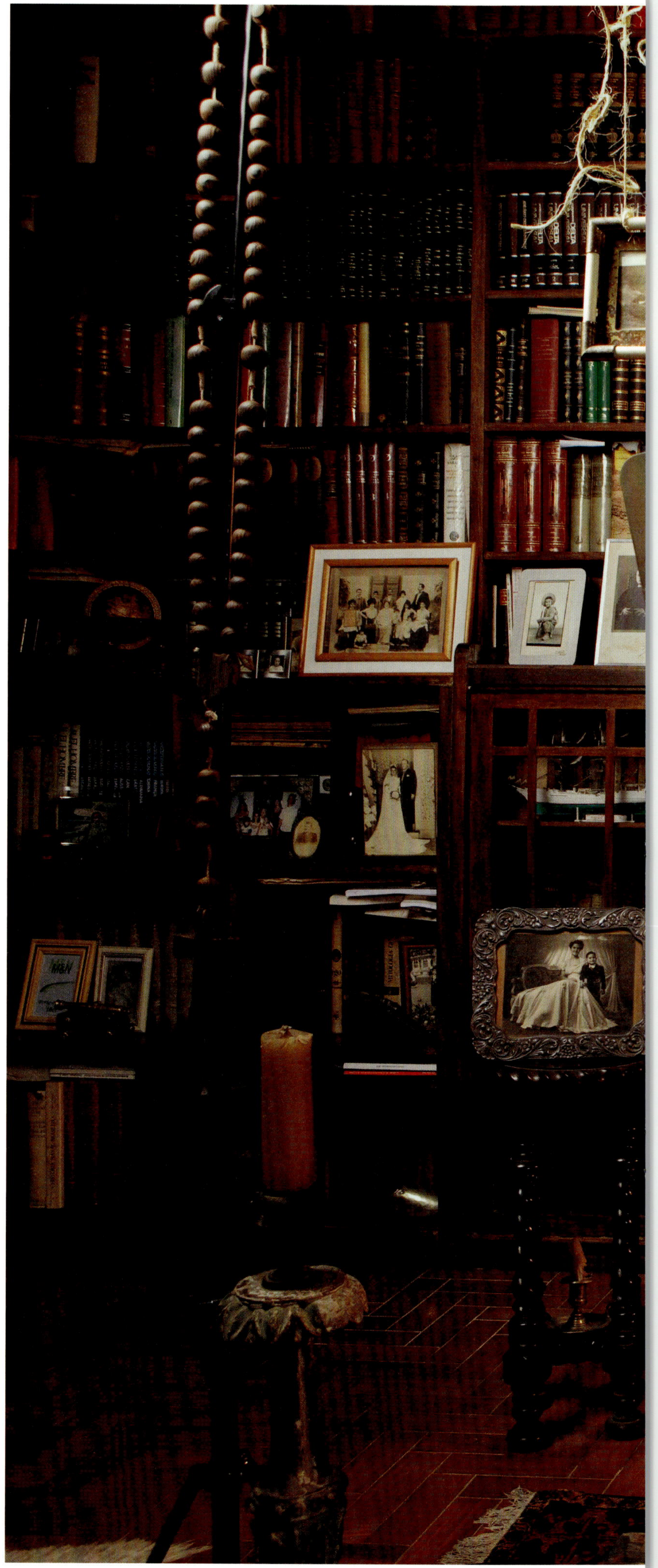

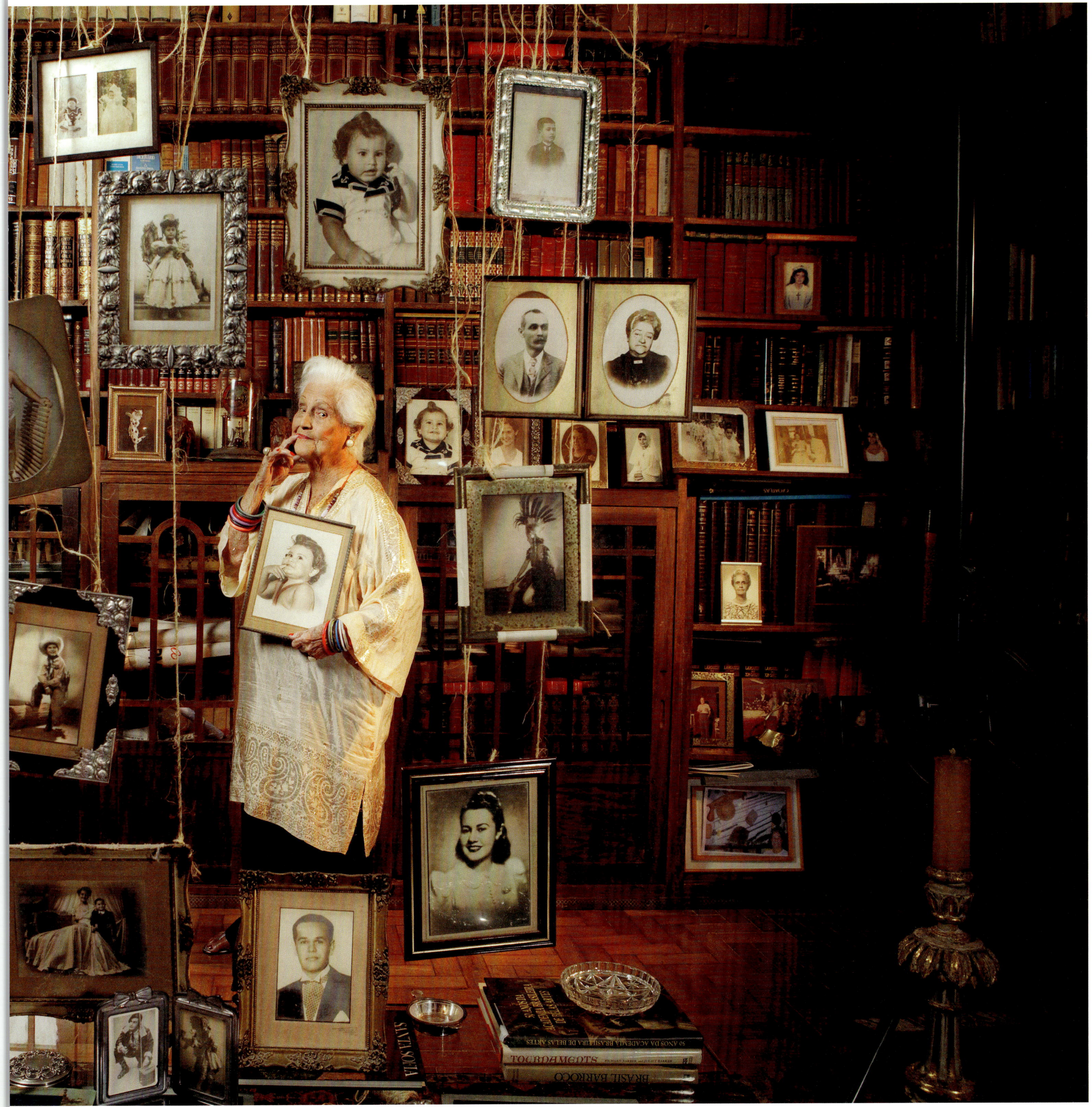
50 ANOS DA ACADEMIA BRASILEIRA DE BELAS ARTES
TOURNAMENTS
BRASIL BARROCO

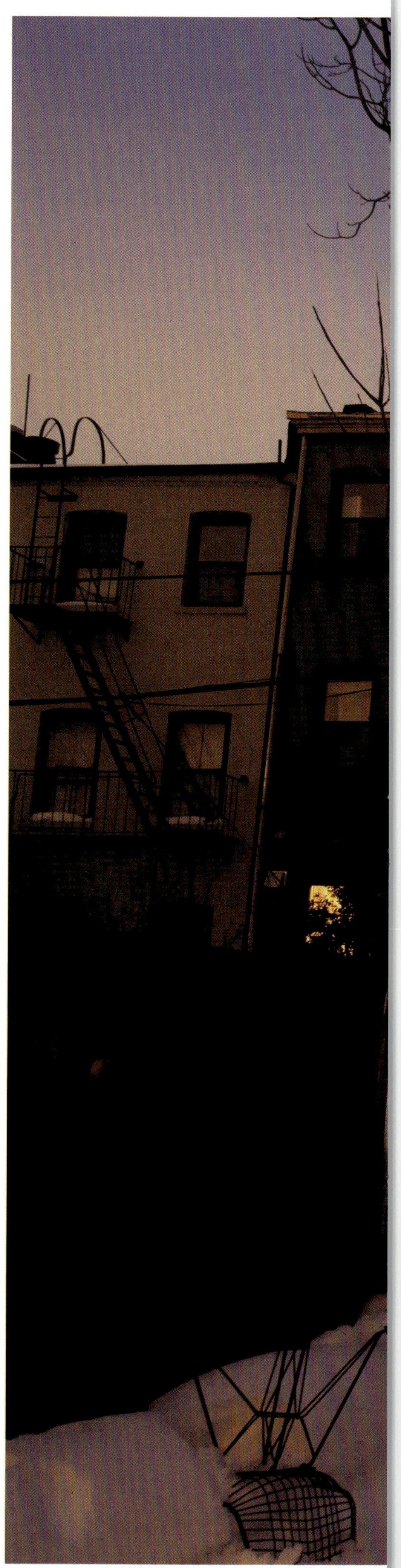

The city connects me to modernity. New York has always been different from the rest of the United States. It is warmth and beauty, organization and anarchy, it is extremes: boredom, excitement, business, culture, competition, but also compassion. Here, dreams are big and people want to stay on top. ¶ I need other people, not solitude. When we are young, we function as a group, we share a workshop, we work together, we throw ourselves into extraordinary creative projects. The older we get, the more difficult it is to cultivate this sense of sharing, to reconcile family life and creative life. ¶ Today, I acknowledge that my son was lucky to have parents responsible for their choices. Creativity is not just a part of an artist's life, it is a way of thinking, of developing positive things. To find a solution to a problem by following one's own emotional journey is a miraculous experience. The important thing is to draw from true emotions, to search inside for how to go forward. ¶ Over time, my work has grown simpler and clearer. You learn a lot as you grow old. It is easier to teach children or students than to go forward ourselves. When it comes to life, I am a better teacher than student.

CARIN GOLDBERG AND HER GRAPHIC CREATIONS, NEW YORK, UNITED STATES.

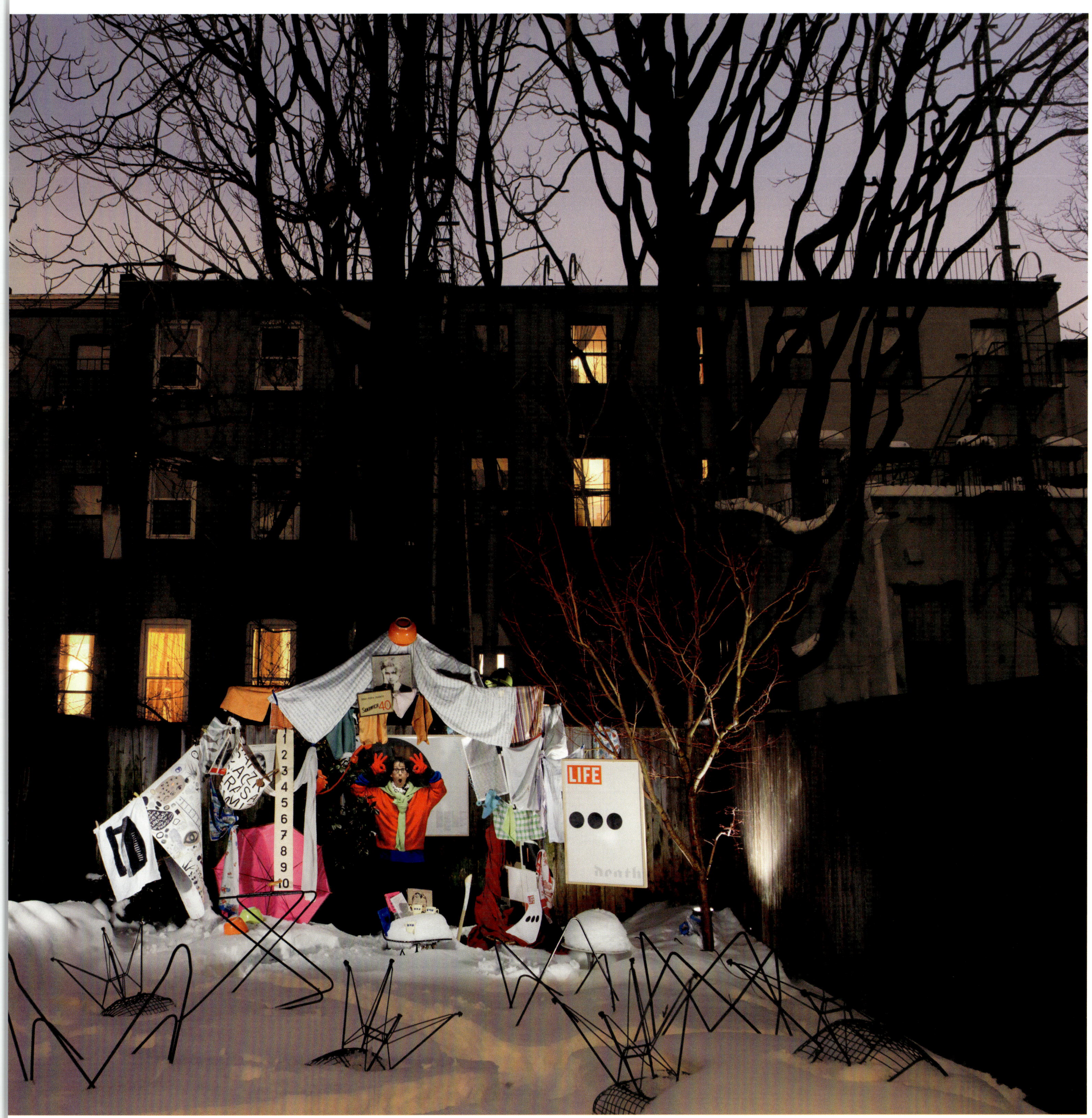
LIFE
death

In the painting above me, my aunt is making stewed guava. Some mornings, the aroma is so delicious that you smile to yourself when waking. I was born in the countryside, to a modest background where our pleasures had the unique flavor of our toils and our authenticity. ¶ Through my music and my paintings, I want to express the life of rural black communities. To share with others the joys and suffering of people who crossed the sea in the holds of boats. Whatever the color of our skin, the memory of slavery is knowledge that gives us the ability to not repeat the same mistakes. Unfortunately, I think history will never shelter anyone from the reign of violence and domination. In books all this seems so long ago, but for us, the memory is still very vivid. ¶ When your consciousness knows there is a need to resist you will not allow yourself to be blinded by the luster of your own possessions. Then nature gives you the ability to celebrate life, the understanding of the energies in the sky and the earth, songs, music and dance.

MESSIA DOS SANTOS, HIS MUSIC AND HIS PAINTINGS, RIO DE JANEIRO, BRAZIL.

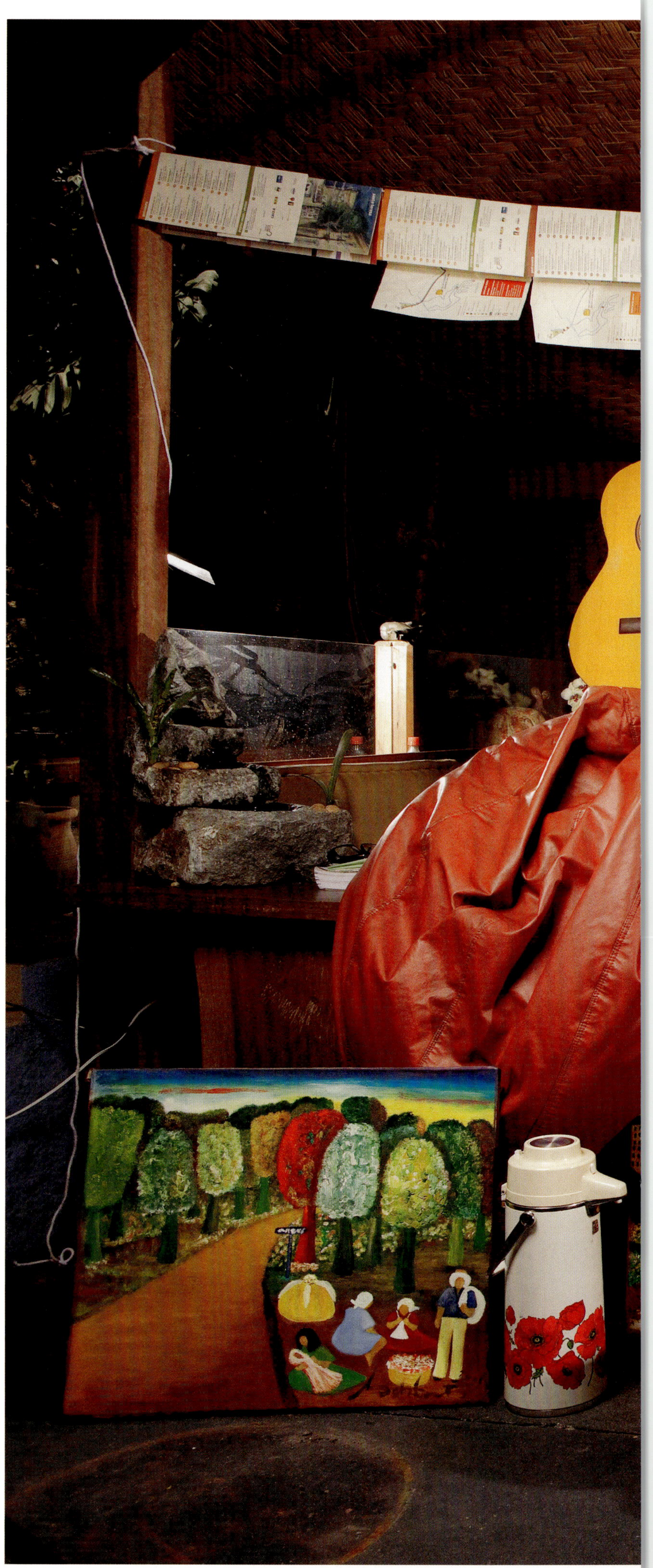

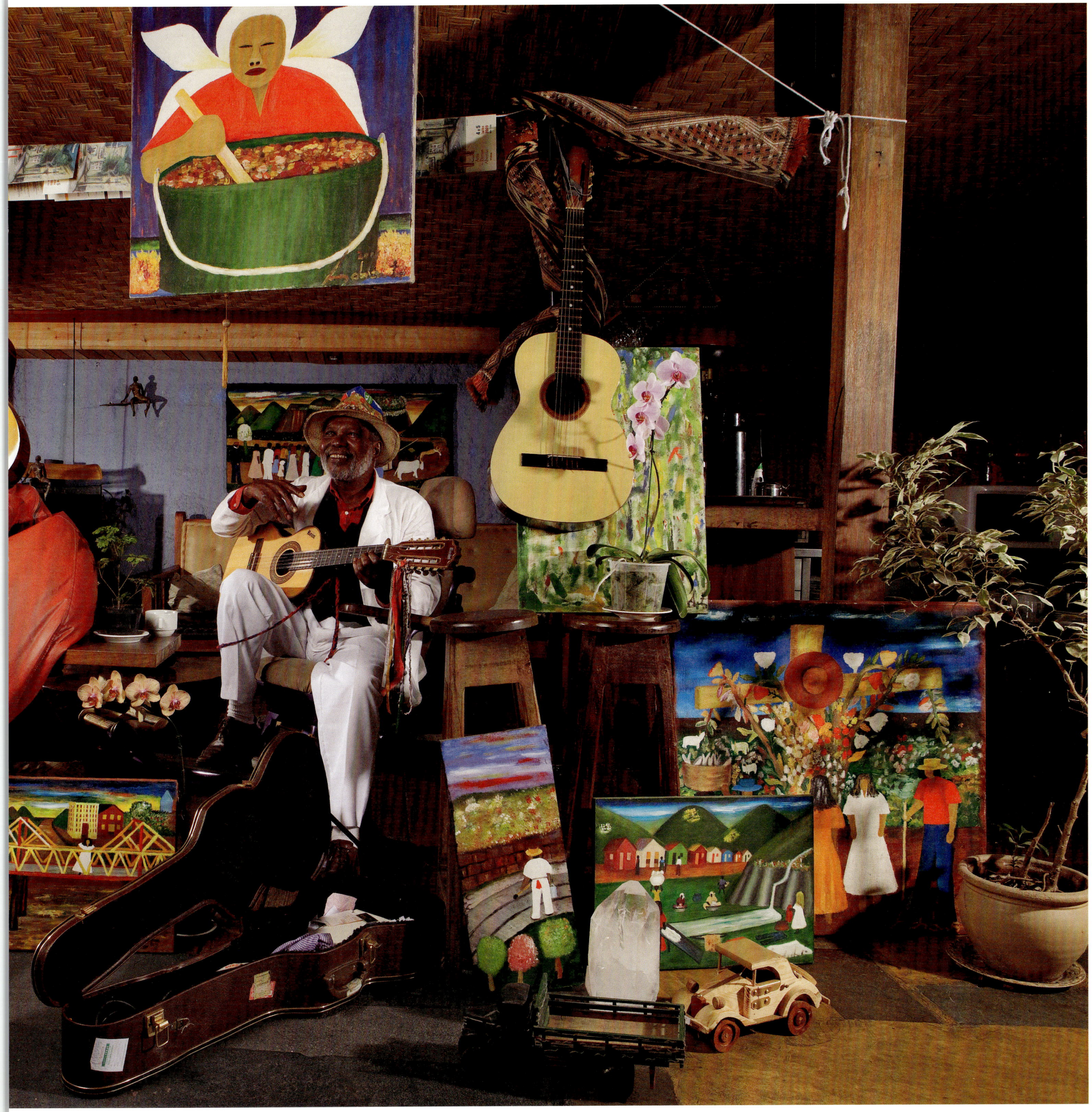

There are three robots at the back of my barn. They turned up there by magic, perhaps just so they could pose with me in this photo. In any case, they are tough and they seem to be having fun. They party with the tractor wheel and one of them even has an arm coming out of his head. ¶ We have worked this land for four or five generations. For twenty years, I have lived in this house where virtually nothing has changed. In the beginning of summer, during the grand festivities, we parade through the village holding up a small red house to bring health and happiness to all of the families in our community. ¶ I can spend two or three days in the city but I can't stay there. There are too many people, too many things, too much of everything, everywhere. I worked for a company, but then I came back to work the land, like many people here. It's a hard life, but I have to be here because the view of the light and the trees gives me abounding joy. In this season, the rice I cultivate is like gold. It's a treasure that I can eat every day without growing tired of it. I love the paddies, like terraces, and behind them, the hot springs where we bathe. ¶ Since the death of my husband, I use machines. They help me a great deal but they are expensive. If, one day, our imagination becomes reality, robots could be useful and help me in my harvest. I am sure that the robots will come and when they do, I hope they will still make me laugh. Maybe they will even stop the critters from eating my garden.

ETZUKO NUMAZAWA AND THE IMAGINARY ROBOTS, YAMAGATA, JAPAN.

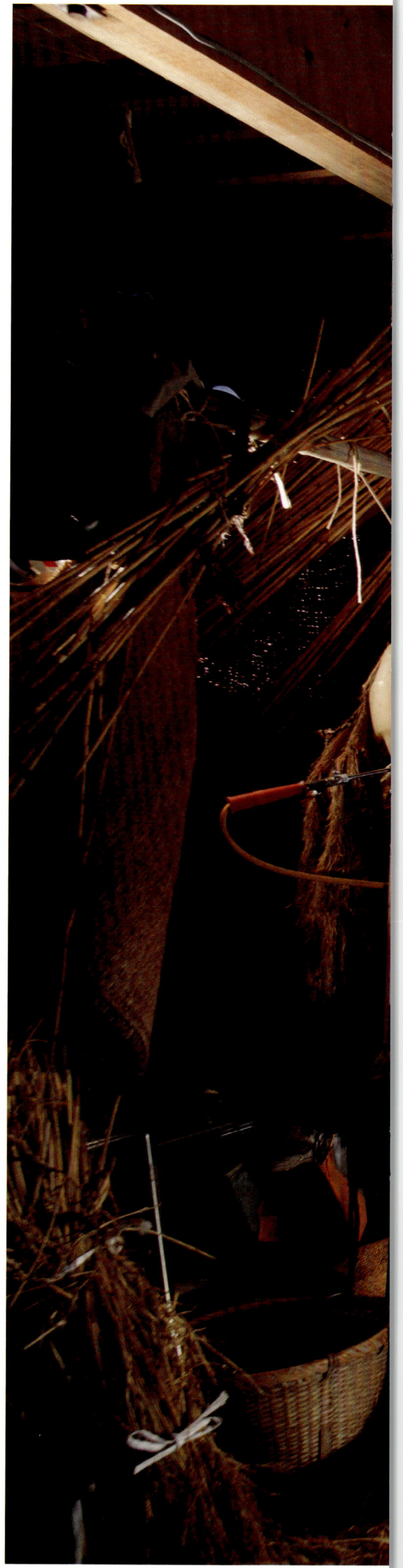

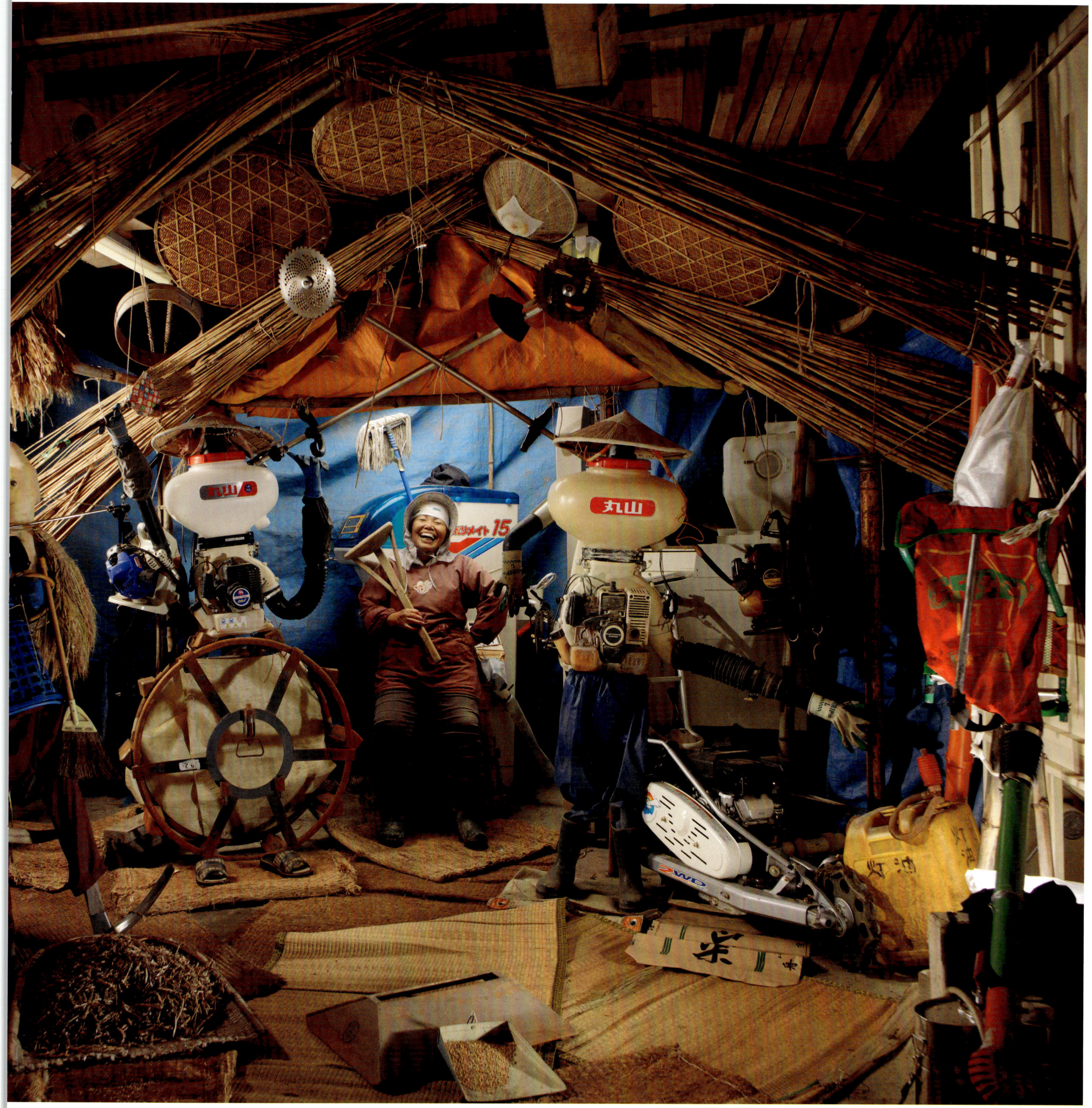
丸山
丸山
灯油

MARIE ET HENRY O'GRADY ¶ HOSHO UMEZU
FLORIAN COLOMB DE DAUNANT ¶ MOHA
CARDOSO HERRERA ¶ DANIEL BOCLY ¶ JOSE
AOUDA AWAD HAWASA ¶ MARIE ET HENRY O
CHRISTIANE GOVAERTS ¶ FLORIAN COLO
SAMSRI RUKSAP ¶ DORA CARDOSO HERRER
ARAI ¶ ANTON PETROVICH ¶ AOUDA AWAD H
UMEZU ¶ VALENTIN ACALO ¶ CHRISTIANE G
MOHAMED HAWAMDEH ¶ SAMSRI RUKSAP ¶
JOSEPH FILANCIA ¶ KOGI ARAI ¶ ANTON PE
HENRY O'GRADY ¶ HOSHO UMEZU ¶ VALENT
COLOMB DE DAUNANT ¶ MOHAMED HAW
HERRERA ¶ DANIEL BOCLY ¶ JOSEPH FILANC
AWAD HAWASA ¶ MARIE ET HENRY O'GRADY ¶
GOVAERTS ¶ FLORIAN COLOMB DE DAUNAN
DORA CARDOSO HERRERA ¶ DANIEL BOCLY
FILANCIA ¶ KOGI ARAI ¶ ANTON PETROVICH
O'GRADY ¶ HOSHO UMEZU ¶ VALENTIN ACAL
DE DAUNANT ¶ MOHAMED HAWAMDEH ¶ SAMS

THE PLAYHOUSE OF LIFE SUPPORT

I love the radio, vegetables, and I have a true passion for local plants. Vegetables are political, I would even go as far to say geopolitical! I like to mix their flavors when I cook and to take care of the land that is my garden, I put a stone under the wooden door to prevent the rabbits from eating my vegetables, I close the other door so the deer don't come in. Sometimes I even cut down a tree to let the light, life, back in. ¶ For a while now I have been learning Arabic. I brought two little cedar trees from Lebanon, wrapped in my clothes. Now I'm waiting for them to grow. It will take two thousand years! Our parents worked very hard to provide us with education. It was in the sixties. We lived among family portraits and horseback riding trophies. When I started to live with the man who later became my husband, our families stopped talking to us because it wasn't acceptable at the time. ¶ But everything changes so fast. Before, it was us elders who suffered. The war and social progress made us heroes but, today, society is starting to see us as a burden. I hope that our children can see their retirement as a place of freedom and a time to develop their passions.

MARIE AND HENRY O'GRADY IN THEIR GARDEN, SUSSEX, ENGLAND.

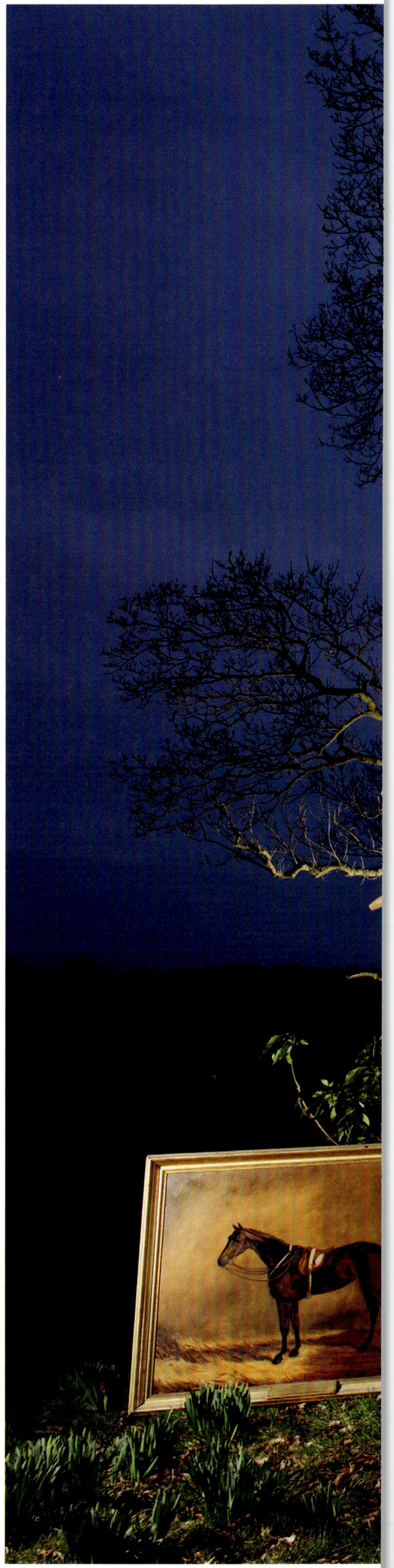

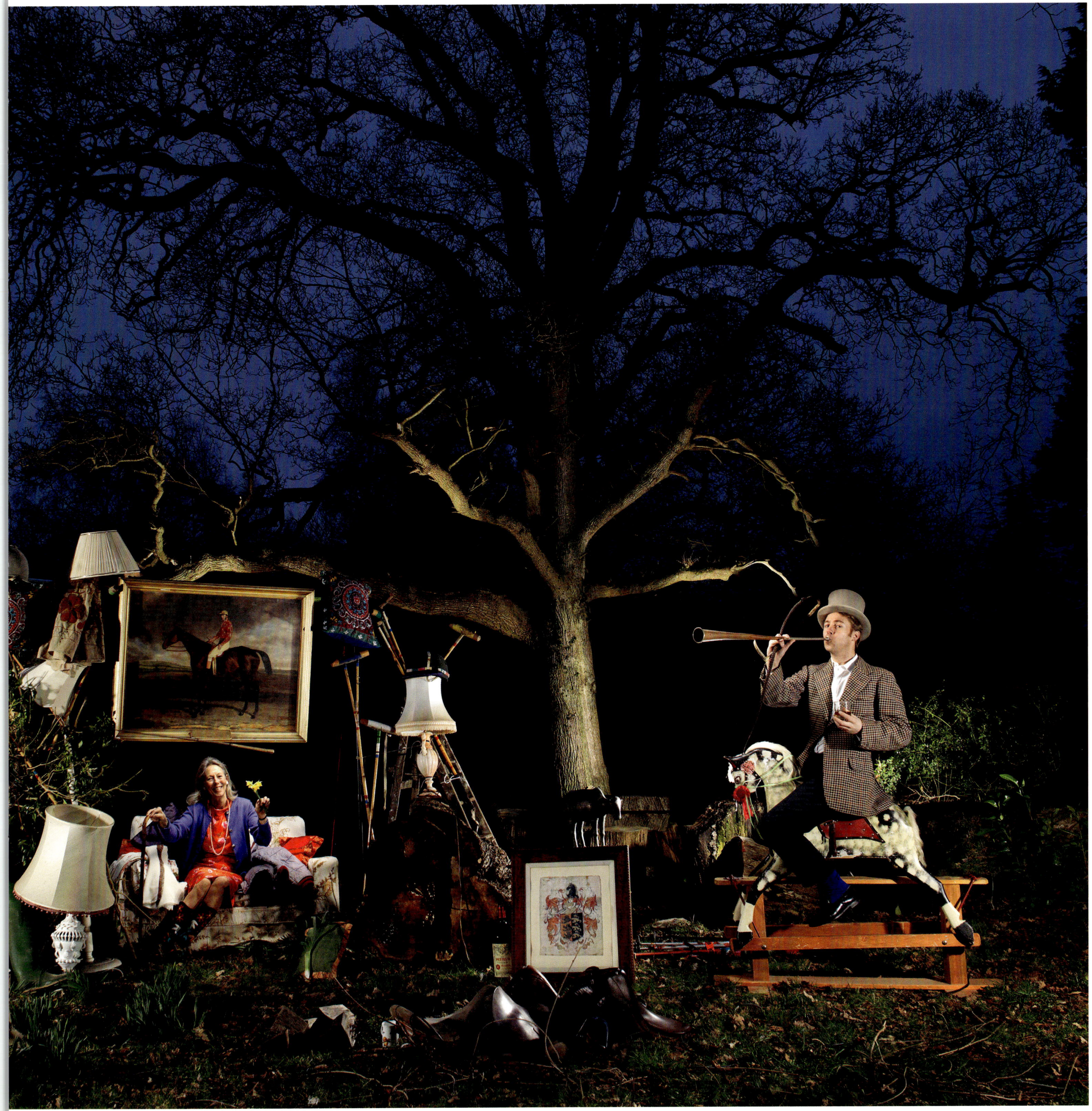

The first time I ever saw the sea I was moved. In my childhood, I only knew about the mountains, the tall trees and the white blanket of fog. Then I discovered the power of the waves and the calm sea on beautiful days. ¶ When I was small, I was very weak. I stayed in the hospital for a long time. One day, there was a huge fire that killed several people. My mother often told me that she had saved me from the flames. That taught me to make the most of every minute life has to offer. As children, we played outside with toys that we made with our own hands. We would spin our wooden tops on a bit of ground and the first player whose top left the circle would lose, like the sumo wrestlers! ¶ When I play golf or go skiing, I am very happy. I like karaoke but I prefer Buddhist chants and the music we play with the bowls of the temple. When I finished my monastic studies in Tokyo, I came back to the countryside. I need the mountains and I like to savor the fruits of my garden. After our wedding, I took my wife all around Japan to taste the products of each region. I told her she could buy whatever she wanted, as long as she would use it to make me fine cuisine. ¶ Here, the monastic tradition is passed from father to son. My father was my master in calligraphy and the three writings. The dead are laid in rest in the cemetery around the temple. We organize the ceremonies and listen to the living, who come to seek advice. I tell children that if everyone is turning to the right, you always need to look left to see things differently. My destiny as a monk is to adapt myself to each person in order to help them follow their own destiny.

HOSHO UMEZU FLOATING IN THE SUNSET OF THE AUTUMN FOREST, YAMAGATA, JAPAN.

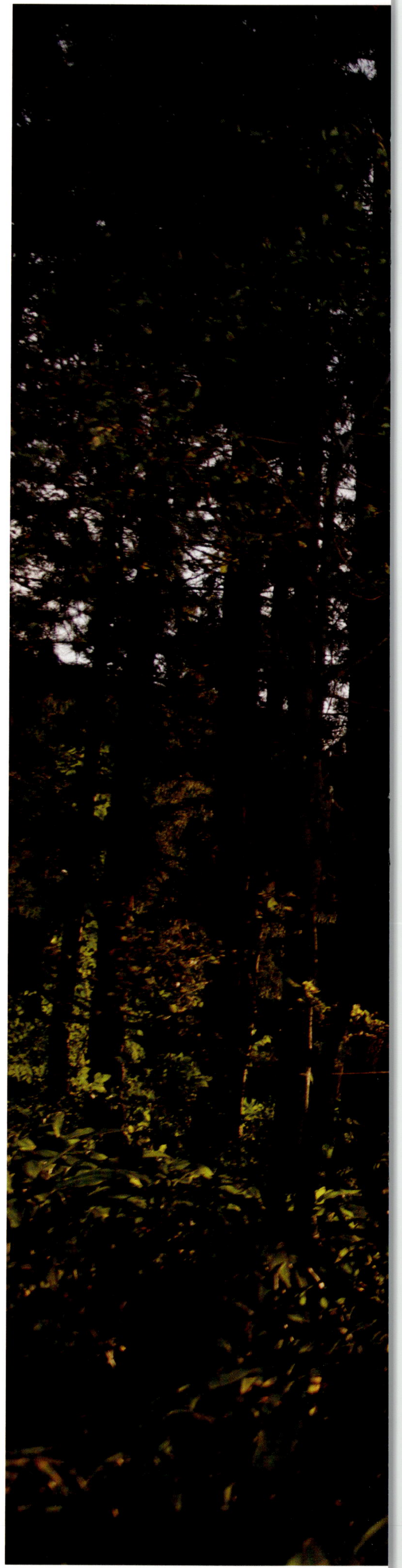

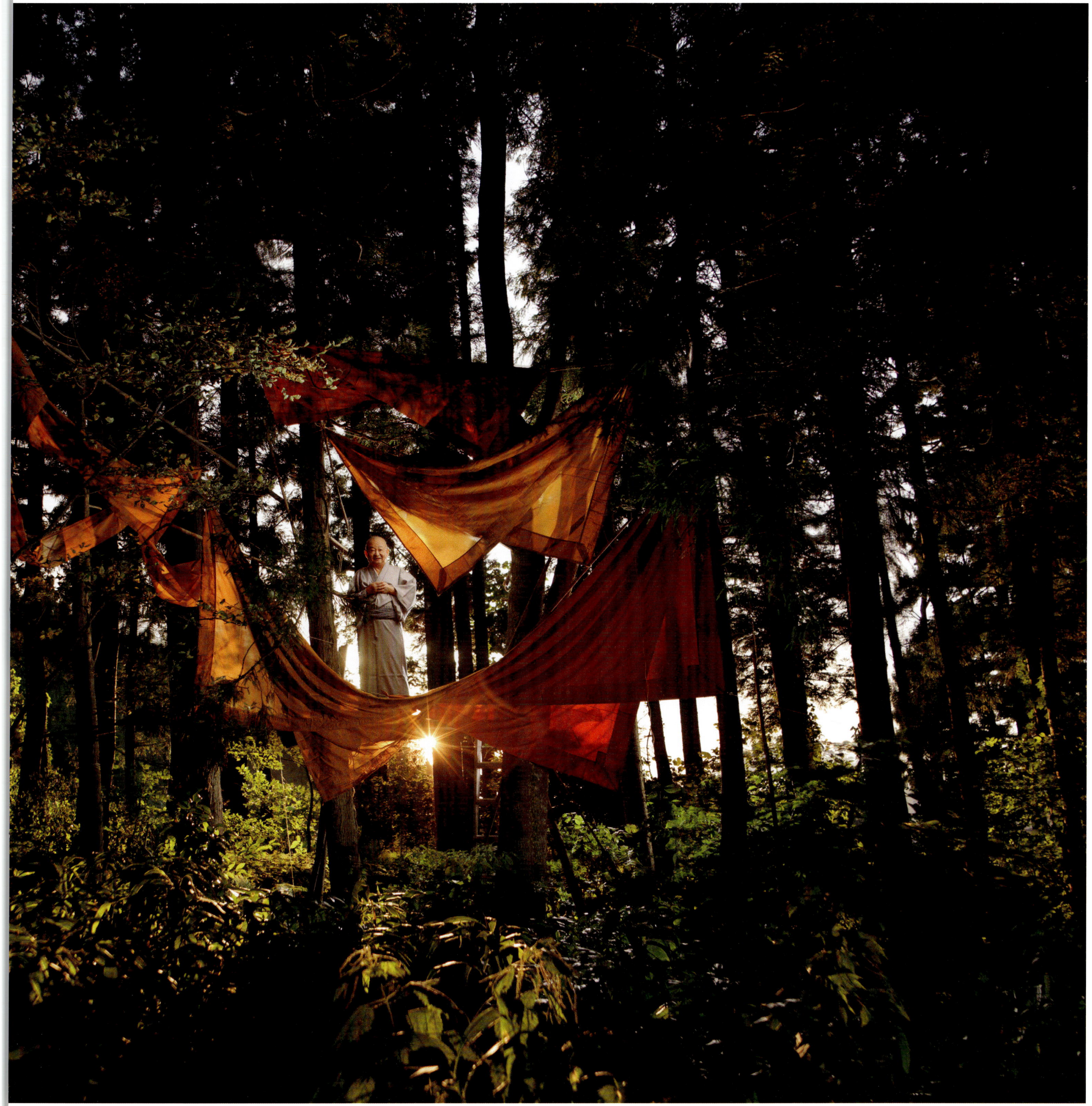

Llamas are part of the family. They are similar to man in many respects. In our cosmology the llama is considered a god. He is very important, like our volcano, Chimborazo, which fertilizes the land and the Inti sun, which makes the plants grow. ¶ I came to cut grass for my alpacas whose wool we spin to keep us from getting cold in the winter. We spend all of our lives with animals. It is this closeness that allows us to endure the harsh climate of our mountains. The llamas give us meat and help us transport fodder. Dogs guard the houses and take care of sheep. Cows give us their milk and their strength to work in the fields. We raise guinea pigs to eat. ¶ Each animal that I've known has its own distinct character. Each makes you think about a part of your humanity. When one passes away, I cannot help but let my tears flow.

VALENTIN ACALO AND HIS FAMILY OF ALPACAS, PALACIO REAL, ECUADOR.

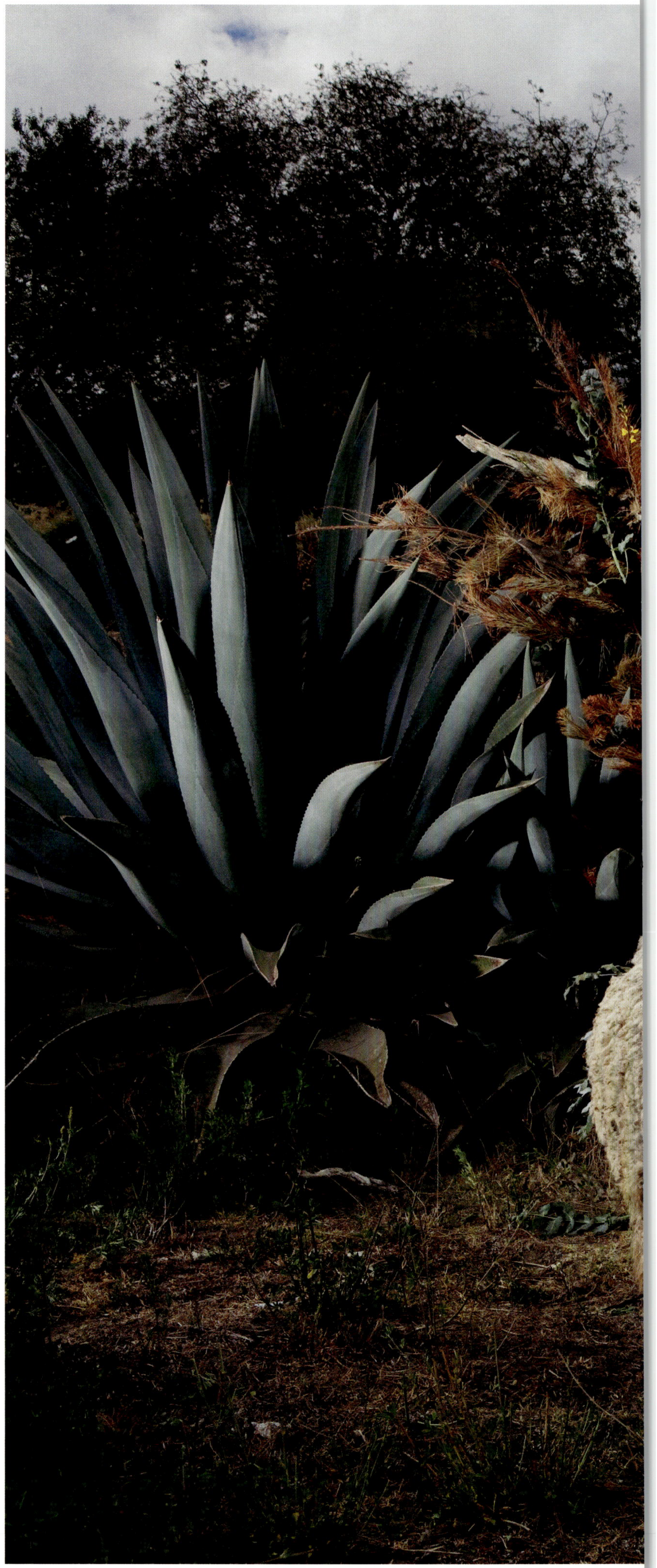

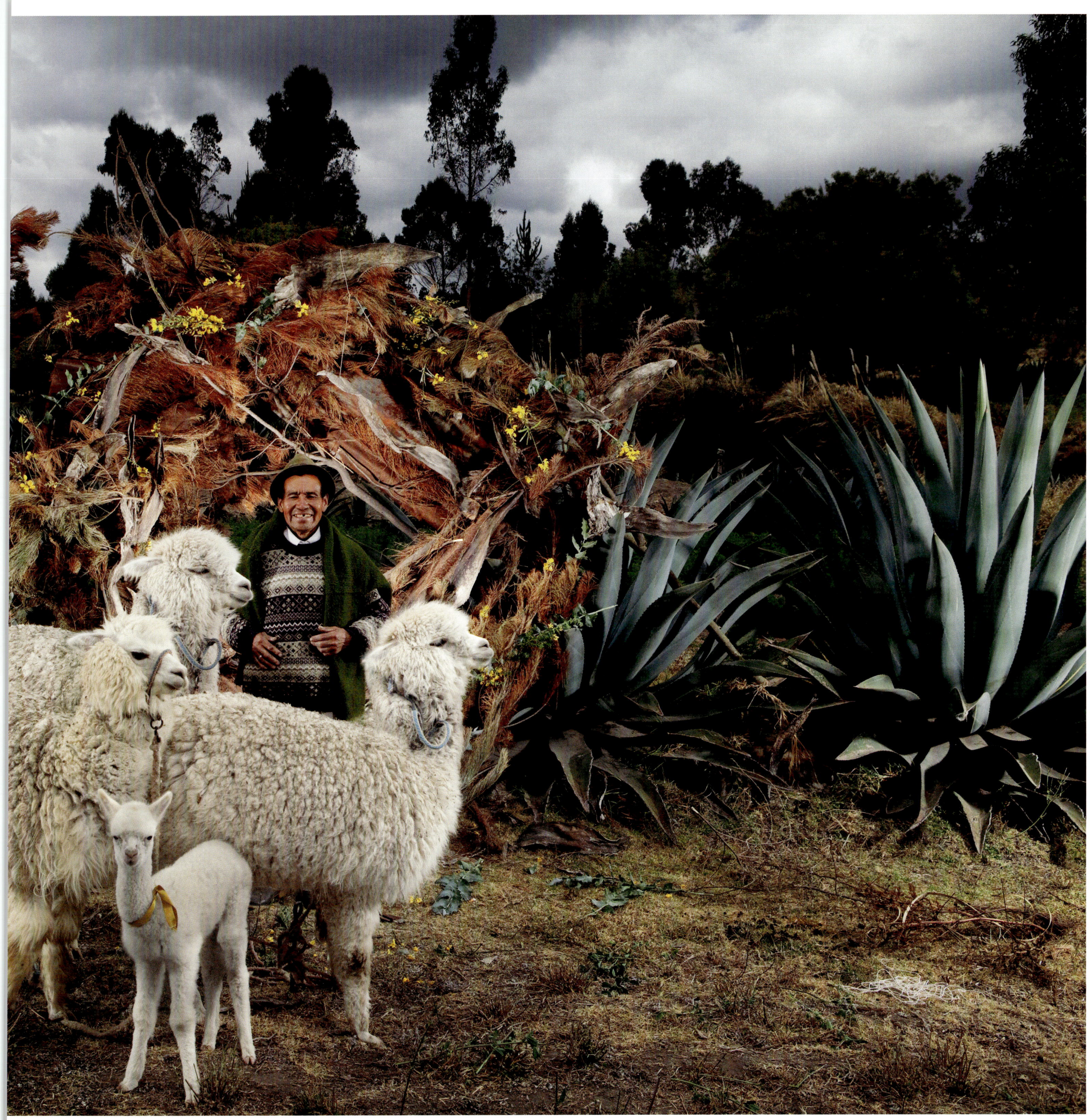

There has always been a Yorkshire terrier in our home. Our Miki has her own little house, surrounded by photos of her mother and grandmother. I have a sincere affection for her. ¶ In life, we don't necessarily say "I love you" at at every occasion. Sometimes we save it for the really important moments. What nourishes our existence is these little things, a look, a smile, a word, a small gesture. It takes but a fraction of a second yet we are rarely mistaken when offering it. A simple human exchange is that instant when we take one another into account. ¶ Just knowing this simple love exists, that which we can give to everyone around us, is something that keeps me grounded. It is the recognition of the Other, with a capital "O".

CHRISTIANE GOVAERTS AND MIKI IN THE GARDEN OF THEIR HOME ON THE BANKS OF THE MARNE RIVER, FRANCE.

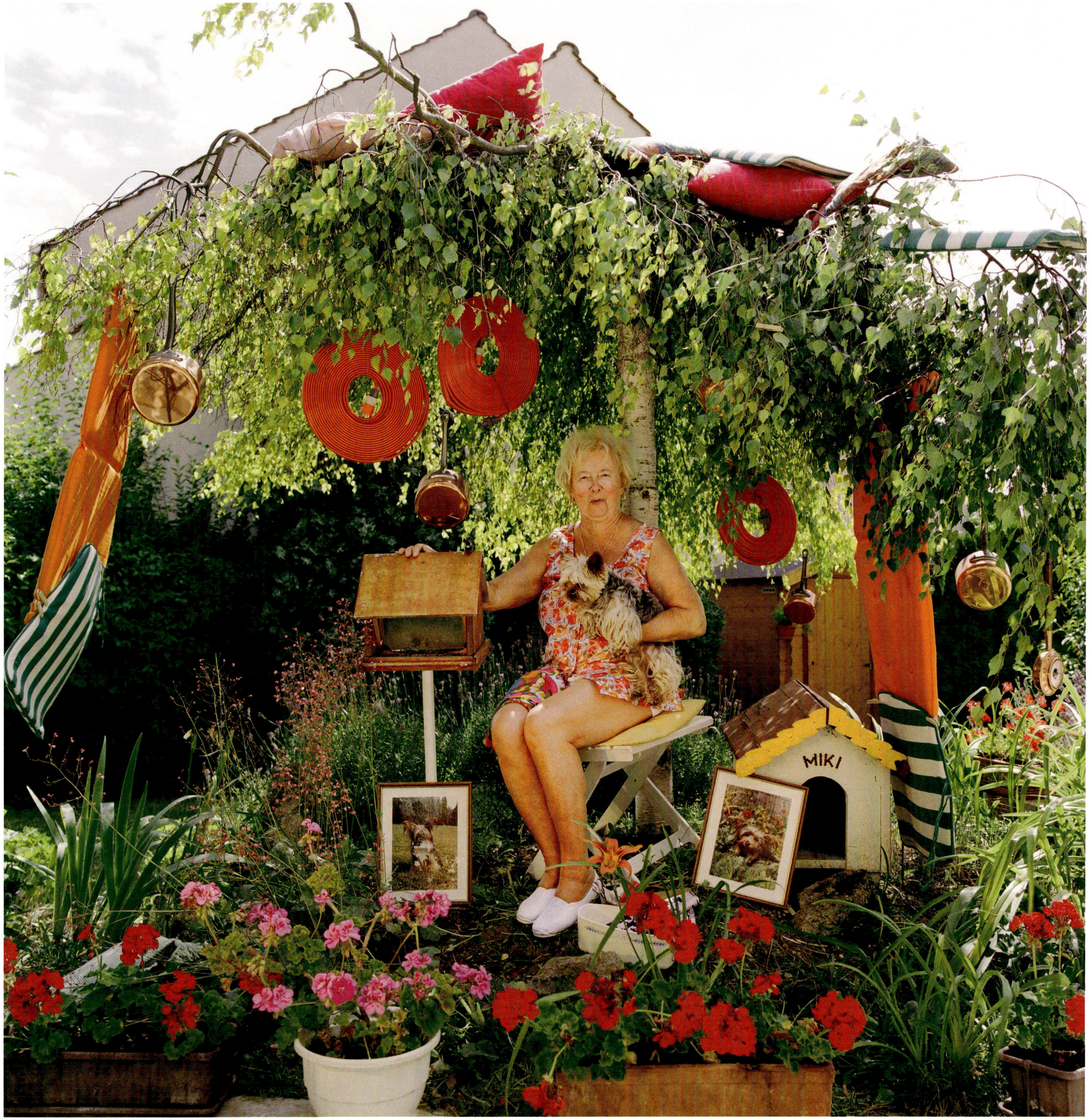
MIKI

To be asea is to engage in a soulful struggle within oneself. I would go for miles and miles, and when a storm arose, it was sometimes absolutely terrifying. Yet, as soon as the calm returned, I was ready to go again. ¶ Nature is also in a cycle of perpetual rebirth. When species disappear, others are created, like what happened when the meteorite fell in the time of the dinosaurs. I think that man will one day use up all raw materials, an inherent problem with overpopulation. That will force us to confront our destiny. ¶ I spent many years at sea, and in the heart of Camargue where the land and the water meld together. Here, I've always felt safe, protected, like a nest in the great, open sky, surrounded by the forces of nature. Like in the shelter of my boat, when the sea is raging. Nature is so much bigger than all of us, but when fear sets in we have to conquer it, not pass it along to others. In the near future, we will have to continuously adapt to change, to be flexible like the reed, not rigid like the oak, which shall one day succumb to the elements of nature, and break.

FLORIAN COLOMB DE DAUNANT AND HIS HORSE, IN THE SANCTUARY OF HIS BELOVED CAMARGUE, CACHAREL, FRANCE.

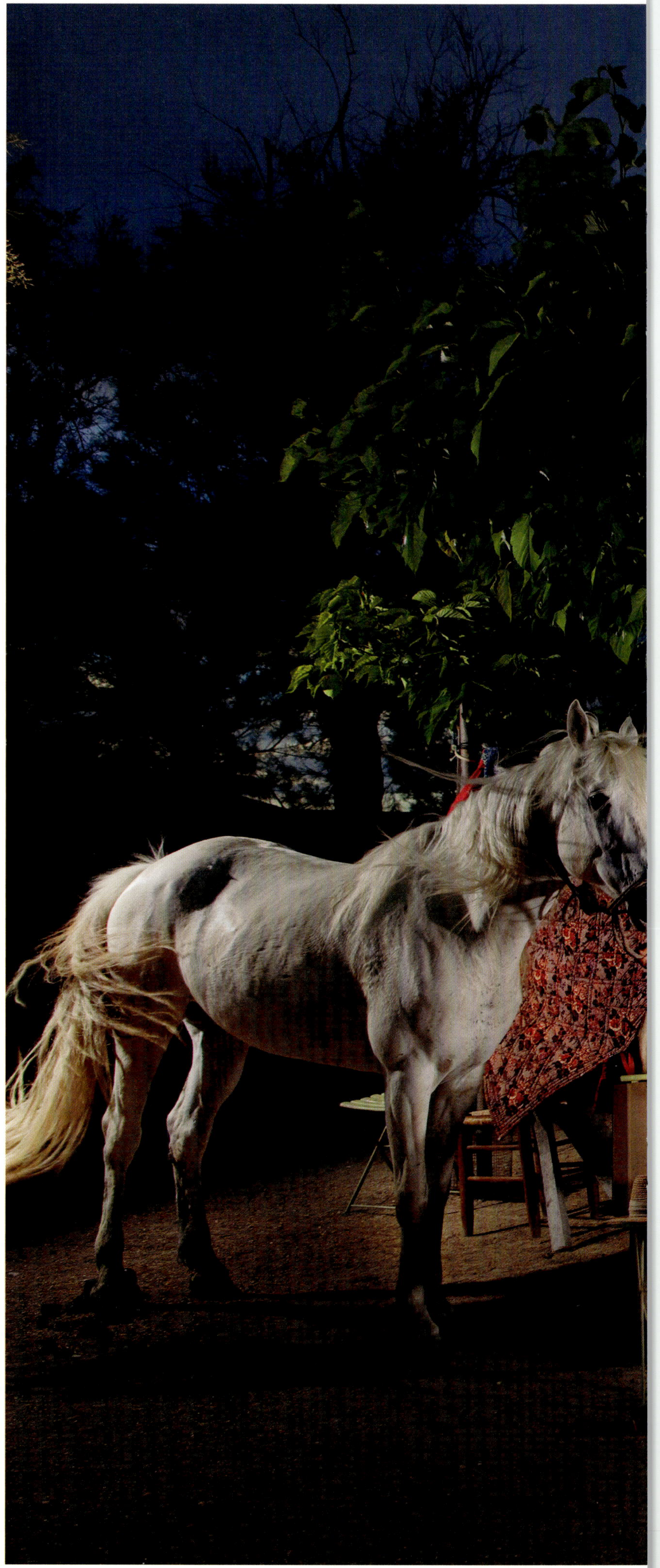

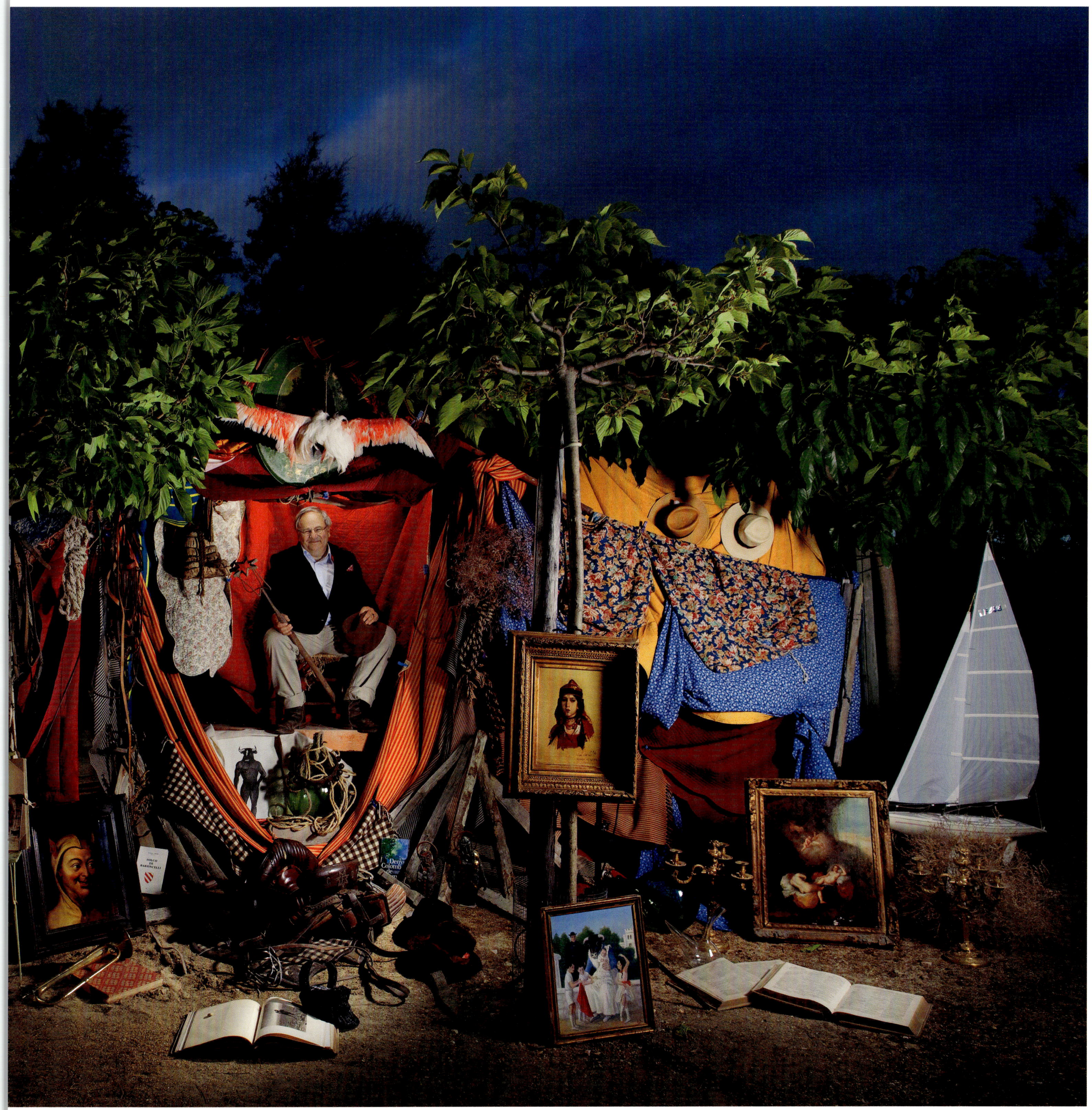

When I was a child

my dream was to build a house with my own hands and to have four wives. I lived my whole life with one wife but she gave me seventeen children. Today I have 115 grandchildren and not one day goes by that one of them doesn't come over to share a cardamom coffee with me. I'm 79 years old now and I've just remarried. Sometimes the memories from my former life make me cry. ¶ When I was young I spent all of my time on horseback. When I was 20, I tended my own flock. One day, I sliced the nose of a hyena with the tip of my saber. We loaded the backs of our donkeys with grapes, olives and oranges that we sold in Syria and Palestine. We formed long and impressive caravans. Today, our village has passed from 1,000 to 60,000 people and there is no land left to farm. If you have animals in your house you will endure the complaints of your neighbors. All we consume these days are products that are brought in by trucks, like this television that has killed our social life. ¶ I prefer to stay at home, chanting tales from bygone times, poems of courage and hospitality, like those we tell women when proposing. They used to resonate when families got together for work. Then, our reunions were those of wheat and barley, the gathering of olives and nuts.

MOHAMED HAWAMDEH CELEBRATING POETRY, SUF, JORDAN.

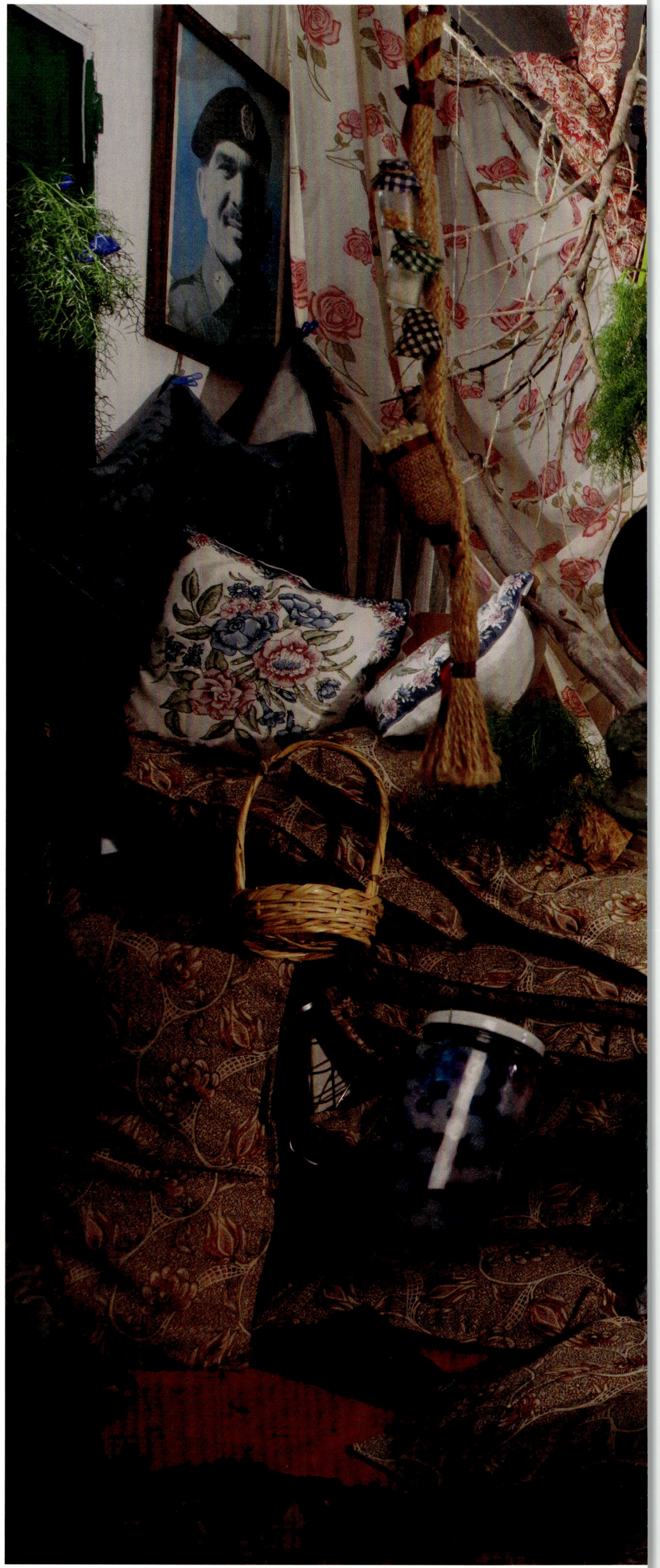

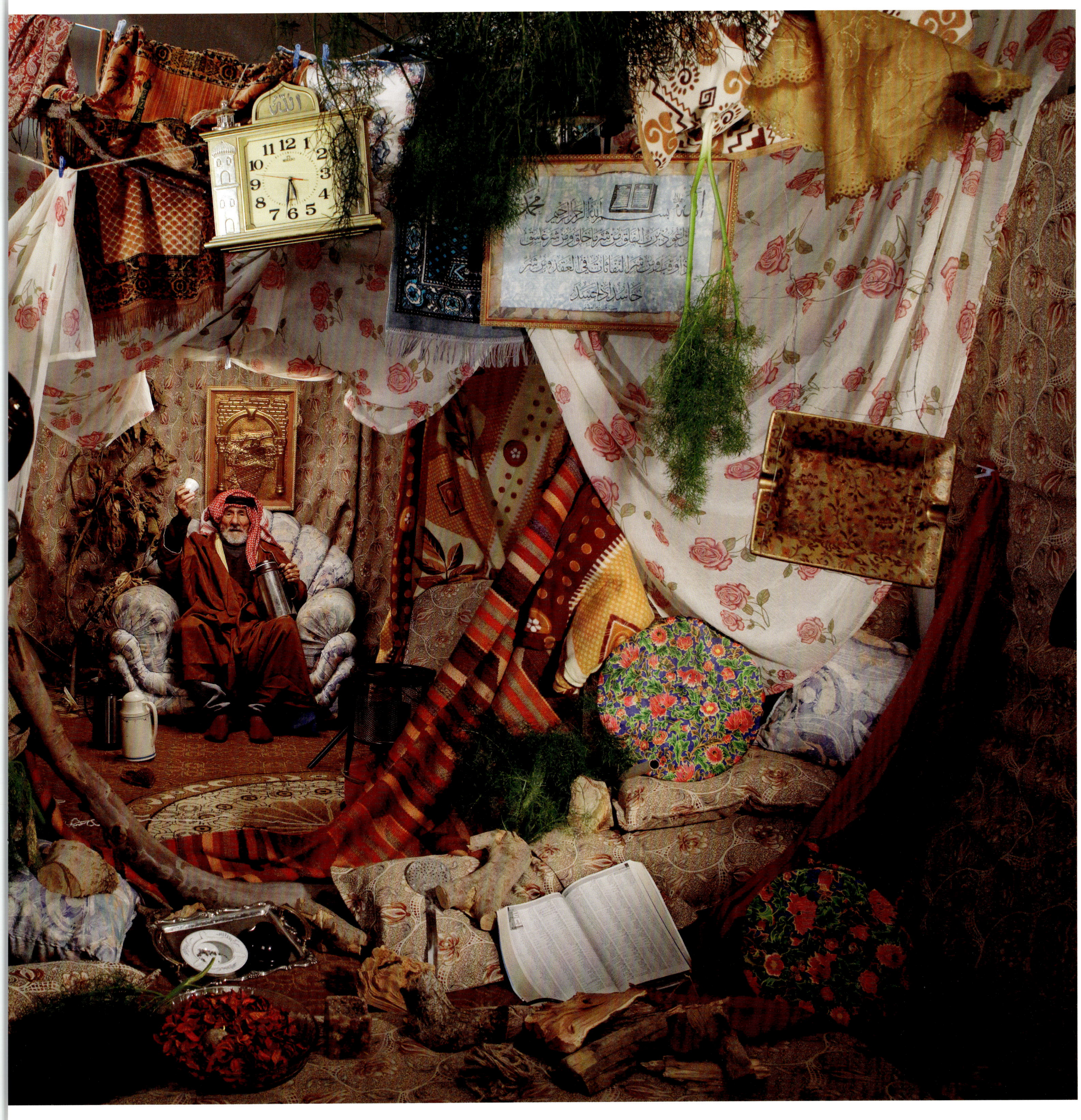

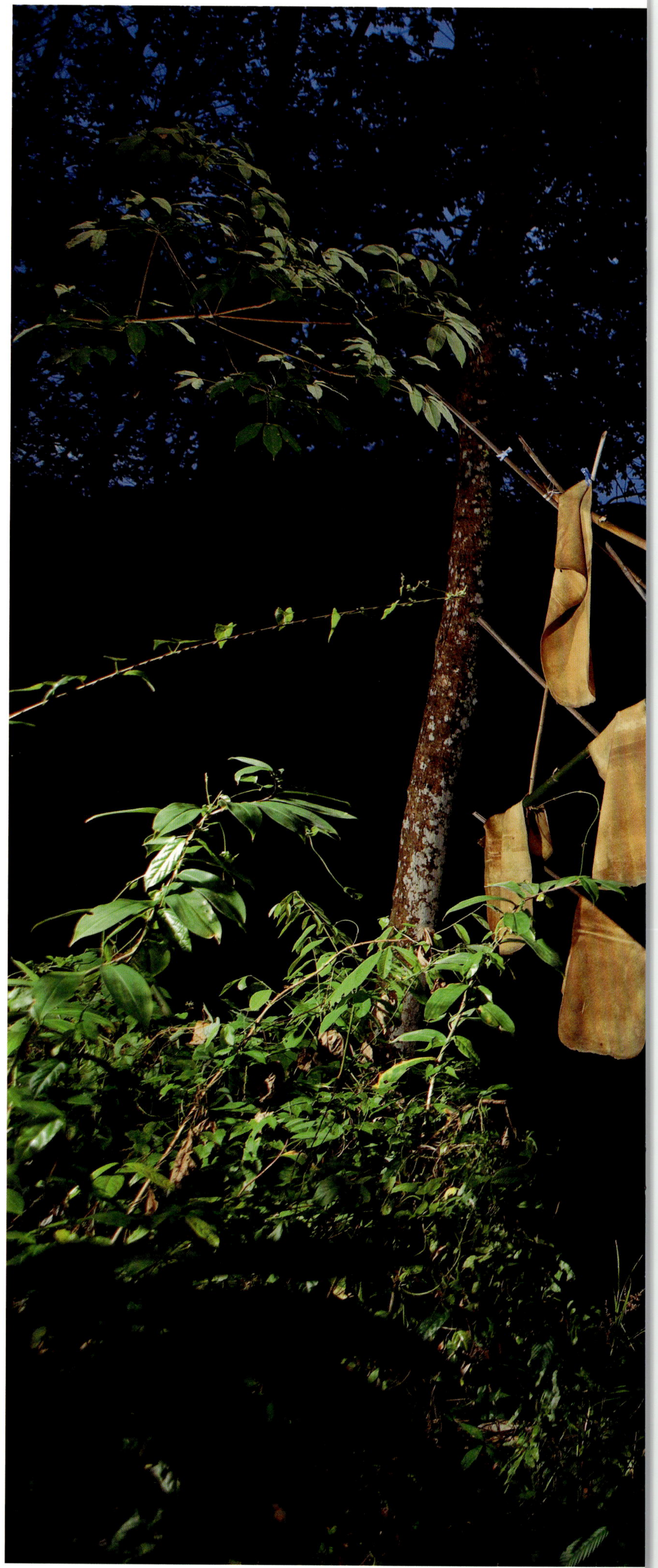

I spend every day of my life in nature. I have 5 fruits in my garden: coconut, bananas, rambutans, durians and mangoes. I go down to the village to share them with other families. ¶ When I first fell in love, my man gave me a bouquet of tantawans. Since then, these huge yellow flowers brighten each day. We bought a rubber plantation and we sell the raw material, which is sent far away by boats. The rubber travels and is processed and you will find it on the other end of this earth, in modern objects like cars and computers. ¶ I have always liked the rain that nourishes the soil. After the tsunami, we rebuilt our village far from the sea and we put up water reservoirs. It's good to have water in the house and not to have to transport it anymore. In front of my tanks, I am like a queen, with my sheets of rubber that all of the children in the neighborhood gathered together to hang up.

SAMSRI RUKSAP IN THE RUBBER PLANTATION, KOH MUK ISLAND, THAILAND.

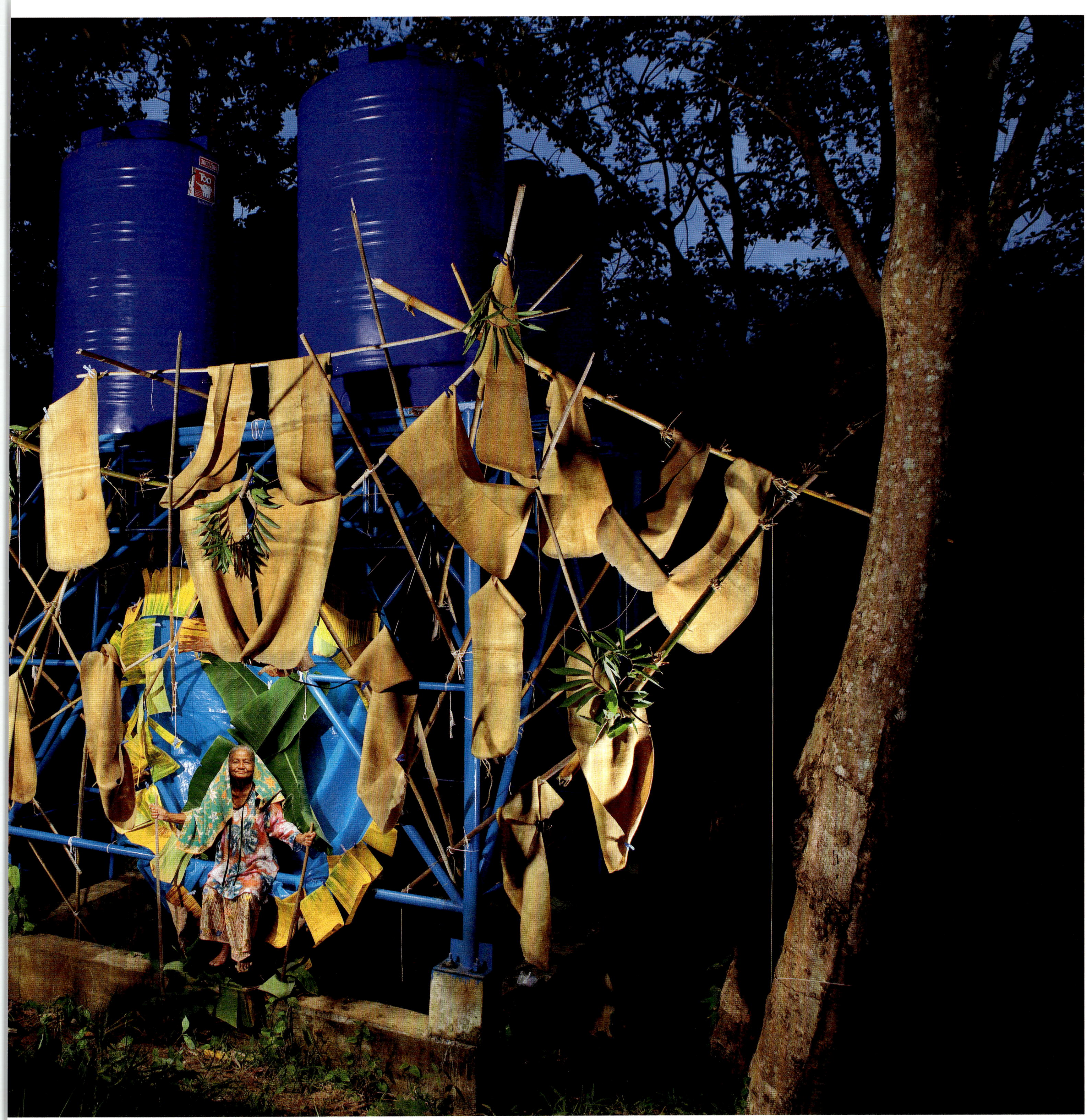

I met my husband under the outstretched arms of the Rio Christ. Each of us had just passed before the flashes of a camera. We first found ourselves side by side in the same photos. I remember saying to myself, what a charming man! When he saw me in person he made the first move, and we both laughed. We became friends and we had a simple but wonderful wedding. ¶ I came from the countryside where my older sister had taught me to sew. She was always my accomplice in everything. As children, we liked to slide down the slopes of the green gardens on banana leaves. ¶ When I came to Rio, I was frightened by the city's clamor. In the beginning I found everything to be violent and characterless. Then, one day, for the New Year, we went to the beach surrounded by a crowd of people all dressed in white. There were people of all ages and colors singing samba songs in chorus. At the seventh wave after midnight, we tossed a rose into the sea. We could have been in paradise. Our wish had been to have children, and it came true. Since then, I take care of them while embroidering beautiful colors onto white linen.

DORA CARDOSO HERRERA AMIDST THE WHITE LINEN OF HER APARTMENT IN RIO, BRAZIL.

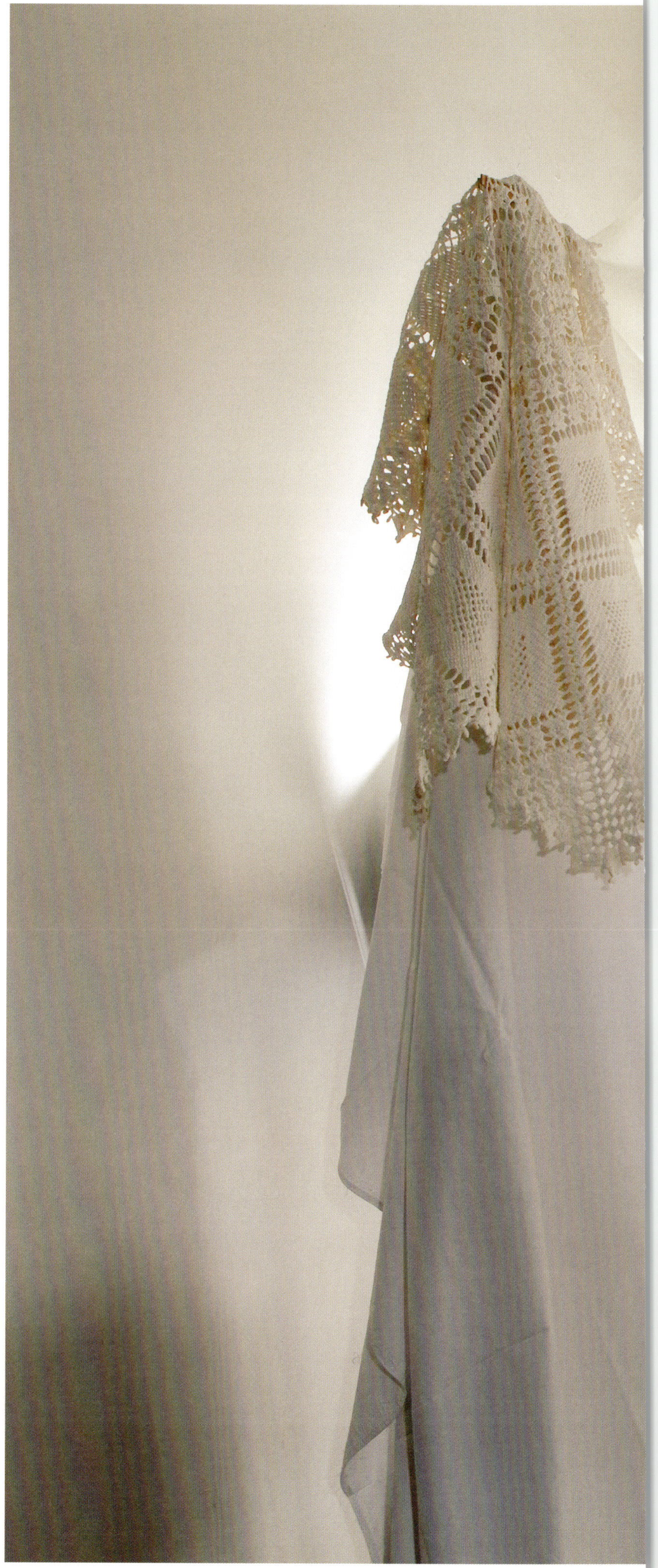

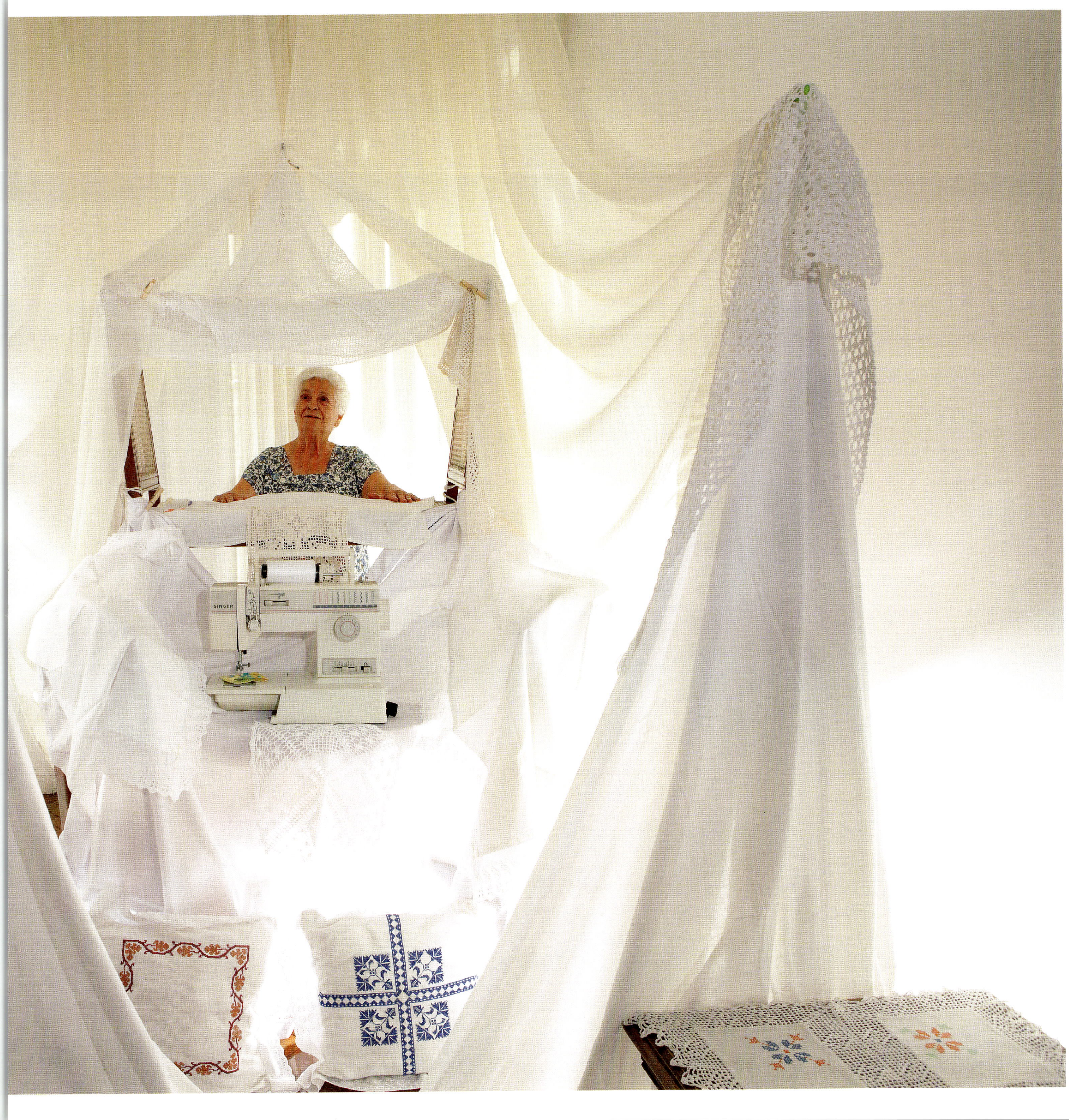
SINGER

The United States,

for Europeans, has always been a dream of freedom. D-day landings, Kennedy, Westerns and Jazz. I have lived in New York for 27 years. I am surrounded by curves and charts. I play the stock market, especially oil, a real thrill. In the same way that my father would buy a car on Monday and sometimes sell it on Friday. He produced superb films. Like *And God Created Woman* with Brigitte Bardot. Then, one day, he lost everything in a huge production disaster. ¶ For my part, I built myself a house with a concrete cellar and heavy wooden doors, a safe place with a strong foundation, where my daughters could always come home to. It's important to do stupid things when we are young because we are elastic, we bounce back, and we bend with the wind. The more we go forward in life, the more visible we become. ¶ I think life is easier these days. The world isn't perfect but we are fortunate to be here, there is no war within our borders. And we have progressed considerably, especially in the face of pain; today there are pills to ease the suffering we had to endure in our childhood. Back then, one plane out of a hundred fell from the sky, now it's more like maybe one out of a hundred thousand. ¶ I have taken a lot of photos and produced numerous films in my life. To me, a picture is sometimes worth more than a thousand words.

DANIEL BOCLY IN HIS PARK AVENUE SITTING ROOM, NEW YORK, UNITED STATES.

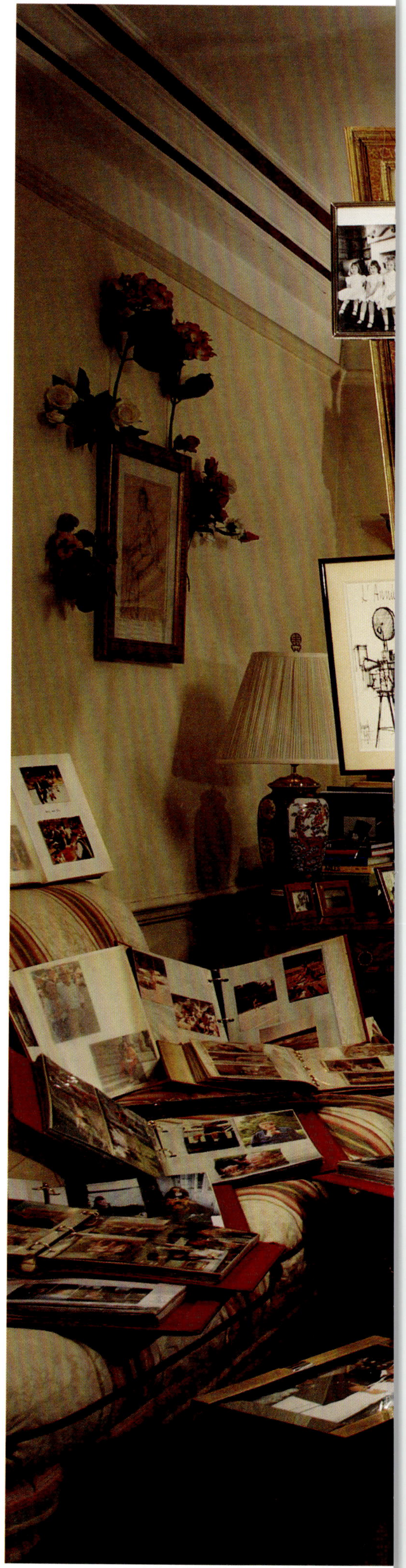

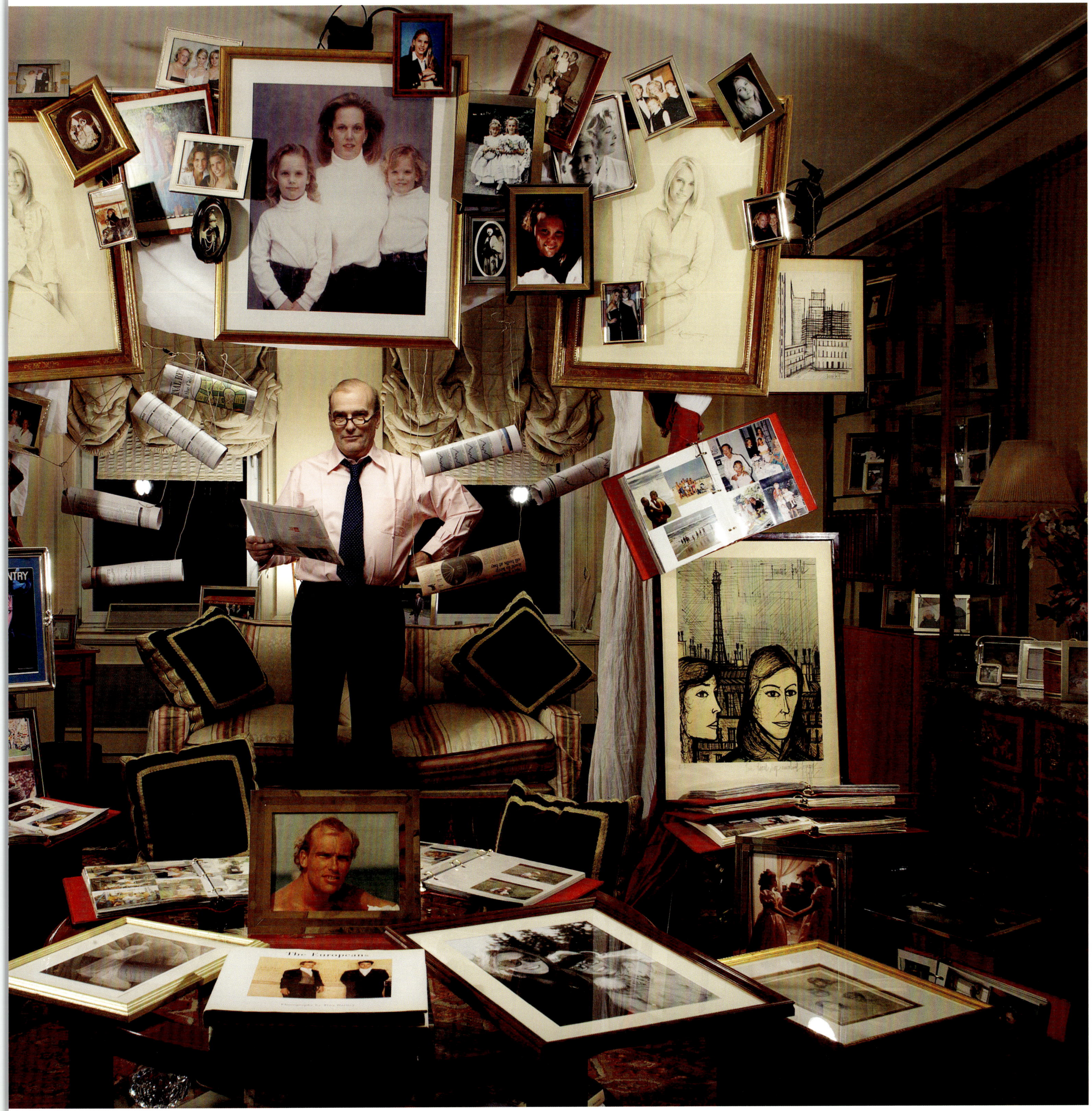
The Europeans

I have two loves, the sea and Pauline. That's the name of my wooden fishing boat, and that of my wife whom I've loved for years. Each morning, I set out at the first light of dawn, and each day, we eat the fruits of my labor. This is the best job in the world. We live off nature, this is our passion. The sea changes every day, and once you fall under its spell, you cannot leave it. The emotions and beauty that it brings are perpetually refreshed. ¶ The light and the water guide me. When the 4-meter high waves crash around me fear takes over and I think the end has come. When this happens, I speak softly to the elements, explaining to them that it's not yet the right moment. I address the sea directly, the sea who has always kept me alive so that I might come home to a loving household. ¶ The tails of the fish undulate, carrying them afar. We, the fishermen, follow them, sometimes far, far away. I've even gone all the way to Corsica following their wake and nourishing presence. For me, the secret to happiness is a simple life where each day seems new.

JOSEPH FILANCIA, THE SEA AND HIS FISHING BOAT, SANARY, FRANCE.

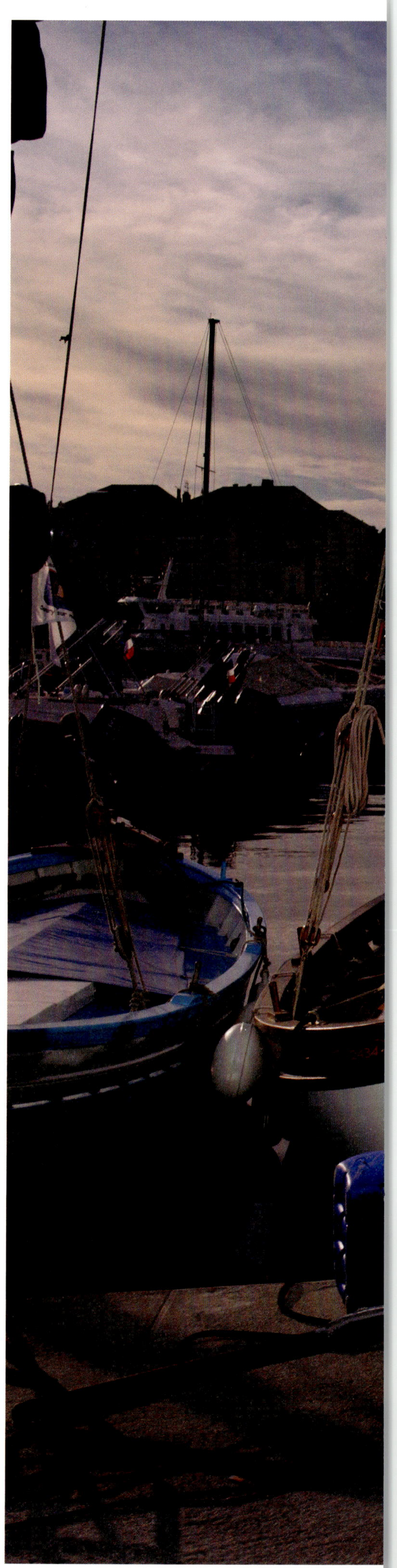

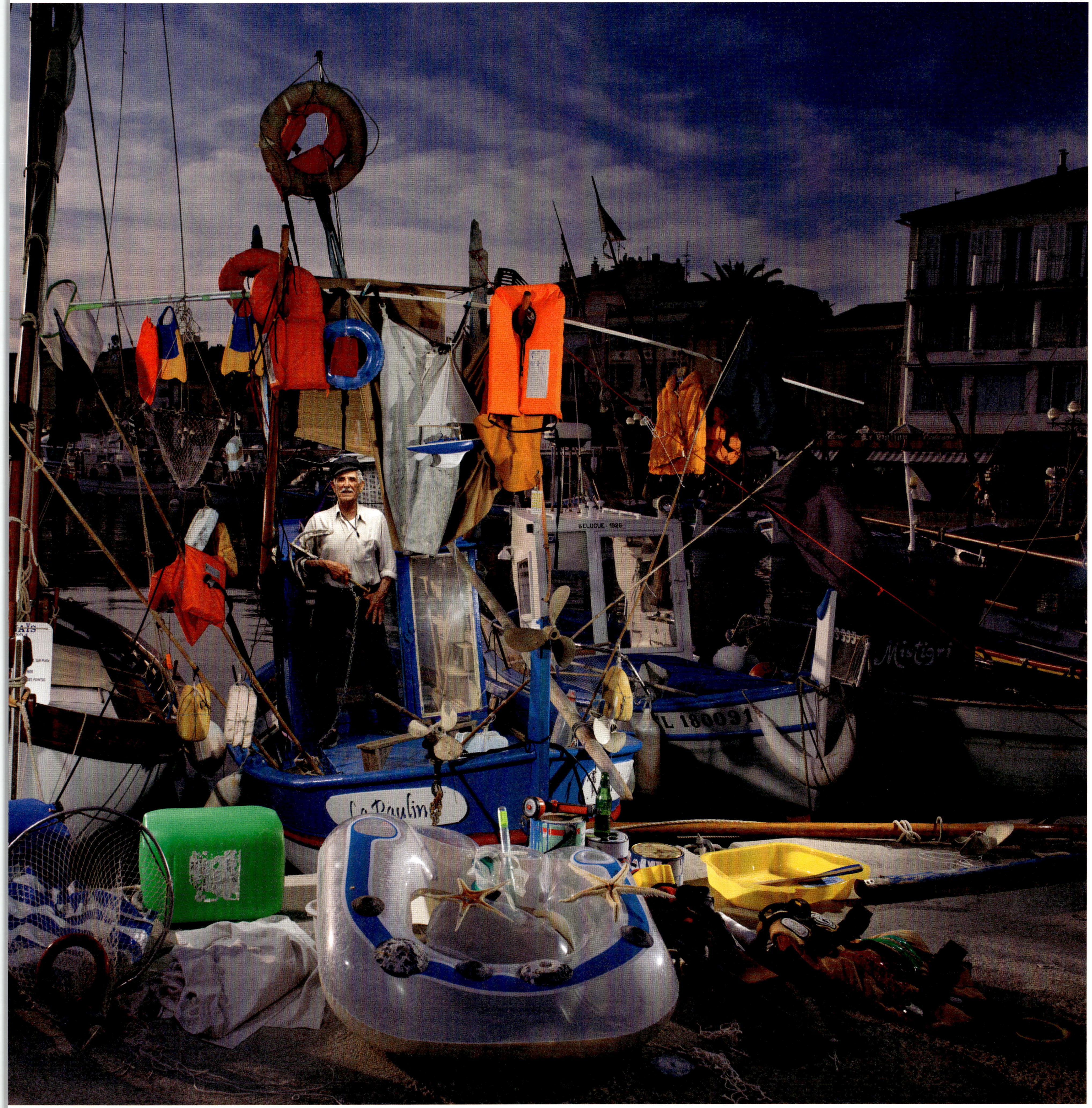
Mistigri
L 180091

I don't like when things change. I steer away from the television. It brings too much news about the world and its upheavals. It brings them closer to home, as if invisible doors were opening into other countries, other people's worlds. ¶ As the head of a company I was constantly under stress. I don't drink alcohol. But I have a passion for antiques. I take great comfort watching objects grow older. The shine of a bronze bowl as it tarnishes. The earthen pottery as it browns. I have simple pleasures. What makes me happiest is to be next to my wife. We're complementary. As I am very selfish and she takes care of others, we get along very well. She speaks far too much, but she is very nice. That makes up for it. ¶ I like to invent new techniques, new machines. In a small company you work for your country, you make everything on site. For me, creativity is very important. The thousands of gloves in our hangar are symbols of safety and the care we put into our work. All my life, I've lived amongst the roar of machines, a mask on my face and dust on my hands. Today, I am contemplating the peace that has settled in my heart.

KOGI ARAI AND HIS WORK-WORN GLOVES, YONEZAWA, JAPAN.

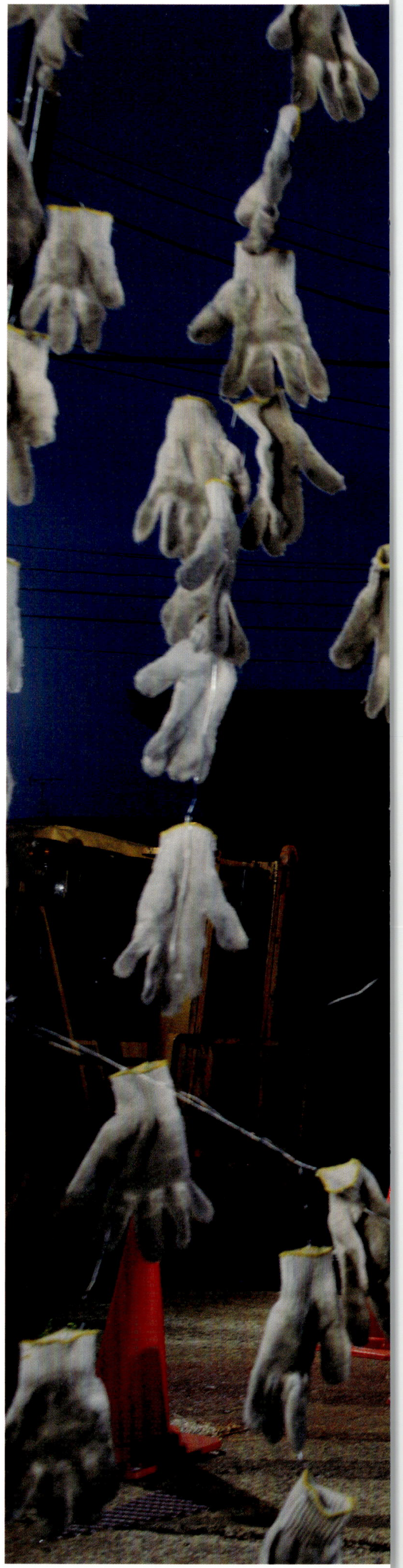

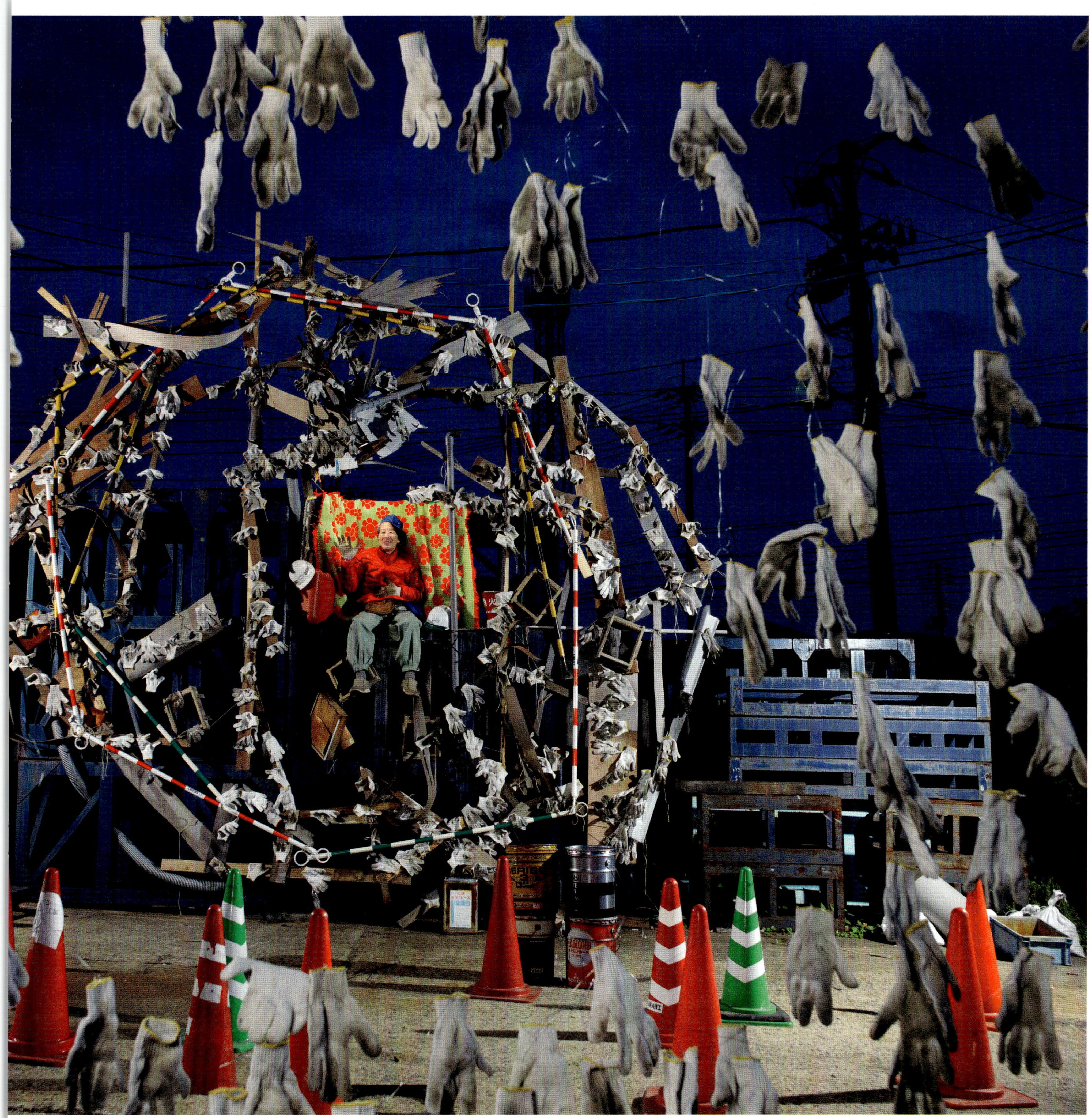

There have been two great days in our lives. The first was our victory in the Second World War and the second, the day Gagarin went into space, for that was the fruit of all of our labor. Before we listened to operas on the radio, great music that stirred us with passion. The television today is full of vulgarity, the programs have no interest. We would do better to take more of an interest in literature and music. ¶ In any case, I cannot say that the way people live today is my idea of living. "Business, Business!" that's all we hear. Me, I say that it's not money that brings progress. Socialism, despite its faults, at least enabled everyone to have something. Capitalism means only a few are wealthy and buy themselves yachts and luxurious houses and sports cars, while the others have nothing. We didn't give Socialism enough of a chance, we just destroyed it. Whatever the regime, man is not just, that's human nature. ¶ The goal in life is to give more than you take. That requires having a conscious and courage. Me, I don't smoke, I only drink a bit of vodka, I work a lot in my library and my money all goes to buying books. My way of being useful is to publish my creations so that everyone can benefit from my inventions, machines steeped in technical imagination. I want to share them with everyone, without expecting anything in return. That is how I live.

ANTON PETROVICH AND THE MEMENTOS OF THE COMMUNIST ERA, MOSCOW, RUSSIA.

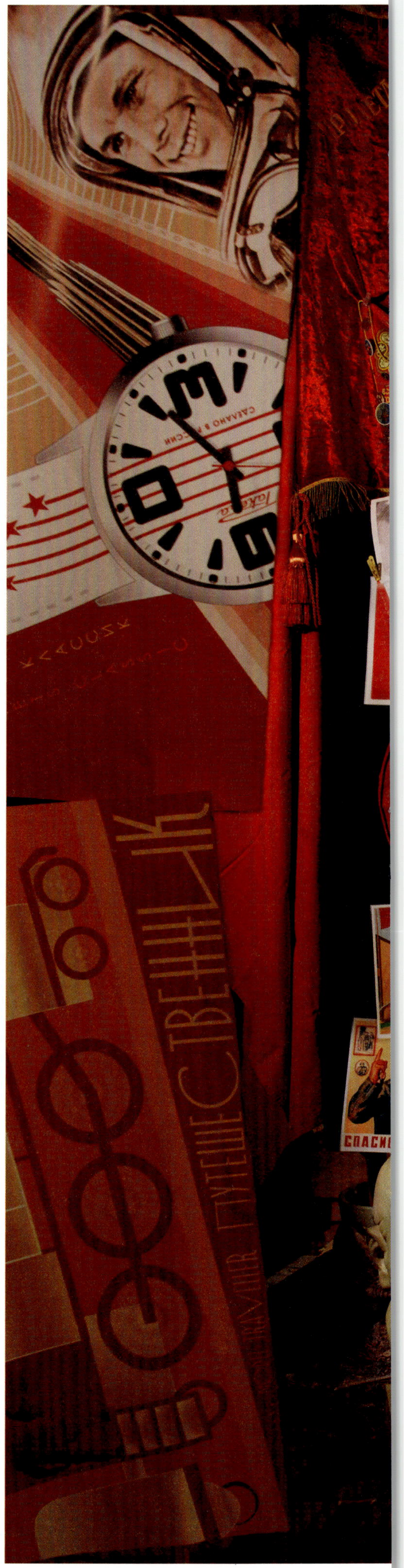

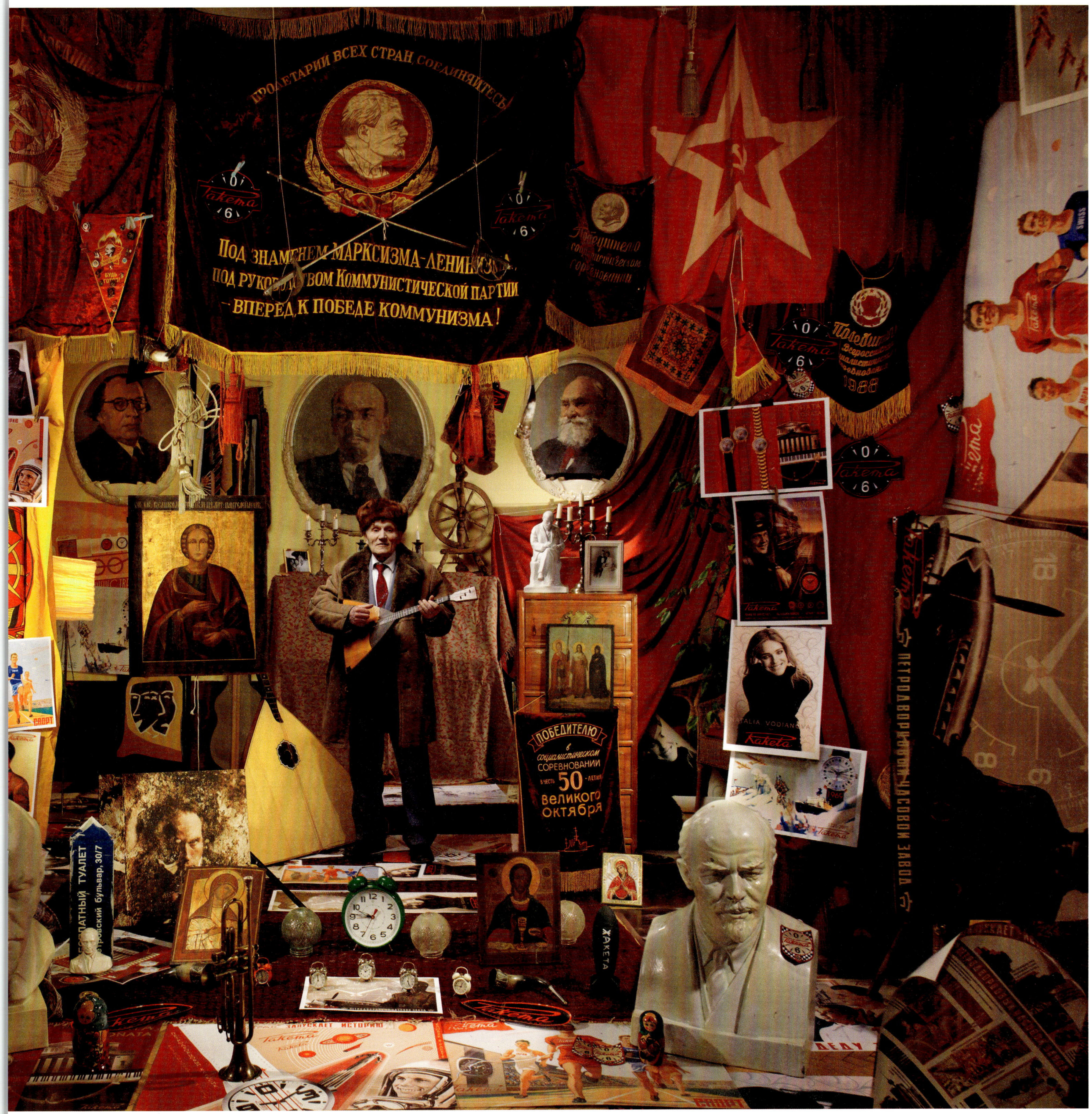
ПРОЛЕТАРИИ ВСЕХ СТРАН, СОЕДИНЯЙТЕСЬ!
ВПЕРЕД, К ПОБЕДЕ КОММУНИЗМА!
ПОБЕДИТЕЛЮ
в социалистическом
СОРЕВНОВАНИИ
50
Великого
Октября
ПЛАТНЫЙ ТУАЛЕТ
Ракета

Our King Abdullah brings us peace. He has built safe homes for our children and his image is displayed in every household. Our religion is a promise we have made to welcome and help all human beings. To a stranger, you offer hospitality. You give them tea. With those who enter your tent, you share a meal. We know the names of our ancestors as far back as ten generations. We are one big family. Beyond our borders, we greet each other by invoking their names; that reminds us that we are all cousins. ¶ I spend my time between mountains and desert. Tonight, the moon will be full and my heart will rejoice. My dog cares for our goats and protects us from wolves and hyenas. The city is far away, with its lights and vanities. For me, life has not changed since the time of my parents. I have only a radio that brings me news of the world. ¶ Before, we had fewer things but more friendship. Each day, we would gather together to talk. Today, I continue to savor life through respect for nature. It is vain to trade the presence of others for futile pleasures, and to destroy the creations of God.

AOUDA AWAD HAWASA BEFORE HIS TENT IN THE DESERT AT THE FOOT OF THE MOUNTAINS, WADI'ARABA, JORDAN.

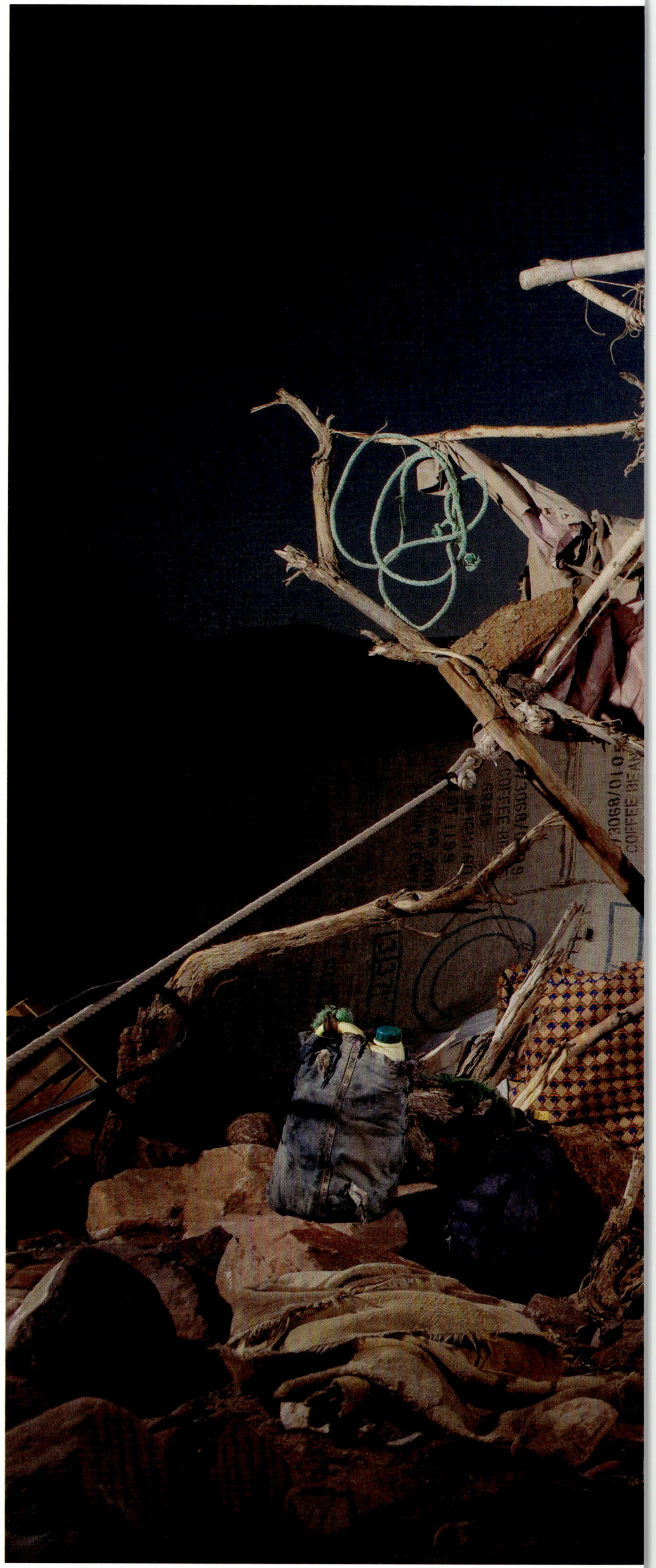

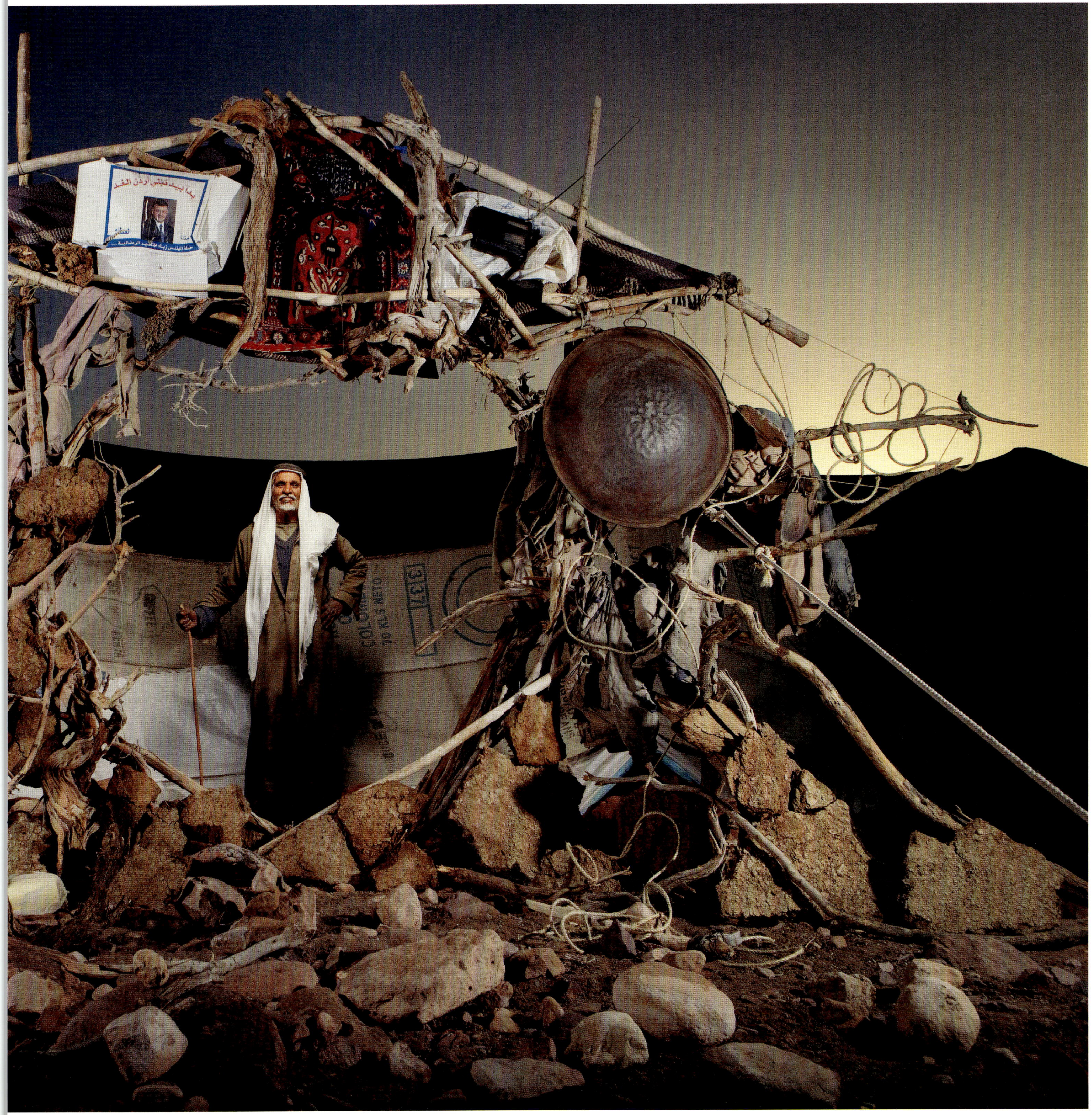
يدا بيد نبني أردن الغد
70 KLS NETO
337

GERARDO COCA ¶ MANUEL ZATAN ¶ WANG X
KAZUKO SHIRIASHI ¶ ABETA YASHIKO ¶ OLG
MARIKI ¶ LULAMA JIM ET NANCY WITBOOI ¶
BOUDHAKUMARI DHAKAL ¶ GERARDO COCA
KIM HENG ¶ DANNIS BARNES ¶ KAZUKO SH
VEDERNIKOV ¶ TETEA AROUA MARIKI ¶ LUL
TENESACA ¶ PATRICK JAMPO ¶ BOUDHAK
ZATAN ¶ WANG XIAO ¶ YUJI SATO ¶ KIM HENG
YASHIKO ¶ OLGA ET NICOLAÏ VEDERNIKOV ¶
WITBOOI ¶ CONCEPCIÓN TENESACA ¶ PATRIC
COCA ¶ MANUEL ZATAN ¶ WANG XIAO ¶ YUJ
SHIRIASHI ¶ ABETA YASHIKO ¶ OLGA ET NICOLAI
ET NANCY WITBOOI ¶ CONCEPCIÓN TENESAC
GERARDO COCA ¶ MANUEL ZATAN ¶ WANG X
KAZUKO SHIRIASHI ¶ ABETA YASHIKO ¶ OLGA
TETEA AROUA MARIKI ¶ LULAMA JIM ET NANCY
TENESACA ¶ PATRICK JAMPO ¶ BOUDHAKUMA
WANG XIAO ¶ YUJI SATO ¶ KIM HENG ¶ DANNIS
OLGA ET NICOLAÏ VEDERNIKOV ¶ TETEA ARO

THE PLAYHOUSE
WHERE HOPE BLOOMS

On those evenings

when the moon is full, our dreams fill up the night. The desert of salt, which burns our skin, is drowned by the rains. ¶ When cometh the season of flowers, when branches bend beneath the weight of blooms, the earth gives us fruit. Days pass by in those instants of beauty where we sow and we give life. Faithful dogs lead the sheep beneath the shadow of the fig trees. We seduce women with our perception of the world, rid of jealousy and the fever of possession. ¶ And so, I fall asleep in the vast expanses, on the footsteps of my childhood, until the wind and the morning laughter gently wake me.

GERARDO COCA ON HIS BED IN THE ATACAMA DESERT, CHILE.

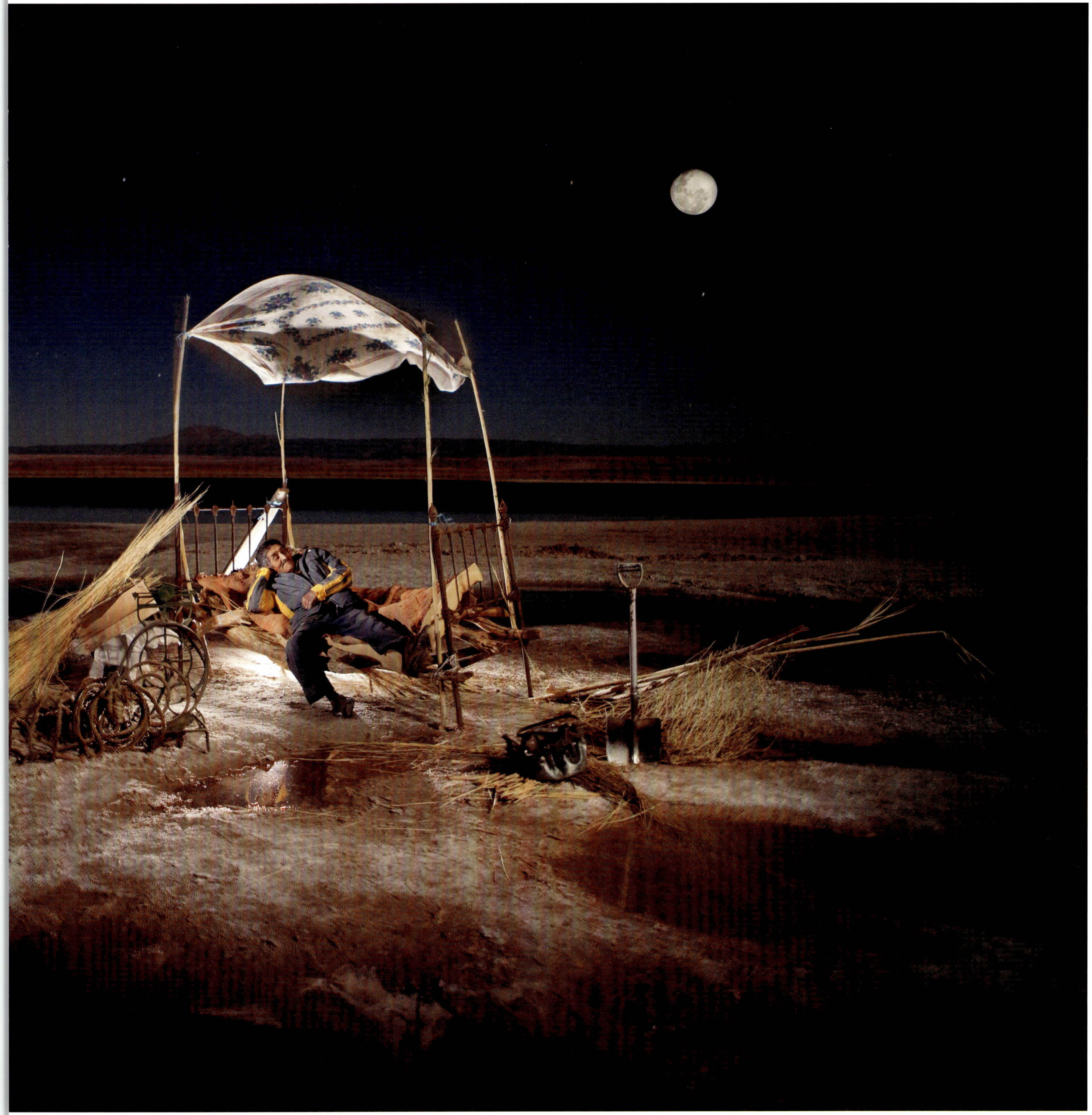

In the evening, when I wander through the village, the lights glow from the houses like the ricochets of laughter and the drama of all of these inaccessible lives. Here, we live in great poverty. Our cinder-block homes with sheet metal rooves are nothing like those of the soap operas our wives and children watch all day. ¶ I never went to school. Our generation had neither dreams nor opportunities. We were content with helping our parents with their farmwork. Happy and carefree, we looked upon the valley, sown with other villages, like miniature buildings from a far off miniature world. Only the present existed. The evenings were lively with songs when up into the dark sky rose the columns of smoke that heralded the wrath of our volcano. ¶ We survived a period of such poverty that the llamas disappeared for several years. We had to wait for the 60s before our community could come together. Today, we have a chief who speaks with the government. Together, we brought the llamas back amongst us.

MANUEL ZATAN AND THE HOUSES OF THE MOUNTAIN, THE ANDES, ECUADOR.

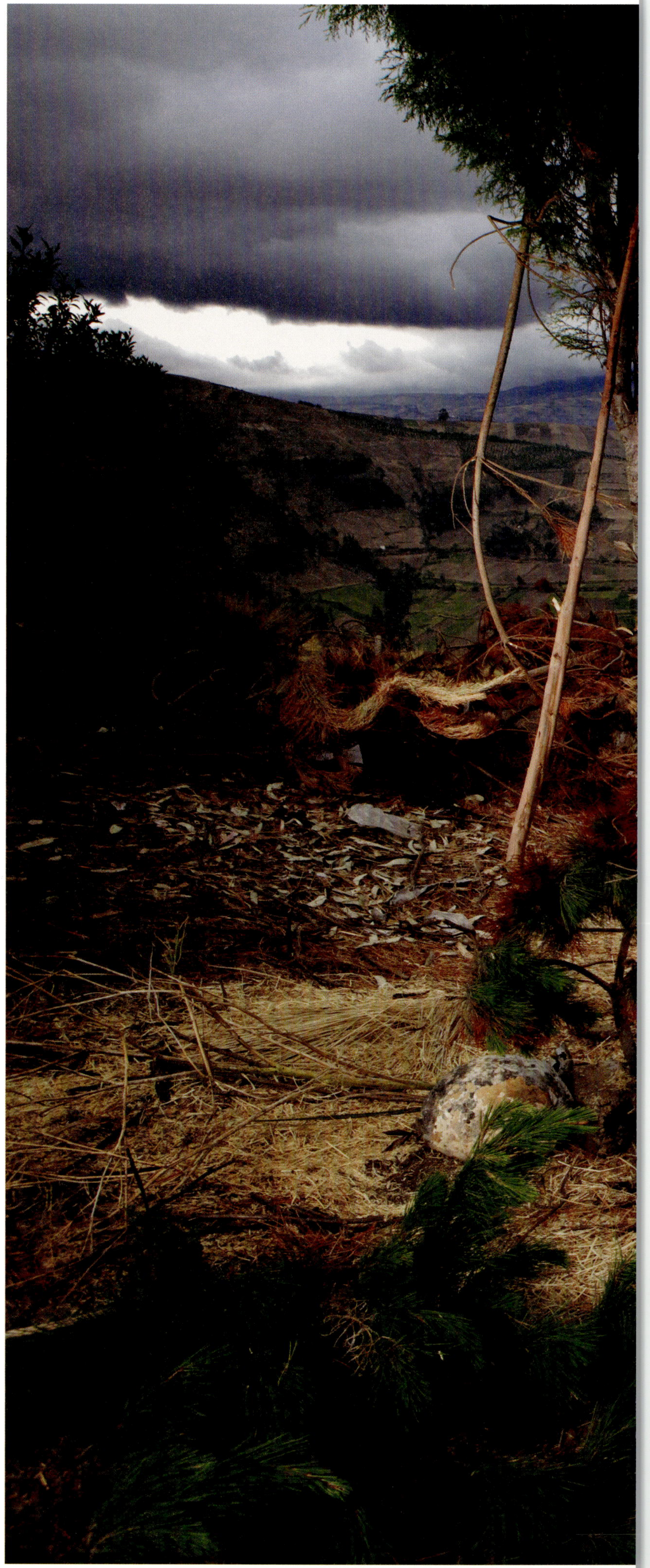

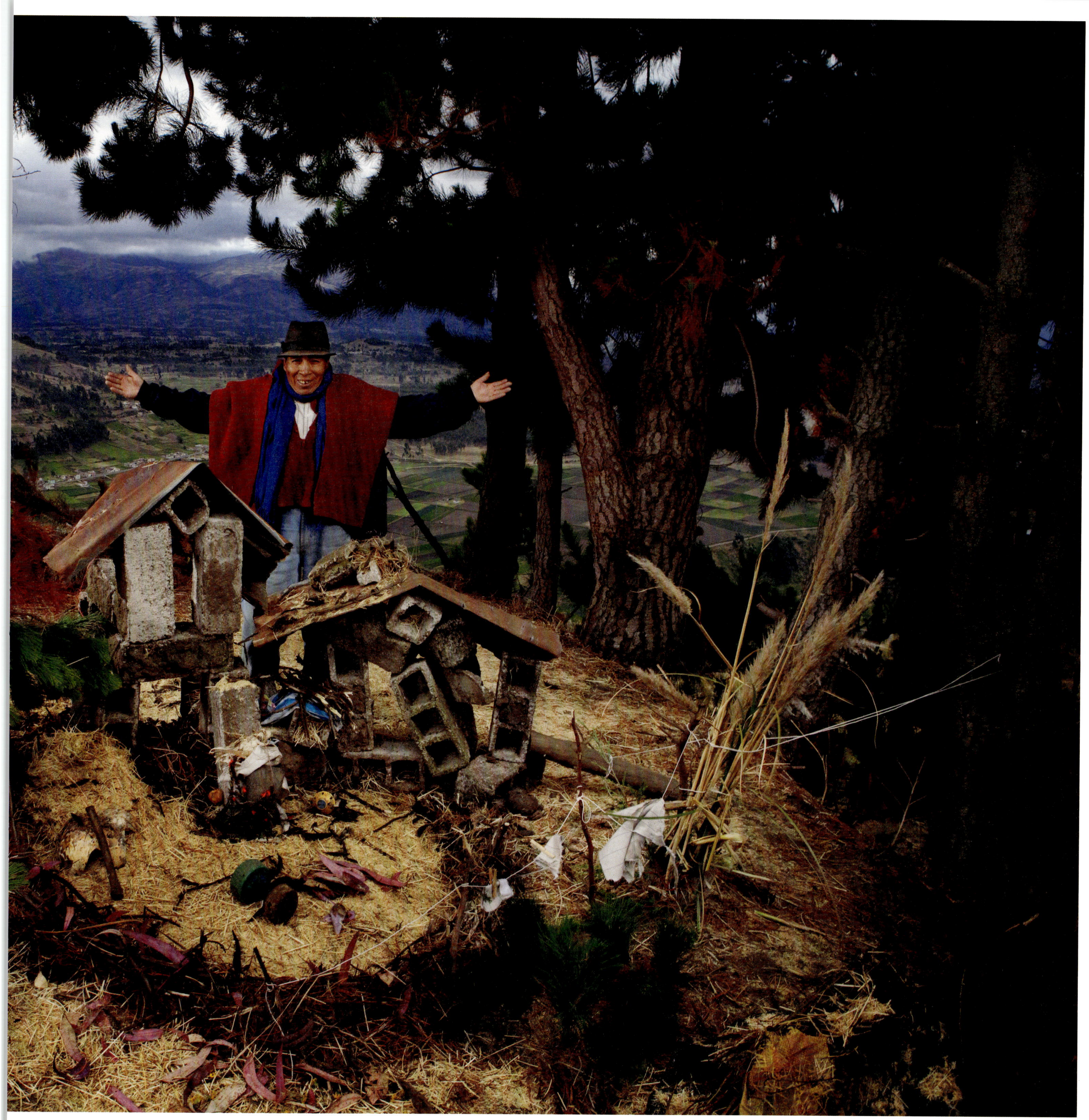

With the strength

of our own two hands, we have built these towers of light so that men in suits can live inside them. It is a country for their dreams, like a landscape from another planet, inside a television. We, the workers, live in camps made from canvas and bamboo. With my friends, some stones and a few pieces of wood, we have built our own city, in the image of the city that was built by all kinds of workers, the big and beautiful Shanghai skyline. Our piles of pebbles are their skyscrapers; our weeds are their giant trees that reach like arms up to the sky. Here, with one simple movement, I can make the most extraordinary works of architecture. ¶ I call upon my grandchildren to join me in this dream. Thus, they will grow within the echo of my own game and I can finally rest at the foot of the tree, rocked to sleep by their laughter.

WANG XIAO WITH HIS SHOVEL ON A CONSTRUCTION SITE, SHANGHAI, CHINA.

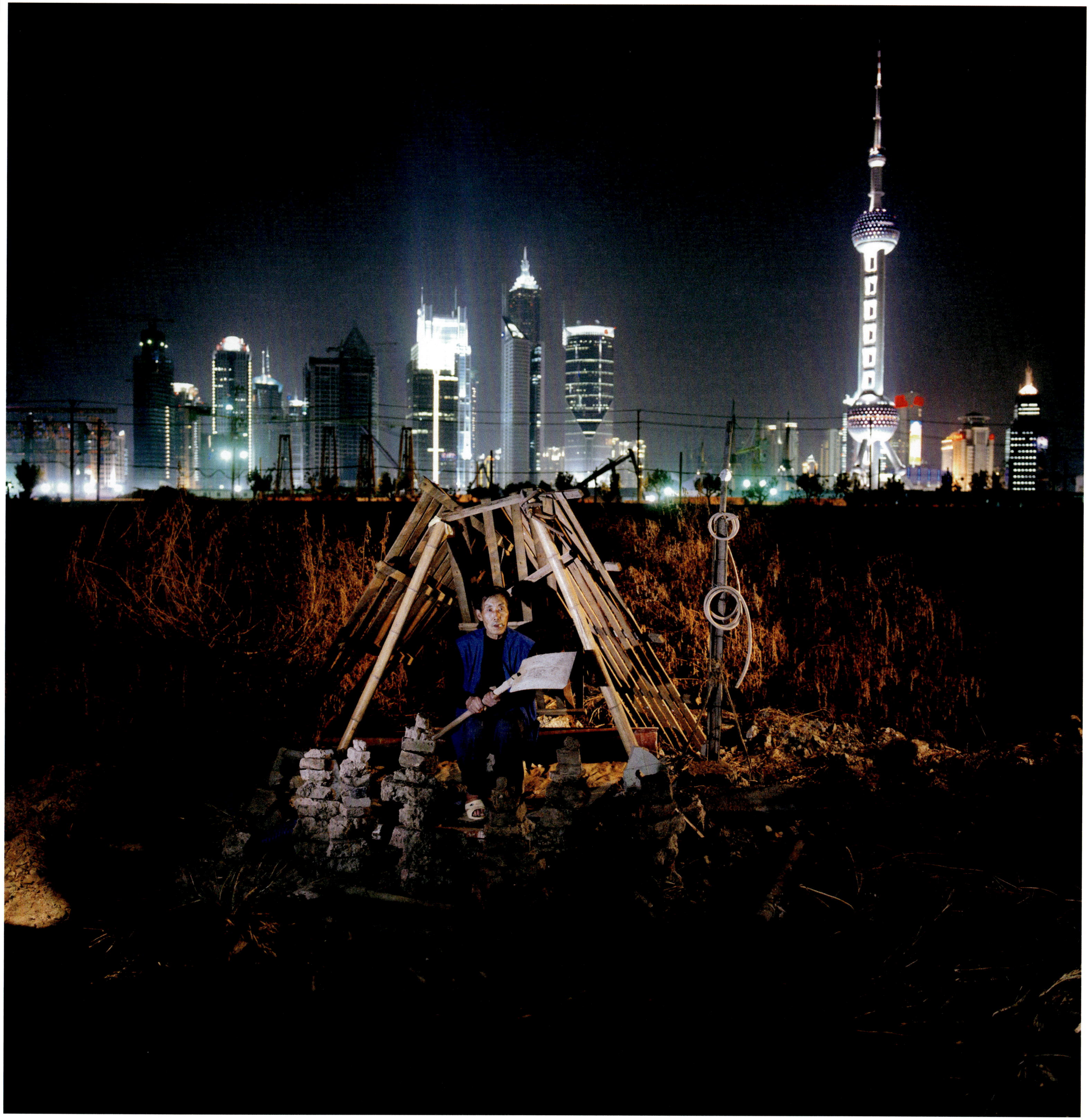

I come from the city of Tokyo but during the war, I was sent to the countryside like a lot of other children. I was about ten years old. My family stayed back in the city, where bombs were falling. Everywhere, fire and destruction, and me, there in the middle of green fields and beautiful forests. It was there that I discovered the play of light as it dances on the grass, the clarity of the night sky. The glacial silence of forests and of softly falling leaves. I discovered nature. It was an incredible encounter. ¶ After the trauma of Hiroshima, the first thing that I did was to stand up and speak out against the war. I chose to create images with meaning. That was all I did: graphic design trying to change the world for the better. ¶ We have gone very far in the destruction of nature. I have seen contaminated rivers and the sea thick with pollution. I have seen entire populations of fish wash up onshore, seen their silvery backs, their open mouths. One single A-bomb can lead to the end of the world. Since Japan's defeat, we no longer have the right to have them, but today our voices are rising against that law. Insidiously but quickly man is retracing the path of his former errors. ¶ Younger and new generations are completely assisted by technology. How are the young going to find their way? We give them what they want, prepackaged solutions, so much that they never learn how to break out of the model that is shutting them in. ¶ You have to know your body, not just your head. You need to touch, feel, get closer to nature. That is the only way that we can continue to develop new perspectives and ideas. You need to reconnect your body to your brain. You need to stay vigilant, and clairvoyant. To be wise enough to be able to take a step back, to identify the group of people who stand up in resistance, and to find in yourself the capacity to join them in revolt.

YUJI SATO, HIS HOUSE, HIS CAR AND THE POSTERS BEARING HIS MESSAGE, TOKYO, JAPAN.

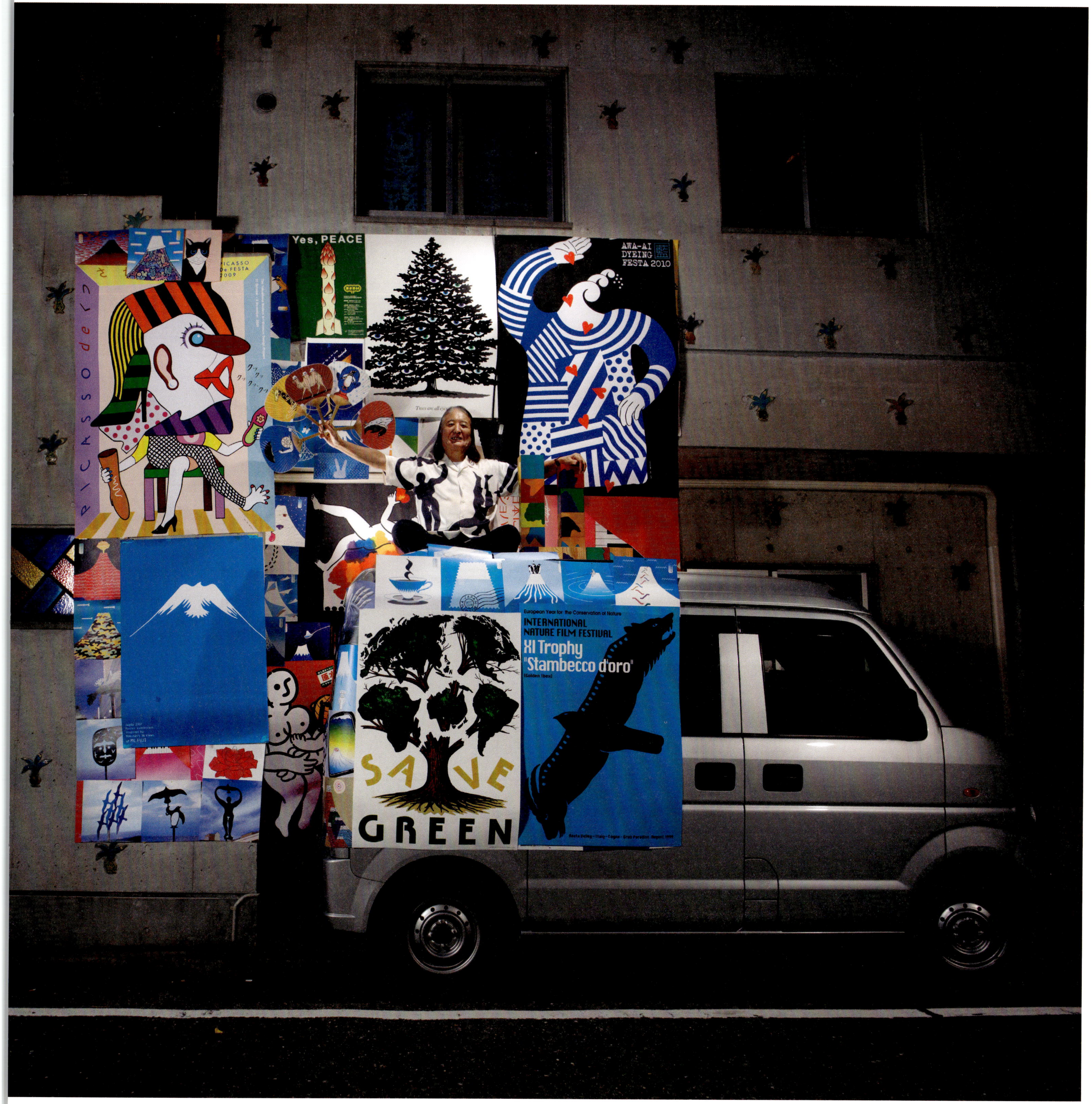

Yes, PEACE
AWA-AI DYEING FESTA 2010
PICASSO de
INTERNATIONAL NATURE FILM FESTIVAL
XI Trophy
"Stambecco d'oro"
SAVE
GREEN

When we were young we'd swim in the Mekong. Our laughter would echo off of the circles formed by drops in the river. ¶ In our little village my uncle was a great carpenter. Thanks to him, I learned this trade and could offer services to everyone around me. I carried all sorts of materials around by bike. Roads gave villagers the ability to ride about, but at the same time, they allowed huge trucks to take trees from our mountains in order to sell them to strangers… ¶ My life changed when I saw the fight where my elder brother was killed. After that, I lived in utter fear. At that time, it was kill or be killed. As I became a career soldier, I went from camp to camp, from war to war. I had to go where they sent me, or else be executed. I saw many atrocities. The hardest times were those of war. In addition to the pain and suffering, people didn't have the chance to study, or even work. So poverty set in everywhere and an entire generation was sacrificied… ¶ Then, the day I became a dad, my perspective on the world changed completely. I worked hard, seeking a different life. I left everything behind when I set out for Phnom Penh. I started working with wood again in an art school and then became a set decorator for the theater. I have one child who became a tailor, another an electrician, another a chemist and the last one works in a casino. They will never come back to the villages. They are the result of my choices and my transformations.

KIM HENG IN THE TREE FULL OF HOUSES, KAMPONG CHHNANG PROVINCE, CAMBODIA.

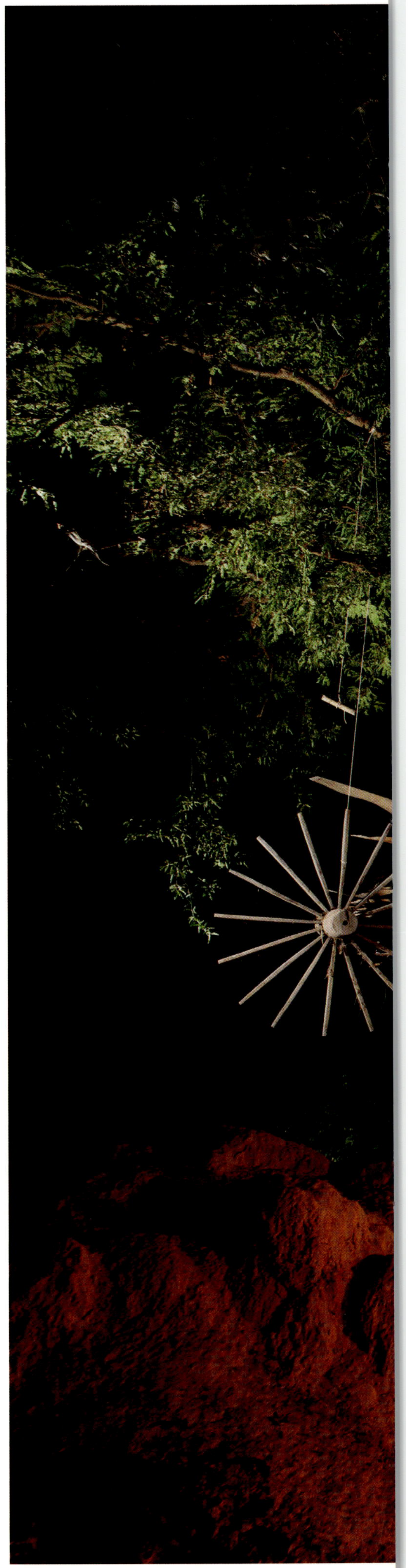

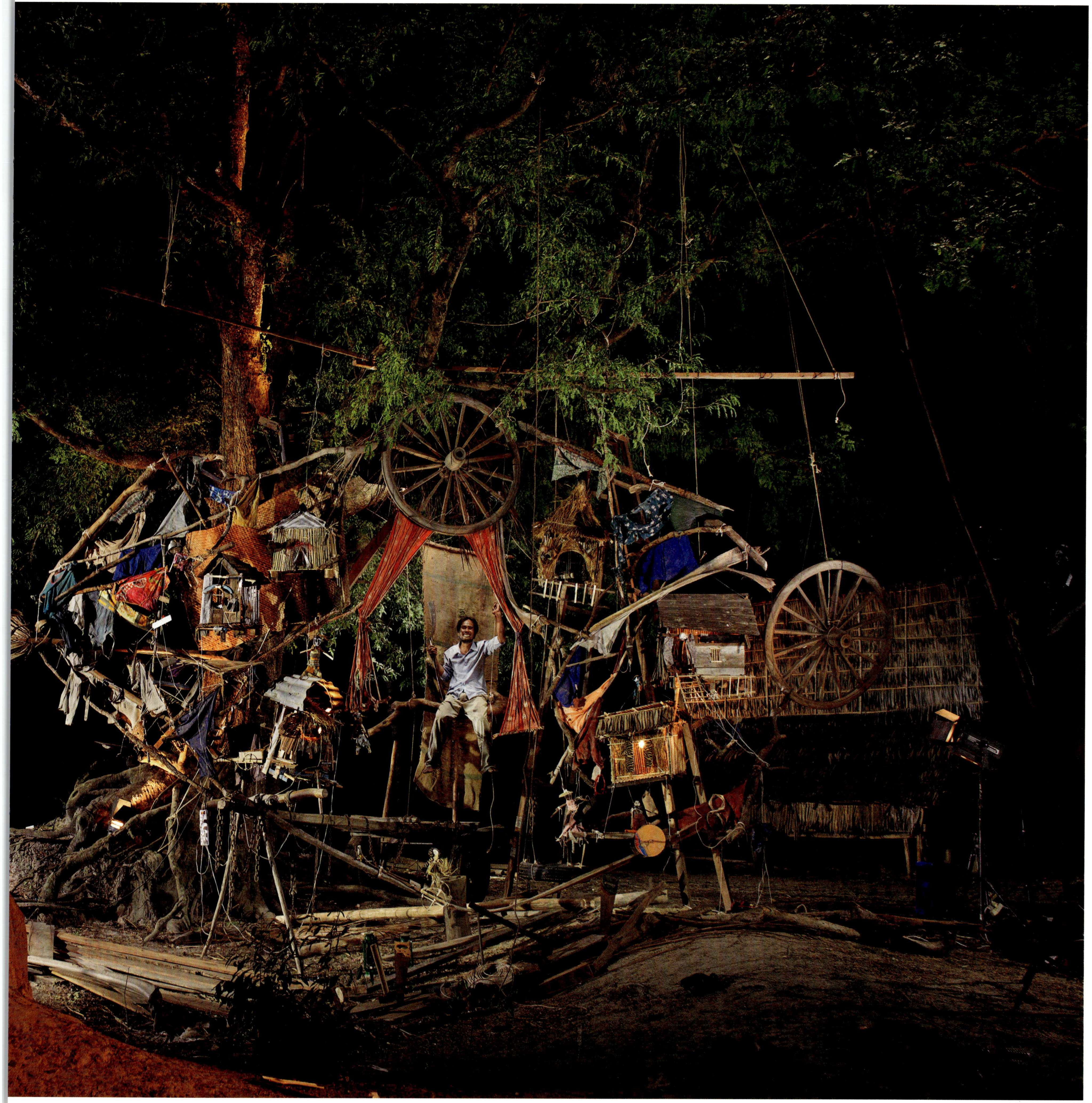

A long time ago, a small dolphin by the name of Opo and his mother came to live in the bay. People came from afar simply to see him, to watch him play. We would go to the bus stop to watch all the well-dressed men and women arrive, those wearing hats and shoes who would dive into the water like children as soon as they saw him. Sadness set in amongst all of us the day that we found him dead, killed by man. ¶ I became a soldier and went away. In the jungle of Malaya, I learned to survive amid the violence of war. When I came back, there was only nature to heal my wounds. When one works the land, its energy comes to live in us. It expands inside you like it does with plants, it flourishes in the hands of man as it does in the leaves of a tree. It gently soothes the anguish of bad memories. Only then can we devote ouselves to the joys of raising children. To guide them, watch them grow up like trees. To listen to one's wife so that she will stay near. To look contemplatively out to sea and to rejoice in the life created by enduring love.

DANNIS BARNES IN HIS GARDEN BY THE WATER, OPONONI, NEW ZEALAND.

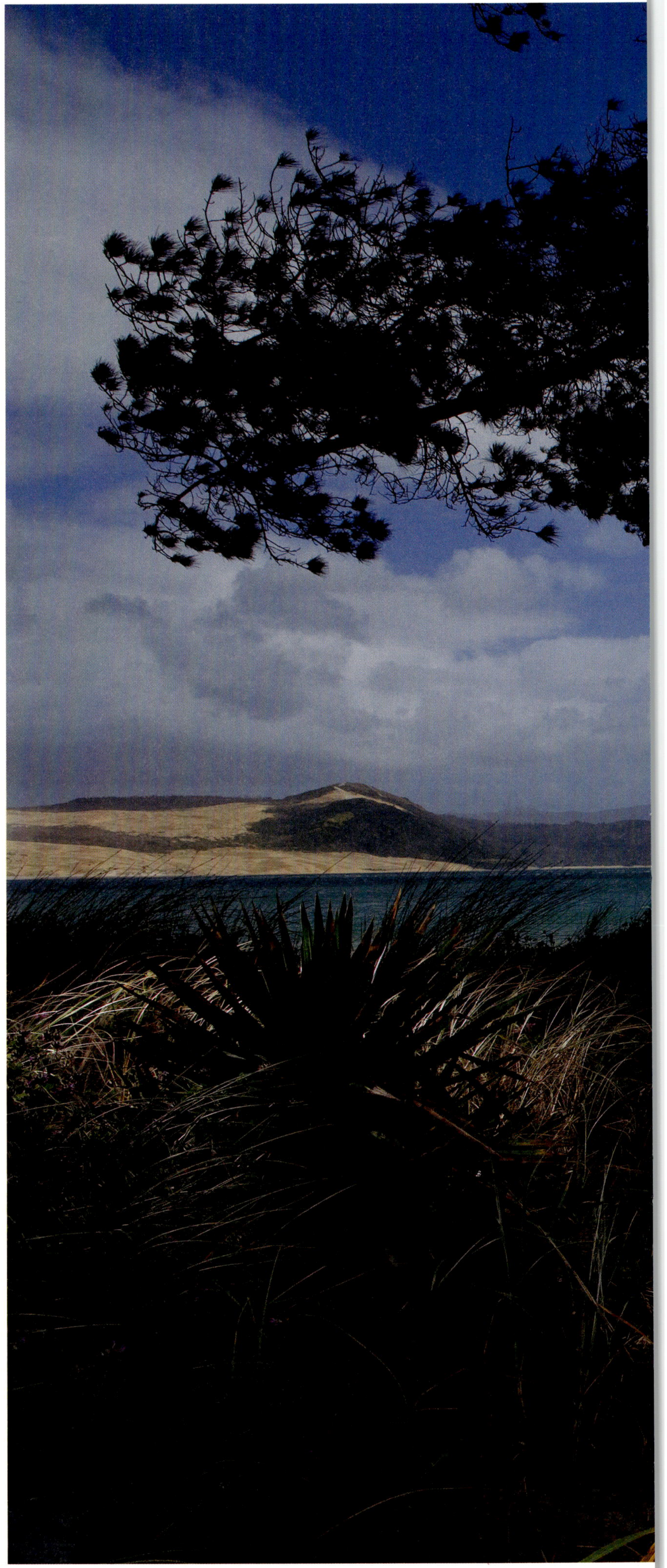

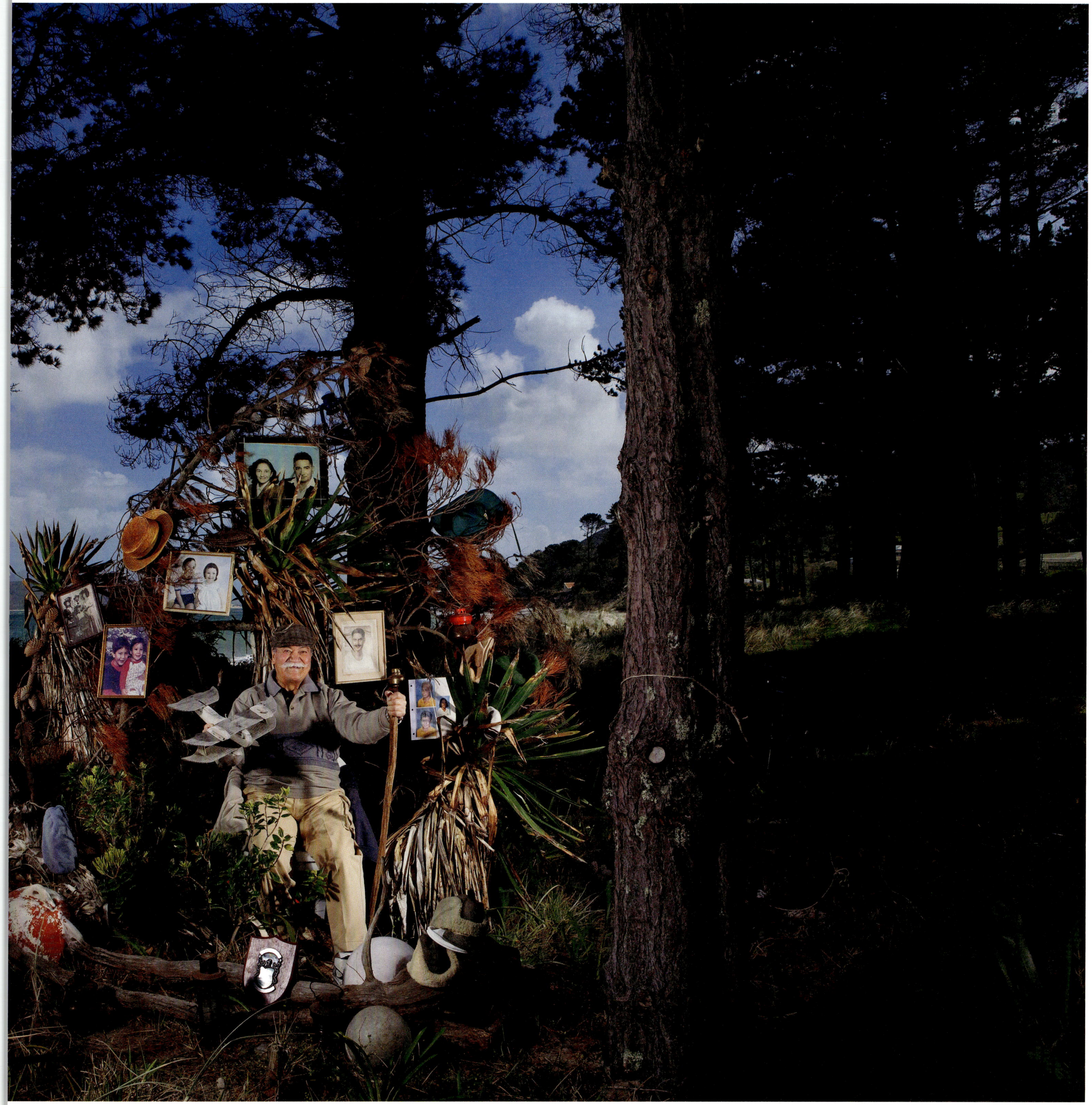

We live in a large house. At the beginning of the war, bombs fell in my garden, right in the middle of the green grass. We had to flee in order to survive. ¶ At that time, children didn't have the opportunity to study. They had to work in factories to help their family. I was there, my hands kept busy but my head dreaming of elsewhere. I was there building my future; I just didn't know it yet. ¶ One day, we were finally able to return home. The war was over. Calm had returned with the freshness of a new spring. I walked through the garden. I climbed the steps and entered into my childhood home. There, I read a book. My first. It was *Howling at the Moon* by Sakutaro Hagiwara. Then I read *The Flowers of Evil*, by Baudelaire. After that, I never stopped reading. At 17, my first poem was published, one about eggs that fell on a town.

KAZUKO SHIRIASHI IN HER FOREST OF POEMS, TOKYO, JAPAN.

Football Player ¶ He's a football player ¶ Kicks a ball, everyday he kicks a ball ¶ One day ¶ He kicked love high into the sky ¶ And it stayed there ¶ Because it didn't come down People thought it must be the sun ¶ The moon or a new star ¶ ¶ Inside me ¶ A ball that never comes down ¶ Hangs suspended in the sky ¶ You can see it becoming flames ¶ Becoming love ¶ Becoming a star

Taken from the collection, *Seasons of Sacred Lust*, published by A New Direction Book, with the author's kind consent.

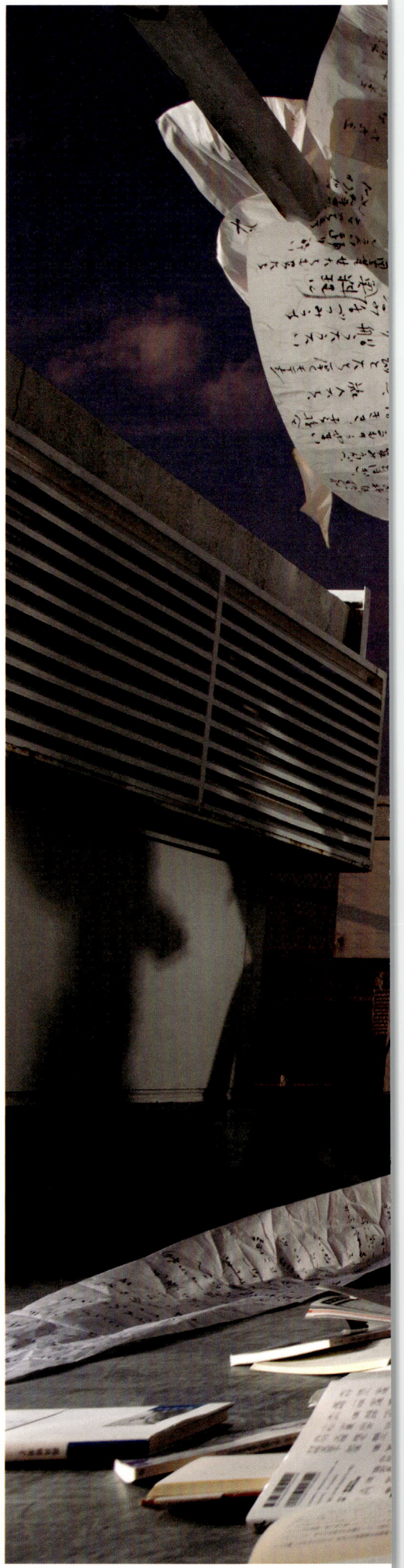

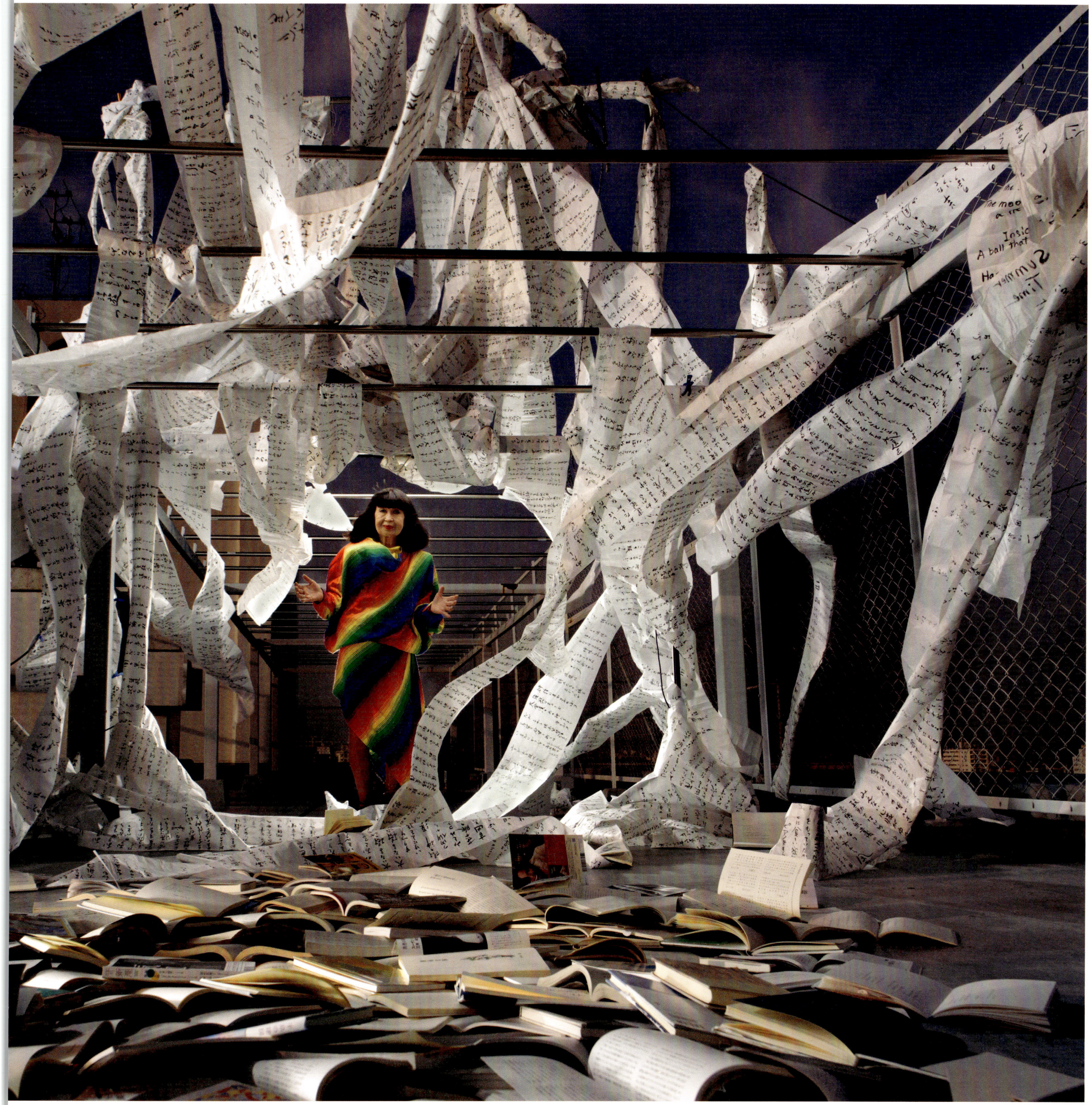
A ball that
Summer
Time

I like to work with my hands. I divide my time between the trees and the stage sets for the Biorman shows we're putting on in Tokyo. There are acrobats who jump on trampolines while giant monstors attack them with their flashing colored lights. ¶ At one time, I drew wild forests. Then I left to research them, to find out if they really existed. I didn't find my forests but I found a garden. Now I draw the vegetables I grow. That is part of my quest. ¶ I give my children organic produce. The most important thing for our family is to eat well. It is also food which feeds the brain and makes man the way he is. In making them eat well, I ensure their good health. I don't know what kind of work they will do but this will give them the energy to do it. I think that our children are capable of surviving because their bodies are accustomed to dirt and dust, and to confronting nature. ¶ Whatever our passions may be, the first most essential thing is to preserve our health, the second, our relationships, and the third, the wisdom that grows with the coming of years.

ABETA YASHIKO UNDER THE CANOPY OF HIS CHESTNUT TREES, YAMAGATA, JAPAN.

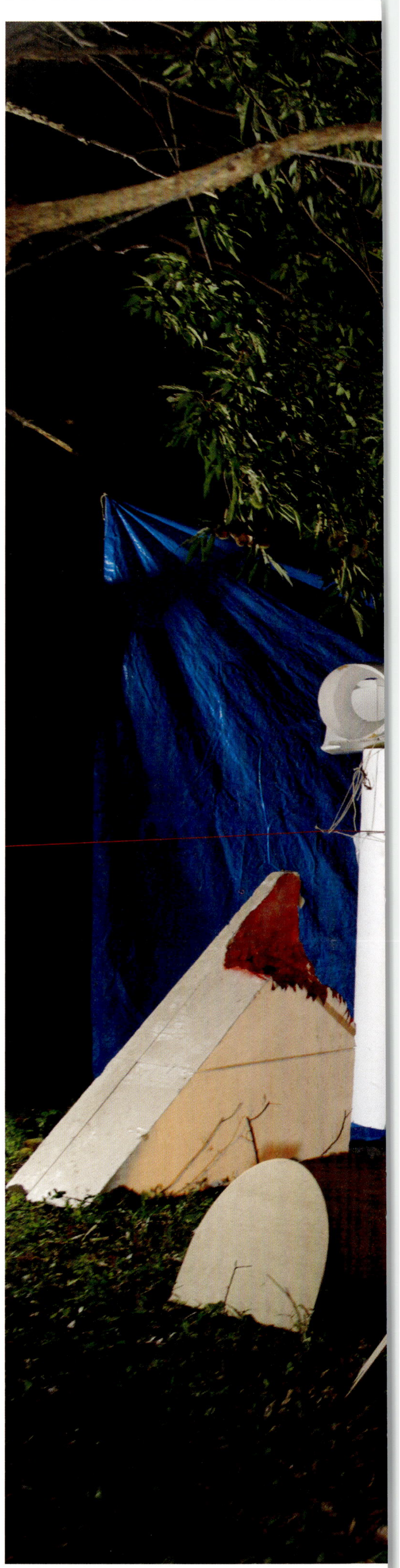

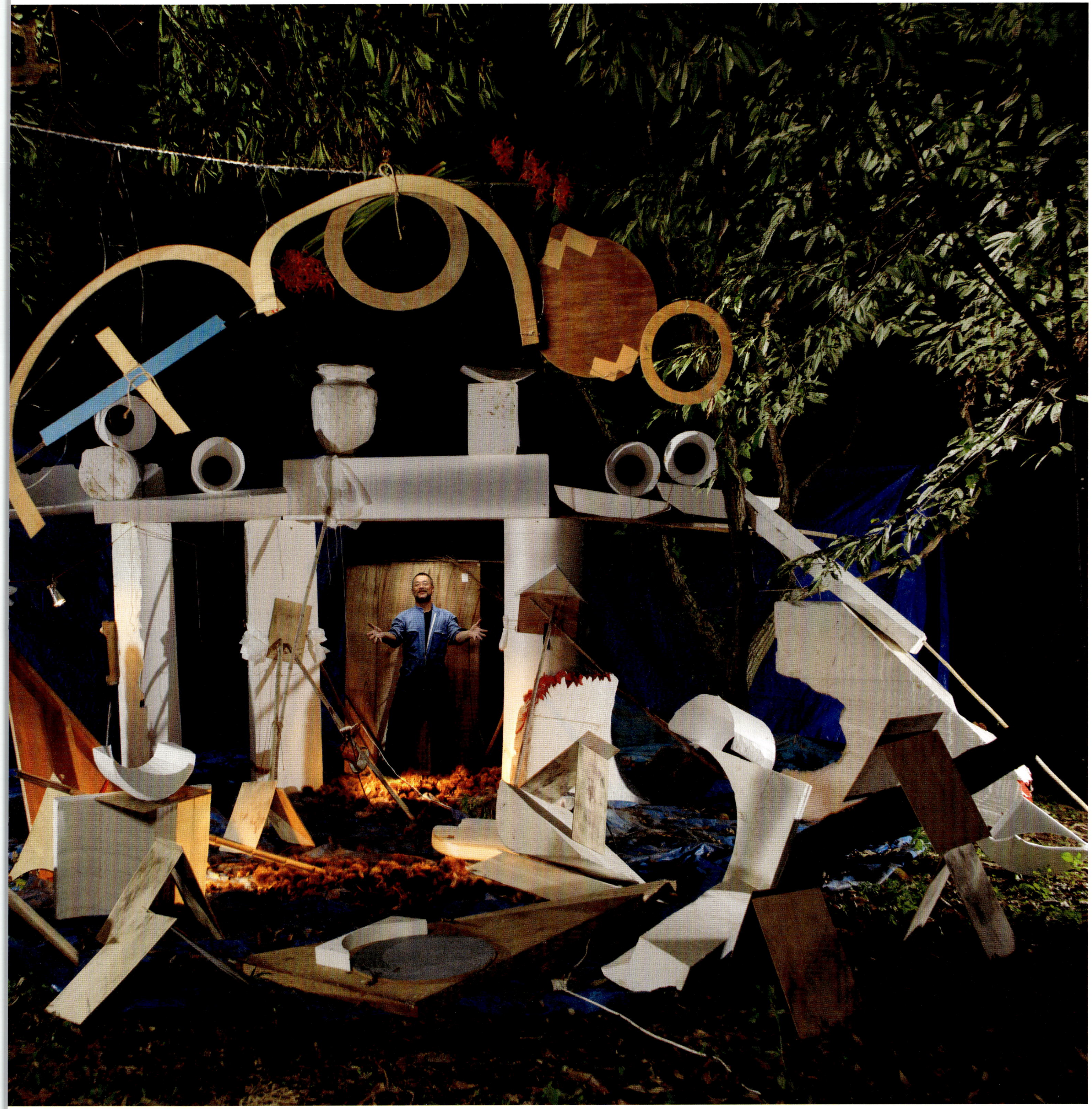

We were born in a small village, between Moscow and St. Petersburg. We met each other as children, cradled by the experiences that make up our shared memories. When our family sang together, people would stop outside, under our windows. Sometimes, we even took the tables out into the street and neighbors came to sit with us. We loved that, the long evenings spent with friends, open doors and open hearts. At that time, we would say that Russia was the heart of the world. ¶ And then, we decided to follow a dream. We left for Moscow. There existed more opportunities. We wanted to give our children a brighter future, a European lifestyle, with better jobs and a real chance at success. This may have been a mistake. Each country has its own specific traditions and in Moscow, under the shadow of globalization, they disappear more and more. Advertisements cover the city walls and hide the beauty of age-old buildings. Everywhere, there are expensive boutiques, yet so many people who have no money. Today, we live according to the "law of the jungle." People only think about business and themselves. ¶ It's true that, as you grow older, you become nostalgic. In our language, there is an expression which says, "when the trees were big"… We thought about it all the time, reminiscing about that lost epoch, when life was cold and snowy. Nostalgia grew and grew until we eventually we left the city. We returned to live in a village near the forest. We built everything with our hands. Sometimes, we sing our songs to the elders who live here, in the middle of nature. Like in our childhood. Like before. At the heart of the world.

OLGA AND NICOLAÏ VEDERNIKOV AND THE FROZEN TREES, IN THE DACHA'S GARDEN, RUSSIA.

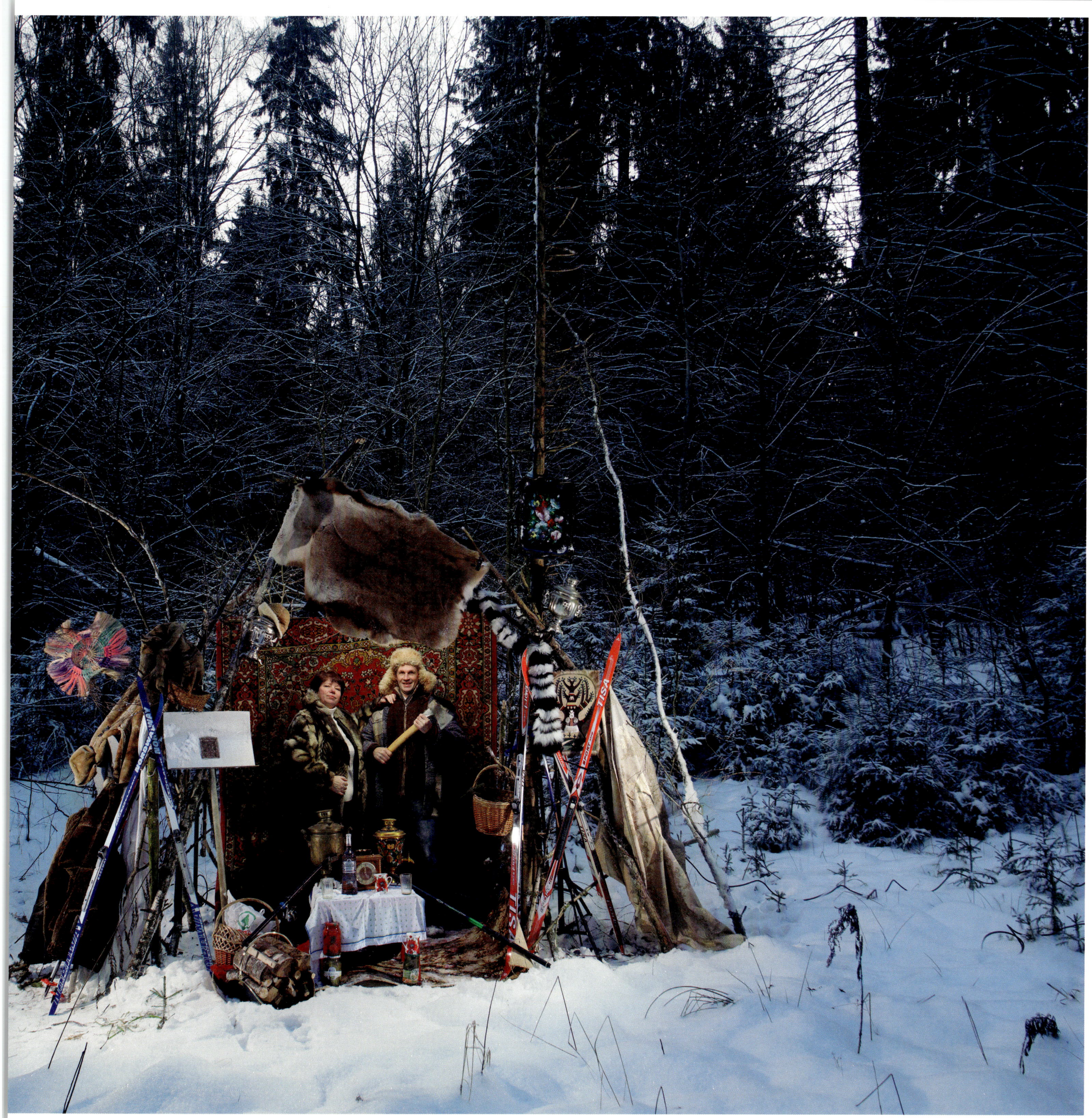

The most beautiful thing I've ever seen was in my childhood, my family gathered together. Sharing the activities, like gathering corn in the garden, and women's conversations admist the peelings and leaves. My father would come back in the evening with a huge sea snake and my mother would accept it as a gift, cooking it in the smoke of the hot stones. ¶ School inspired me to travel, to live elsewhere. It was dance that brought me to the continent. I was offered a tour of the world but I preferred to ask for a scholarship to learn medicine and teaching. Among the Mapuches, "the men of the soil" in southern Chili, I found a new family. I shared their struggle against the deserting of the countryside, for better health conditions, for more developed education. ¶ I returned to my island to work the land. I share the solitude of the wind-swept plot of land where an old dilapidated bus protects me. I have joy in my heart for I see the community of my people maintaining ties with our land. The vast sky rustles with the murmurs and conversations that chase each other with the memory of our ancestors.

TETEA AROUA MARIKI AND HER GRANDPARENTS, RAPA NUI, CHILE.

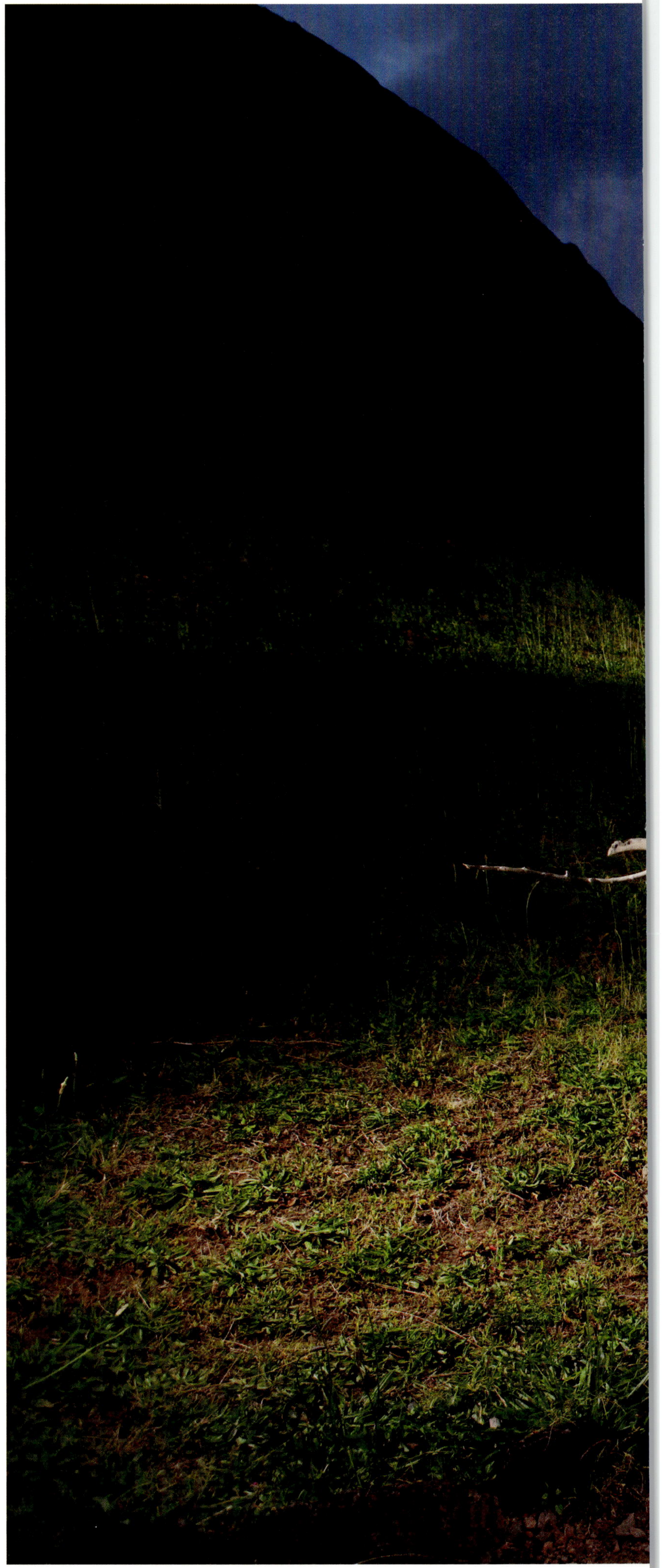

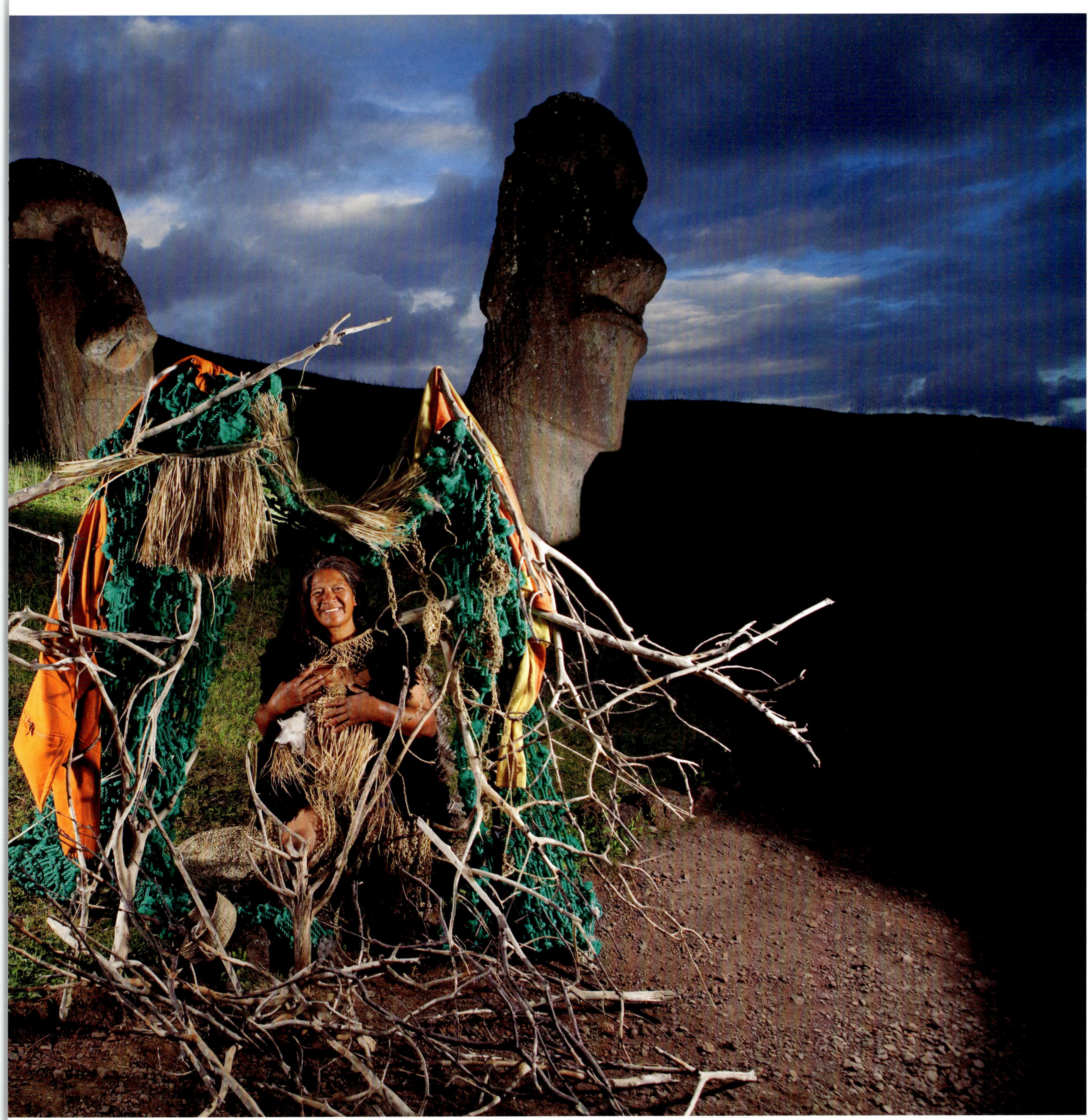

Here it is the grandmothers who work hard! In olden times, there were fewer diseases for we ate more wisely, the fruits of our own harvest. It was much better than that of the supermarket, that which, in any case, we couldn't afford. So, the grandmothers got organized. Today, we grow vegetables and we give them to the elders, to the children and to those suffering from AIDS in need of vitamins. ¶ In the beginning, I nearly ran away! The work is too hard. But I learned to watch the vegetables grow and to God I give thanks. I breathe life into them. And it keeps my body in shape, a natural form of exercise. ¶ The young today are ashamed to take care of cows and fields. We need to negotiate with the police in order to have some delinquents with us. They have a choice between the garden and prison! Some are really lazy guys and others steal our vegetables. When they get out of their cell they're so hungry they eat anything and everything they find. We teach them that food comes from rain and from the earth that we walk upon. Maybe one day, they won't steal anymore because they will grow their own gardens.

LULAMA JIM AND NANCY WITBOOI IN THEIR COMMUNITY GARDEN IN THE TOWNSHIP OF PHILIPPI, CAPE TOWN, SOUTH AFRICA.

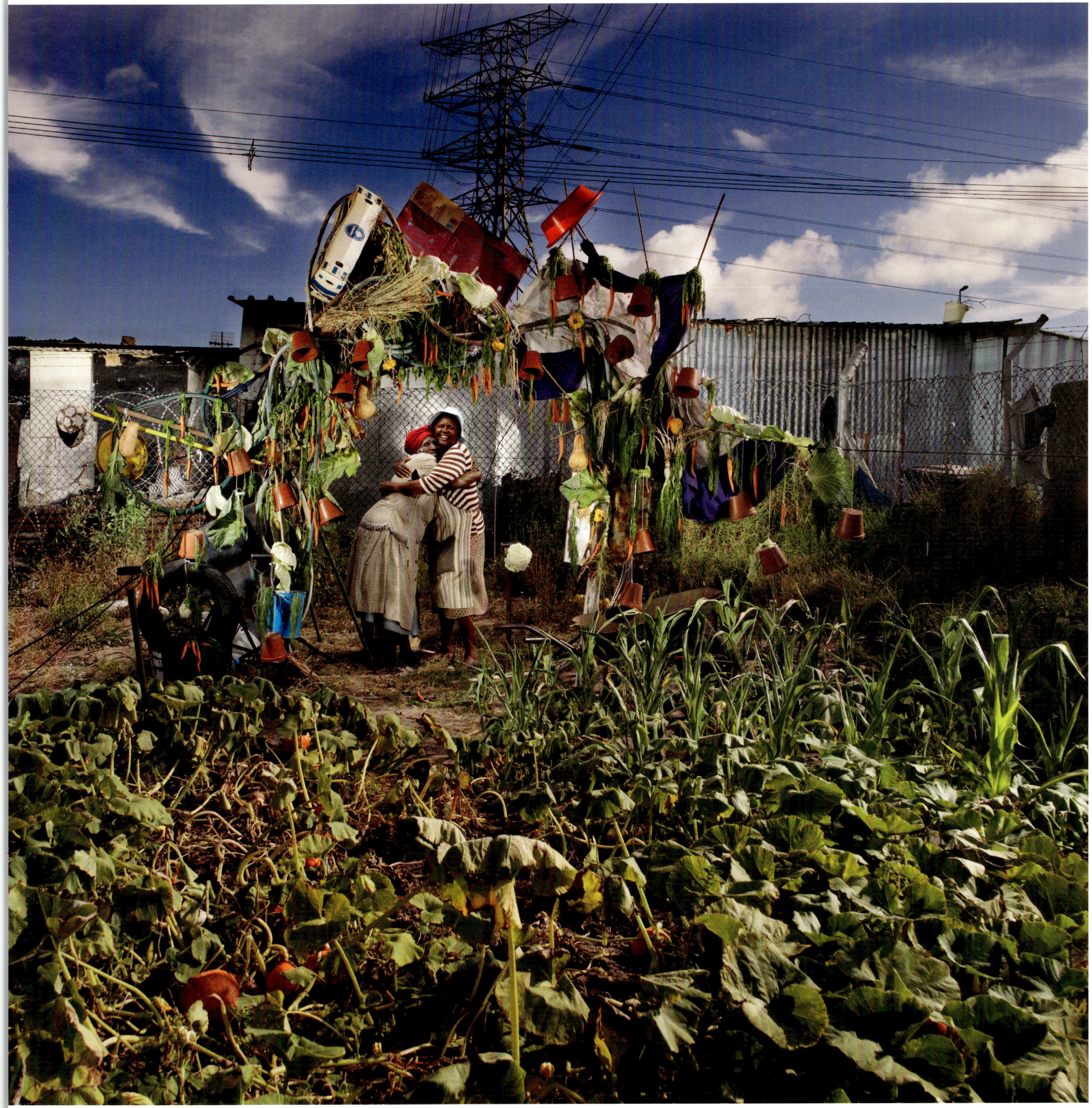

The hat I am wearing comes from my parents. It is as white as the snows of Chimborazo, the volcano that protects us. The two black bands symbolize the mourning of the Incas. ¶ When the Spanish came, they took our land and the Puruhaes people were forced into slavery. During this painful time, a man crossed over the mountains. Dressed like a beggar, he walked with a heavy wooden box on his back, from community to community, without ever tiring. This man, we called him the mailman. To bring us our mail he had to constantly go back and forth between Quito and the mountains. Since no one had addresses, he had to speak with everyone and he quickly became a friend of all of ours. One day, while climbing to the house of a rich and powerful man he noticed the severed heads of an entire Indian family. He was chased by a pack of dogs and had to take refuge at the top of a large tree. ¶ The postman got out safe and sound but he was never the same. He started to help us organize protests so that the Indians could legally occupy their land. For years he wrote letters for our illiterate families. It is thanks to the men like this simple postman that, with time, we have been able to recover our lands for the future of our children.

CONCEPCIÓN TENESACA SPINNING WOOL FROM HER LLAMAS BY THE FIRE, ANDES, ECUADOR.

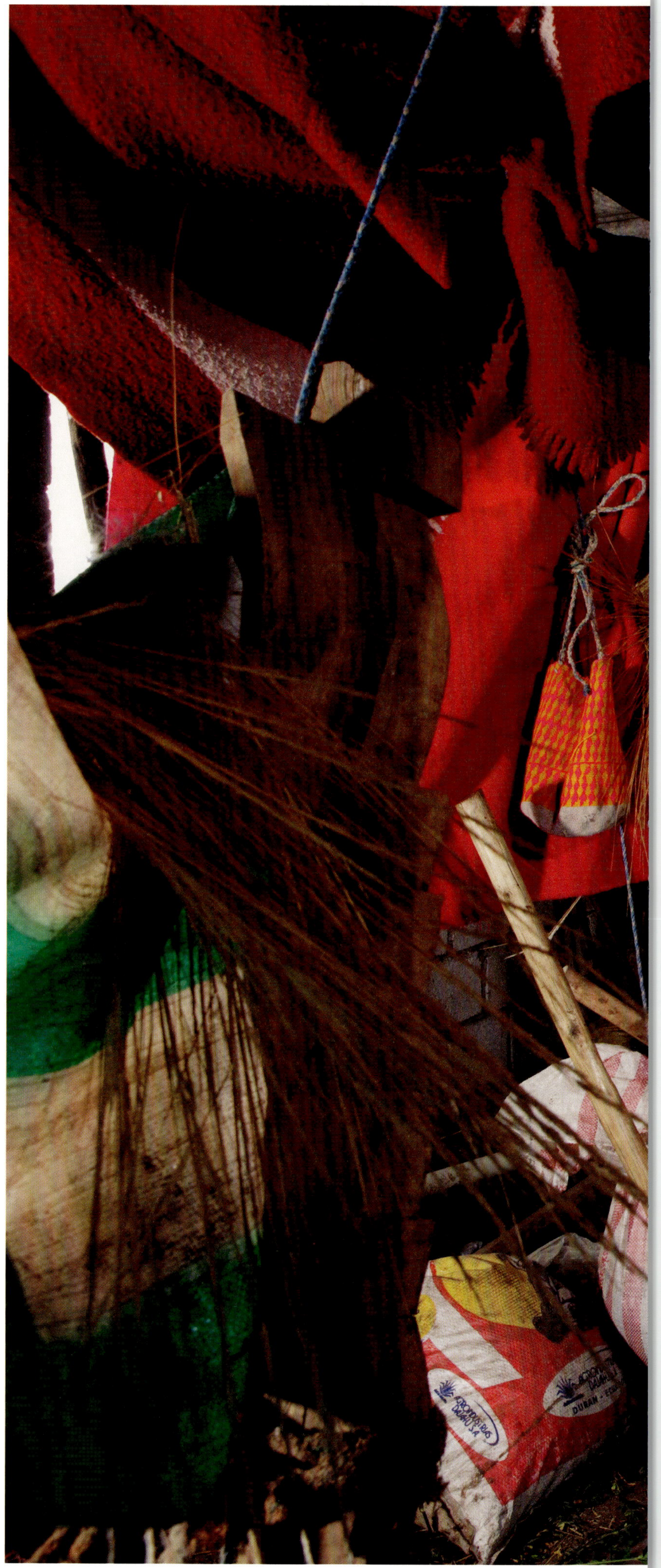

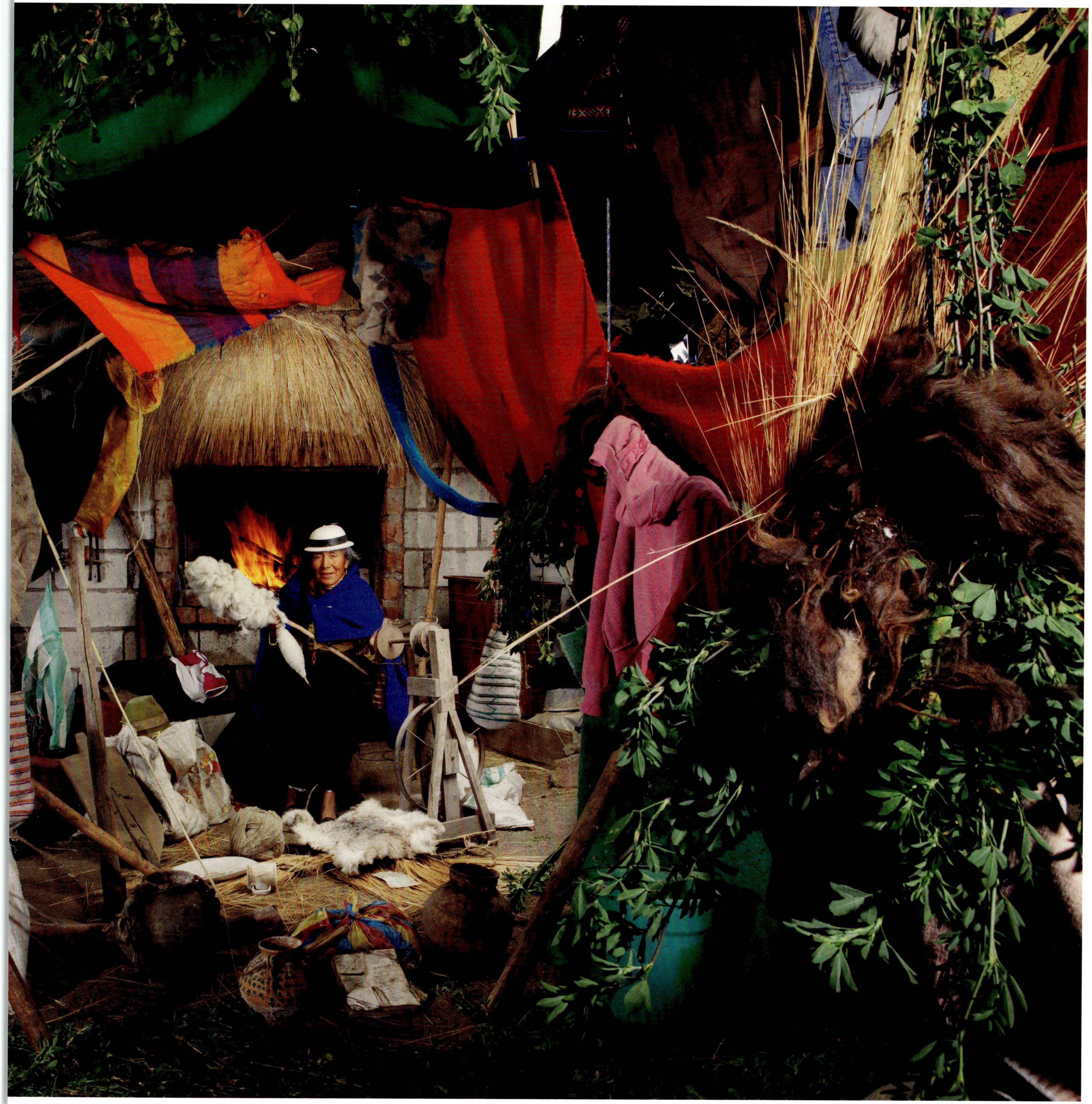

It took us quite a bit of time just to get to the point where we could play football. For the kids to have shoes and uniforms. Here, everything is a challenge, even the slightest thing. To speak to children and their families, it takes hours. Negotiate, convince, try to help them. We fight for everything but the game, the beautiful game of football, teaches us to go beyond our errors, to accept our losses and move on. Thanks to this, some of us have escaped poverty. And those who make it to the big teams become ambassadors for their towns. Our pride. They are cheered by everyone, helped, supported, and when their turn comes they will be the ones who will aid the others. ¶ Here we do everything together. That's how we struggle through in the face of adversity. When someone dies the whole community comes together to help those left behind. We are united together like the fingers of a hand. A clenched fist, raised and ready to fight. ¶ In 1998 we had had enough of squatting in shacks made of sheet metal, with no water nor electricity. We didn't have land. We didn't have anything. So, we all sat together and chatted. Everyone gave a bit of money, whatever they could afford. It wasn't much, but there were a lot of us. Finally, we were able to pay a lawyer who fought for us. We were displaced but they found us new land. We built our own houses.

PATRICK JAMPO, THE FOOTBALL TEAM AND THE DOG, "DAT COM", CAPE TOWN, SOUTH AFRICA

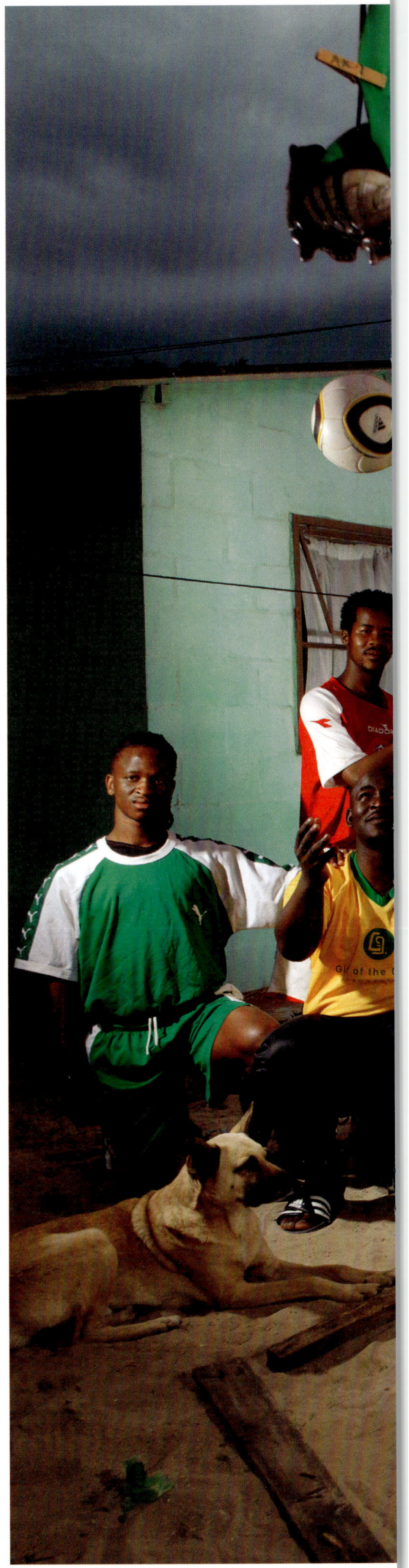

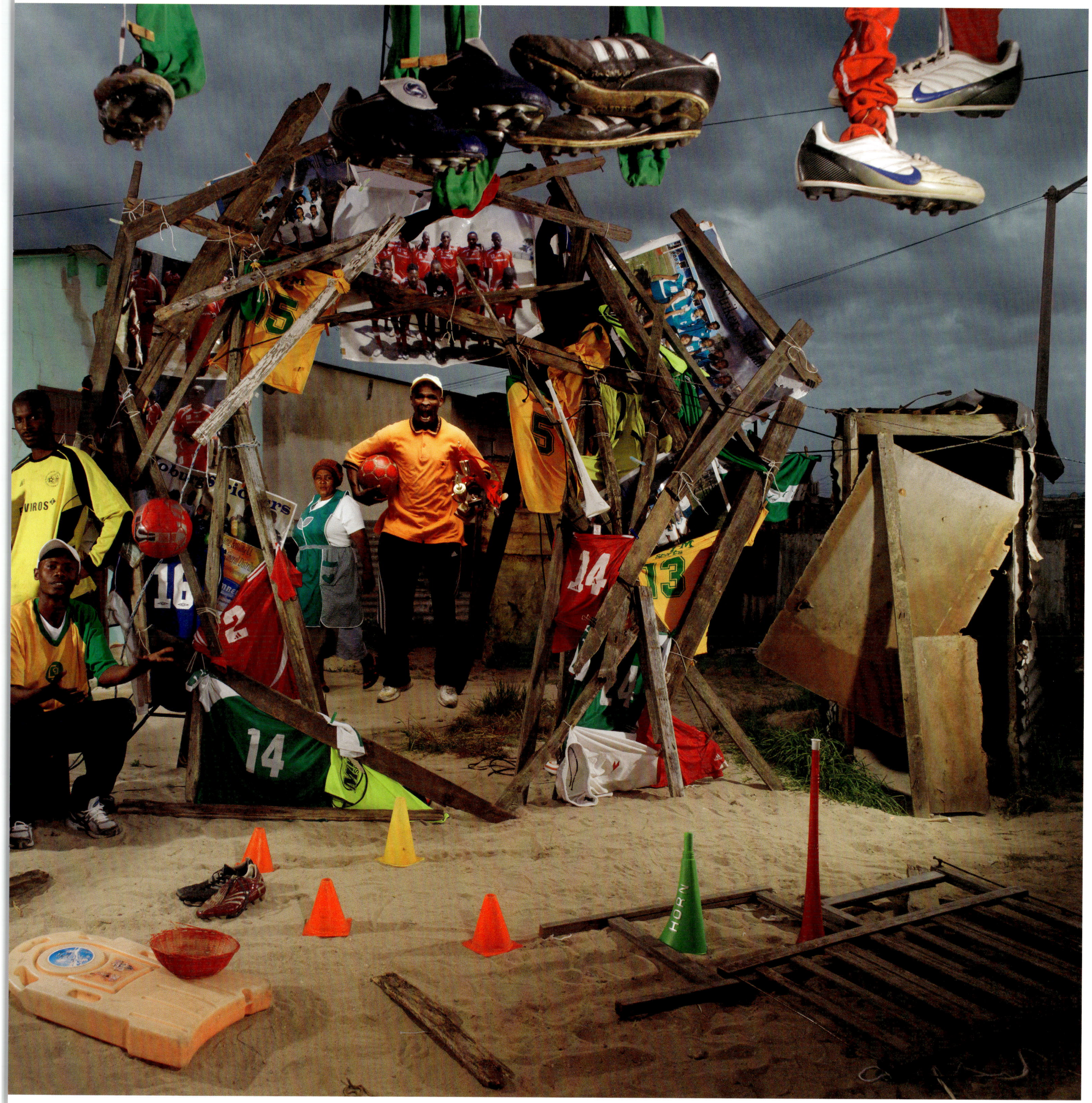
HORN

The "Chuwa" is a tree of two seasons: the season that carries the leaves and the season that awaits their renaissance. Its sacred character comes from the stones gripped in its roots. Out of respect we only walk around it when following the path of the sun. Each day I visit and greet it. At its feet is a small stone that we paint orange to please the gods. My prayer is my companion wherever I go, accompanying me in my daily tasks. ¶ Today, it is the Hindu holiday of Magesakanti. All the members of families in our village have come; some of them have traveled all day to be here. Some from as far away as Kathmandu. "Chuwa" carries our prayer into the wind through the red saris of all the women here. Sometimes with the overflowing of our joy, our laughter can be heard from one end of the world to the other. ¶ We know not loneliness as there are children in every home. Harmony with nature reminds us of the beauty of eternal rebirth. *Om Mani Padme Hum.*

BOUDHAKUMARI DHAKAL IN THE SACRED DURALI TREE, NEPAL.

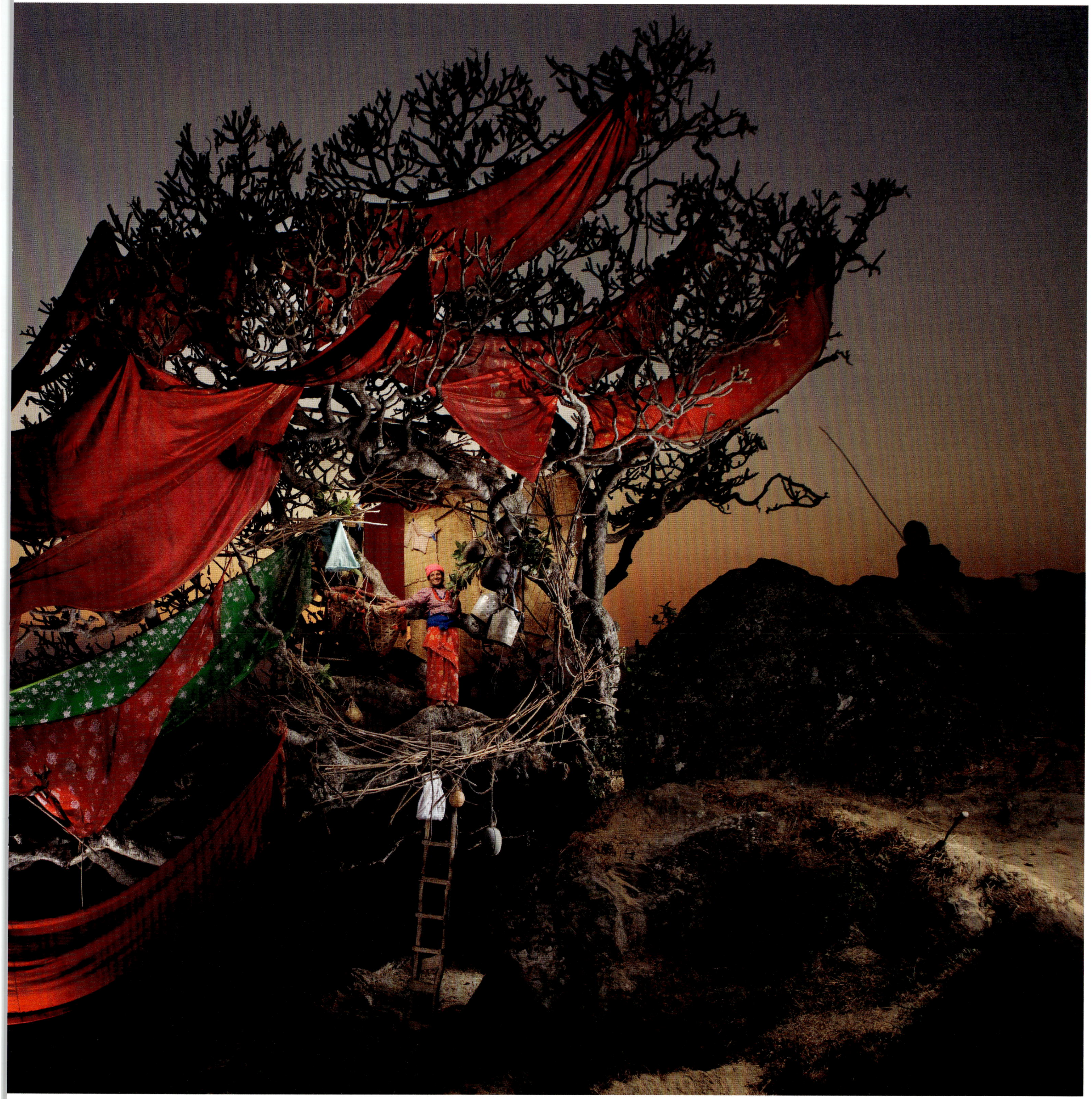

TABLE OF CONTENTS

I would like to thank

All the grandparents from all over the world for their enthusiasm, laughter, benevolence, and their ever-present understanding of the values I've tried to convey through this project. ¶ All my translators, interpreters and the hundreds of people around the world working as ad hoc set designers who helped me construct the Playhouses. ¶ Thomas Millet, Ayumi Morita, Louis Hubert, Virginie de "Groland" and Intagrist Ag Mohamed Mitta for accompanying me on my wild expeditions. ¶ Yann Arthus-Bertrand, for the strength of his convictions and his affection. ¶ Sibylle d'Orgeval and Baptiste Rouget for whisking me away on the *6 Billion Others* project and for sharing a profound commitment to encourage freedom of expression. The Good Planet Foundation, Florent Gilard, Anne-Laure de Pazzi, Dominique Lorens, Chloé Henri-Biabaud and Isabelle Vayron. ¶ Patricia Ricard for her boundless generosity and precision of thought. ¶ Marie-France and Roger Daniel Henry who taught me the importance of commitment and its demands. ¶ Geneviève and Jacques Giraux, my grandparents who laid the first stone. ¶ Sylvain Tesson, Hélène Gaudy and Sybille d'Orgeval for supporting me in writing the texts. ¶ Bernard Marcadet and Christian Boltanski for their reflections and faith in the *Playhouses of Our Grandparents* project. ¶ The partners who supported me and who had faith in my approach. Défi Jeune Yvelines, the Orpea retirement home group and the Ricard family, as well as my brother Guillaume Henry, copyright author. ¶ Actes Sud, Anne-Sylvie Bameule and Nathalie Démoulin, as well as Jean-Paul Capitani and Marie-Marie Andrasch. ¶ Quentin Clausin and the team of *Billions Star Hotel*, a film that tells of the Playhouse adventure which takes place between New York and Cambodia. ¶ Matphot, Marco and Picto, Pierrot for their technical support. ¶ Michel de Paris from "Connaisseurs du Voyage". ¶ Fanny Dupéché and Priscilla Telmon for their pure souls and constant support. ¶ Jane Peck for her colors and overflowing enthusiasm. ¶ The Premier Regard gallery as well as Henri Jobbe Duval and Bénédicte Lessieur, Catherine Christin and the Gallery 1161 team, the Fondation Paul Ricard, the Palais de Tokyo and the Comptoir Général. ¶ Jean-Luc Monterosso and the Photomed team, Jacques Rocher, Florence Drouet and the Gacilly team, Wall For and Herbert Hufnagel for welcoming my exhibitions. ¶ Frédérique Babin from *Monde 2*, Agnès Grégoire from *Photo Magazine*, Cyril Drouet of *Le Figaro* as well as *Clé*, *El Pais*, *Courrier international*, *Azart Magazine*, *Flair*, and more. ¶ Serge Richard for the magic of his sound compositions. ¶ Dom and Val of "Contramundo" in Redonda, Brazil, and Carla Talopp for her precious contacts. ¶ And everyone else, too many to mention, but above all Sima, Patricia and Mathilde for their generosity and tolerance of my numerous departures.

PRODUCTION: KARIMA CHABAUD
PHOTOENGRAVING: TERRENEUVE (ARLES)
PRINTED AUGUST 2011
BY EBS PRINTERS (VERONA)

ISBN : 978-2-330-00084-4

PRINTED IN ITALY